P9-ARG-780

Children Who Say No When You Want Them to Say Yes

ALSO BY JAMES WINDELL

Discipline: A Sourcebook of 50 Failsafe Techniques for Parents

*8 Weeks to a Well-Behaved Child: A Failsafe Program for
Toddlers Through Teens*

Children Who Say No When You Want Them to Say Yes

Failsafe Discipline Strategies for Stubborn and Oppositional Children and Teens

James Windell

Macmillan • USA

MACMILLAN
A Simon & Schuster Macmillan Company
1633 Broadway
New York, NY 10019

A catalogue record is available from the Library of Congress.
ISBN   0-02-860817-8

10   9   8   7   6   5   4   3   2   1

Printed in the United States of America

Book Design by A&D Howell

To my son, Jason—as a boy, firmly resolved and unyielding; as a young man, never afraid of trying new and challenging directions

Contents

Part III   Stubborn Behavior in Special Situations

┌Acknowledgments┐

I would like to thank several people who gave me encouragement or assistance in the early stages of this project:

Psychologist Linda Kaiser was kind enough to read the original proposal and make many supportive and encouraging remarks.

Vicki Timms, who shares my enthusiasm for training parents, listened to my ideas and supported them.

Julian Gordon often made insightful comments about oppositional and defiant youngsters, which helped clarify some of my own thinking and forced me to view the psychological aspects of such children in somewhat different ways.

School psychologist Kerrie Delevie has always made me feel as if I had something important to say and during the early stages of my thinking about this book made several helpful suggestions related to oppositional children in the school setting. Her thoughts and generous contributions, related to her own experiences as a school psychologist, influenced what I wrote about difficult young people in the classroom.

As I wrote the manuscript for this book, as always, it was the parents in my eight-week parent-training classes who unwittingly made the biggest contributions to my understanding of difficult children. Their willingness to share thoughts, concerns, and experiences from their own day-to-day lives helped me to include anecdotes that I trust will ring true to parents who read this book.

Many of the parents in recent classes volunteered to read portions of the manuscript while it was in progress. Their feedback has been invaluable as I tried to make this book as practical and useful to parents living with difficult children as I could.

Other people who made significant contributions to this book include Mary Pettit, whose two wonderful children, Paige and Broc, have provided plenty of material for this book as well as previous books. Mary's openness in telling me about her raising of Paige and Broc has turned into a seminar for both of us.

My colleagues, Dan and Kathy Cojanu, who enjoyed talking about their delightful six-year-old, Michael, provided several anecdotes, which helped to enliven the chapter on school-age children. And their comments about the chapter were insightful and welcome.

Another friend and colleague, Tim Albertson, was also kind enough to share stories about his son, which forced me to rethink and try to make more practical the chapter on three-year-olds.

Finally, I couldn't have completed the chapter on adolescents if it hadn't been for the experiences I've had with my own children, Jason and Jill, as they passed through that stage of their lives. But almost as important in the past few years is my work with dozens of teenagers who have been in my therapy groups at the Oakland County Juvenile Court. The young men and women in those therapy groups have been constantly challenging, frequently frustrating, and always a source of stimulation.

For the opportunity to learn from my assignment as a group thera- pist with delinquent adolescents, I owe a debt of gratitude to Dr. Pam Howitt, a deputy court administrator, who originally asked me to take on the job. Dr. Bernard Gaulier, the chief of the Psychological Clinic at the juvenile court, has been supportive in allowing me to try different therapeutic approaches.

Introduction

One of the reasons I decided to write this book was my son Jason. As I write this today, he is a twenty-one-year-old college student, but once upon a time he was a very stubborn little boy. The degree of frustration and anger he could provoke in all of our family was quite phenomenal—certainly out of proportion to our little boy's size.

As Jason grew up, I was sure that many of the things we did to cope with his often annoying and sometimes downright defiant behavior were wrong and perhaps detrimental to his healthy development. That he survived as well as he did is a tribute to his resilience. However, the etched-in-my-mind mental images of uncooperative behavior and classic battles of wills still have the power to evoke the anger and guilt of so many years ago, and they serve as one of the primary motivations for writing this book.

In this book, I will describe many other recalcitrant, negative, oppositional, and stubborn children and adolescents. Most are just kids struggling with the usual assortment of developmental issues related to autonomy and independence. Too frequently, their attempts to assert themselves were met by parents and teachers who wanted nothing more than for these young people to acquiesce and say yes instead of a perpetual no.

One of the fascinating things about our son was that he didn't talk until he was almost four years of age. From infancy to toddlerhood and through the threes, Jason was a cute, cuddly, compliant, loving child who often seemed more angel than boy.

We worried about his not talking, but once he began to talk, the words came gushing out in phrases and sentences. His mother said he just needed to locate the right password to activate his verbal system. While I'm sure things were a bit more complicated, I'm equally certain he began to talk when he was ready. At four, he was ready.

Once talking, though, he was no longer so easy to get along with. It was as if he had finally decided to go through the terrible twos. And once started on this oppositional phase, he couldn't stop. It continued for several years.

Jason was not at all like my first child, Jill, who was usually enthusiastic and willing to try anything suggested to her. Jason, on the other hand, didn't like anything. He wouldn't agree with anything. He refused everything. If the rest of the family wanted to go to a restaurant, Jason didn't like the one everyone else chose. Once in a restaurant, he could never find any food on the menu that suited him. He would sit sullenly, refusing to eat anything or asking for something that wasn't on the menu or that he knew he couldn't have.

If everyone else wanted to go to the park, Jason wanted to go swimming. If everyone else thought a movie sounded great, Jason hated all movies. If it was time to do some chore like clean his room, Jason wouldn't cooperate. If it was time to get dressed for school, Jason sat on the side of his bed and wouldn't move.

He hated everything—until he tried it. But rather than admit he liked it, he had to maintain a negative attitude about it. No matter what good ideas or amusing suggestions anyone had, Jason would find a way to sabotage each and every one.

This frustrated his mother and me as well as his sister, Jill, who is five years older than he. While Jason dawdled because he didn't want to go wherever we planned to go, Jill was bouncy and ready to start any new, exciting adventure—and she was always confident she would enjoy it. Her attitude, of course, just made Jason more determined to oppose everyone else.

We thought of Jason as a stubborn, oppositional child. Some of us even said those words out loud, sometimes in front of Jason. All that did was make Jason frown and dig in his heels.

The frustration we as parents felt was frequently unbearable. No matter how much time we set aside for Jason to play out his resistance and to pout to his heart's content, it never seemed to be long enough.

When we ran out of time and patience, we did what most parents do when they reach the end of their emotional ropes: we resorted to threats, coercion, or force. Not that these methods worked any better than the others. But they did help us to vent our anger.

Was he deliberately a stubborn child?

No. At least not at first. When I asked Jason about it recently, he remembers very well being the stubborn, go-against-everything child.

"I always wanted to be different," Jason said when I told him I was writing this book. "I think I always wanted to stand out and be the center of attention and be different from Jill."

The way to do that when you had an enthusiastic, agreeable sister was to be the opposite. The problem, however, was that Jason couldn't turn off his disagreeable approach—especially after he tried something he was at first reluctant to attempt and found he liked it. "I wanted to go along with things," Jason recalls, "but it seemed to be the only way I could get attention. So I couldn't admit how much I wanted to say I liked things."

For Jason it wasn't a negative mood or a desire to frustrate his parents. He remembers himself in childhood as being locked in preconceptions. "I had this preconception about something and I would be damned if I was going to do it. I'd just get withdrawn and stubborn even if a part of me knew my attitude and behavior would make it worse."

Did the family, his parents, sister, and grandparents, understand Jason? Certainly not. Did we stop loving him? No, never, although admittedly it was hard at times. Did we mishandle situations? Jason generously says he understands and doesn't remember some of the reactions that even today can cause his parents to feel pangs of guilt and remorse.

As is typical of many second children, Jason often felt he wasn't loved as much as his sister. He says he knew that it really wasn't true that he was loved less, "But for a long time that's what I felt," he recalls.

The discipline methods that we used with him didn't always help him to feel more loved. He recalls the one time when his irritated and pushed-to-the-limit father (that's me) lost his temper. As Jason vividly remembers the incident, which I frankly don't recall at all, it was a trying afternoon for me because Jason balked at everything that was proposed.

We were in the car and I was close to the end of my patience. Finally he pushed me too far and I shouted something like, "Jason, I've had it with you today!" At the same time, I threw my arm across his chest, pinning him back against the car seat next to me.

He says that I didn't hit him, but it was as close as I came at any time in his childhood. He was, at the time, stunned and shocked by the force of my anger.

There was another time that sticks in his memory. This had to do with his grandmother. Like me, she had been pushed until she was at the point of losing it with Jason.

Uncharacteristically for her she angrily confronted him and laid down the law: "I don't care what your daddy lets you do, you are not doing that here!" she said to him in no uncertain terms. Jason swears that he never told her "no" after that.

Despite what may seem like a series of battles with frustrating outcomes caused by Jason's reluctance and rebellion, there were many times we handled Jason in very good, loving, and appropriate ways. Which is why, I think, Jason was able to grow and develop without getting locked into the role of an angry, stubborn, and defiant older child or teenager.

We tried to be fair, for instance. We carefully worked out systems so Jason got to pick where he wanted to go and do what he wanted to do. We were often extremely patient and tolerant as we waited for him to put on his shoes when everyone else was already in the car.

The family also learned to put limits on him when he was at his most stubborn and defiant stages: "If you're not dressed in five minutes, Jason, you will have to go in your pajamas." And when we said that, we stuck to it. There were plenty of mornings Jason went to school in pajamas and stocking feet.

There were also several times he was allowed to sit in restaurants moping because he didn't want to be there. He wasn't forced to eat or even to choose anything from the menu. When we ate out, he sometimes ended up going home without having eaten. Usually no one made a big deal of it.

Despite everything, Jason became a healthy teenager and young adult. While he knows he still has a stubborn streak, it doesn't get in his way too often. In fact, there's a good side to it that I've often marveled at: he sticks to things when others might give up.

For me, the father who became a psychologist, raising Jason made me wonder about stubborn, oppositional children. I've gone on to work with hundreds of stubborn and oppositional children and teenagers since Jason was a four-year-old. The lessons I've learned from Jason and from so many other young people are what I've tried to convey in this book.

I know I could have been more understanding and patient with Jason. But often how well we treat our children is related to how much we know. That children like Jason, and those much worse, are not intentionally and perversely stubborn and obstinate is particularly important for parents to understand.

In Part I of this book, I explain why children are stubborn and why they often go against authority. I also make some observations about the kinds of parents and adults who are most likely to cause children to react in stubborn, negative, and defiant ways.

In Part II, I give an overview of what children are like at each stage of development from the first year of life all the way into adolescence. These chapters describe what you can expect from children at each stage, including the negative and oppositional behavior that normally appears at these stages, and the best ways to handle this age-appropriate behavior. Each of these chapters also describes especially difficult, stubborn, and defiant behaviors, and the methods parents, teachers, and other adults can use to cope with these successfully.

In Part III, I talk about special situations, such as in the classroom or in isolated circumstances, in which young people may exhibit especially stubborn and oppositional behaviors. In each chapter, I make suggestions about the best ways of managing negative behavior to keep it to a minimum and preserve the relationship between adult and child.

Also in Part III, I discuss children and teens who have more serious disorders of defiance. Since many youngsters go from oppositional behavior to much more serious conduct disorders, which include criminal behavior and violence, I make recommendations for dealing with individual young people and also address how we as a society can deal with the growing problem of violence in our young.

My wish for all parents and teachers who read this book is that they have a greater realization that children who exhibit negative and oppositional behavior do so as a normal part of development. The desire to be independent and autonomous is a natural part of human growth. For children to be healthy, well-adjusted adults, it's important that they be allowed to experience this vital part of their development. For it to be a successful part of their growth requires understanding parents and teachers who know the best ways of dealing with the human need all children and adolescents have to be different, to find out who they are, and ultimately to be independent and autonomous individuals.

I hope this book helps in some way toward this end.

PART I

Where Stubborn Children Come From

CHAPTER 1

Children Who Say No When You Want Them to Say Yes

Stubborn, Defiant, and Persistent Children

"My second son went into the terrible twos and never came out of them," a mother I sat next to at a dinner party said to me.

"From age two on, the only thing we got from Seth was, 'No!' He was so different from my other two boys, who were easy to get along with and easy to raise. They usually agreed about most things and would go along with almost anything. But not Seth!"

Ashley's mother had a similar problem. When she brought her twelve-year-old daughter to therapy, she described her as "The Defiant One." And Ashley herself admitted she did almost anything in her power to defy her mother. "If she wants me to be quiet," explained Ashley, "I won't do it. Why should I? If I'm talking on the phone and she wants to know who it is, I'll lie to her. It's none of her business who I'm talking to."

Five-year-old Mikey was described by his parents as a stubborn boy. "No matter how many times you tell him not to do something or even punish him," said his father during a parent training class, "he goes right back and does it again. It's like he's trying to spite me. He's just a very stubborn child."

Of all the complaints of parents, one of the most frequent and frustrating involves the difficulties of handling the stubborn, oppositional, or defiant child.

Trying to handle the resistant youngster often leads to a power struggle between a child determined to do things his way and a parent

3

equally determined to make sure the child complies with family rules or parental directives.

In the Chambers family, six-year-old Susan was the cause of considerable consternation for her mother. "I was wonderful to my son, who's now twelve," said Debby Chambers, Susan's mother, "but I'm terrible to Susan."

During family counseling Debby described to me how she and her daughter yell and scream at each other. Debby often angrily calls Susan "a little shit" or tells her she's "a stubborn brat." Susan, in turn, screams "I hate you!" to her mother.

Susan Chambers is a strong-willed child, according to her mother, and is always determined to get her own way. "If she wants something," said a tearful Debby, "she'll find a way to get it."

The conflicts between Debby Chambers and young Susan come about because the girl dawdles at getting dressed in the morning, doesn't like to wear certain clothes, and insists on going places that her mother won't allow.

And how does Debby Chambers handle her little six-year-old tyrant? When getting angry and screaming at her doesn't work, she often ends up carrying the crying child to her room. "I have to physically carry her while she tries to clutch onto the banister or chairs," said Debby, "I end up spanking her because I can't control my own anger. She's just a very difficult child and I always do everything wrong with her."

In other families such conflicts with stubborn children are played out over eating, bedtime, homework, chores, or rules. And like Debby Chambers, many frustrated parents resort to force, coercion, or physical punishment in an effort to exert their will or to influence their child.

There's nothing like being faced with a three-foot-tall child who folds his arms, squares his jaw, and says, "No!" that enrages parents and tests their own needs for control or domination. Not only do parents who are engaged in this kind of battle feel the strong emotions of frustration, anger, and resentment, they usually end up feeling inadequate and guilty for their thoughts, reactions, or loss of control.

Is All Stubbornness or Defiance Abnormal?

In recent years we've begun to give more attention to stubborn, oppositional, and resistant children because parents and professionals alike understand that such youngsters often develop more difficult problems. Not only does defiance bring about power struggles between parent and child, but such resistant behavior can lead to adolescent psychiatric disorders like Oppositional Defiant Disorder. At this stage the breaking of rules and laws can land the child in juvenile courts and require psychological intervention and treatment.

The truth is, negative and stubborn behavior is normal and appropriate at nearly every stage of development from toddlerhood through adolescence. In early childhood it is characteristic of children trying to learn how to deal with the rules imposed on them, while they struggle at the same time to assert their individuality.

Indeed, all children are stubborn, oppositional, and negative at one time or another. No child would be human if he didn't have his own ideas, thoughts, needs, or desires which have to be asserted once in a while.

Words That Mean Stubborn

As you may have noticed already, I will be using several words to describe the behaviors of children to whom I have given the overall label of "stubborn."

It's been said that the more words a society uses as synonyms, the more important to the society the idea or the thing the word represents. Such seems to be the case with children's stubborn behavior. Think of the words I've used already—oppositional, resistant, defiant, stubborn—and some of the other words that are applied to difficult young people: persistent, contrary, negative, rebellious, insubordinate, obstinate, noncompliant. It seems obvious to me that this behavior must be very important if we have gone to such lengths to invent so many words to describe it.

In this book I define stubborn as having a firm resolve to stick to a course of action or get one's own way. I will use words such as persistent, resistant, obstinate, and defiant to mean the same thing. Persistence can be seen as a mild and sometimes positive form of stubbornness, while defiance will be reserved for more extreme examples of stubborn behavior.

I use some other words, like independent, negative, and oppositional, to describe behavior that goes against what adults desire or society dictates. In its most positive sense, this going against is an assertion of independence and autonomy, qualities that are not just desirable but essential to the development of the individual. The trouble is, children who are striving for independence and autonomy will often do this through negative and contrary words and actions. At certain developmental stages, the child may see this contrariness as the only means at his disposal. This can be very tough on the parent, who is apt to take all of this personally.

Types of Stubborn Behavior

I've worked with difficult and oppositional young people and their parents for more than thirty years. I've also raised a son who, for much of his childhood, was a stubborn and contrary boy. In attempting to make sense of the kinds of stubborn behavior that I've seen in children and teenagers, I've identified various types of stubborn behavior. These categories, I believe, will help parents better understand the sorts of behavior that so often cause frustration. The categories are stage-appropriate opposition; negativism and persistence as a trait of temperament; occasional or situationally dependent oppositional behavior; Oppositional Defiant Disorder; and Conduct Disorder.

In the rest of this chapter I will describe each type of stubborn behavior. In chapters that follow I will tell you how each type of stubborn behavior develops and give you ideas and suggestions for positive discipline techniques to handle each type. There is one exception: I will not be giving recommendations for dealing with conduct-disordered adolescents. Most parents do not face this type of severe problem and so it will not be addressed in this book.

My experience with delinquent teenagers in group therapy over the past few years has given me a veritable laboratory in which to try various techniques and methods. This experience, in addition to my work with parents in discipline training classes, has given me unique opportunities to learn discipline methods and approaches that can help parents and teachers be more effective with difficult youngsters.

Types of Stubborn Behavior

1. Stage-Appropriate Opposition
2. Negativism and Persistence as a Trait of Temperament
3. Occasional or Situationally Dependent Oppositional Behavior
4. Oppositional Defiant Disorder
5. Conduct Disorder

Defining the Types of Stubborn Behavior

Although in later chapters there will be more extensive descriptions of these five categories, I want to give some brief definitions of each of the five types of stubborn behavior here.

Stage-Appropriate Opposition

All children are expected to exhibit negative and oppositional language and behaviors at various times in their development. If they did not, they would not be able to develop into independent individuals with a sense of their own autonomy and uniqueness.

In Part II, I will describe each stage of normal development and point out what kinds of negative and oppositional behaviors you can expect as your child moves toward adolescence and adulthood.

Negativism and Persistence as a Trait of Temperament

Remember six-year-old Susan Chambers and her stubborn fights with her mother? Susan represents a youngster with temperament traits that lead to resistant behavior.

Stella Chess and Alexander Thomas, the authors of several books on temperament (notably *Your Child Is a Person* and *Know Your Child*), have described nine traits of temperament. Temperamental traits are inborn and enduring styles of reacting to our environment that help shape our personalities. Children with certain kinds of temperament styles may come into conflict with their parents with the result that the child acts in stubborn ways.

Susan Chambers's temperament included a sensitivity to touch and the texture of clothes that led her to resist getting dressed. This made her look stubborn and noncompliant to her mother. Other children may be persistent or have difficulty trying out new situations. These traits will frequently lead to conflicts with their parents.

It is important to say at this point that children with difficult temperaments don't have to become disturbed or antisocial youngsters. With proper parenting, hard-to-manage traits can be viewed in more positive ways and these children can be raised so that their once-difficult characteristics are channeled in acceptable directions.

Occasional or Situationally Dependent Stubbornness

Some young people are generally easy to get along with and compliant except for one particular issue. For certain children and teens that issue may be friends, clothing, a boyfriend or girlfriend, hairstyle, religion, or chores. But that one issue seems to represent for the youngster (and sometimes the parent as well) something so powerful that it is an all-consuming point of contention, contrariness, and strong oppositionalism. This will be further discussed in Chapter 14.

Oppositional Defiant Disorder

When children are very stubborn, contrary, and defiant, and this behavior lasts more than a few months as part of a stage, they may be classified as oppositional or as having an Oppositional Defiant Disorder.

In its strictest sense, Oppositional Defiant Disorder (ODD) is a diagnosis that may be determined when a young person (often, but not always, an adolescent) meets certain criteria. These criteria include extreme negative, hostile, and defiant behavior that persists for at least six months. The youngster diagnosed with ODD will display, in exaggerated form, the rebellious and defiant actions usually associated with difficult teenagers—for example, talking back to adult authority figures, insubordination, and failure to obey rules and reasonable commands. Young people with ODD tend to be very argumentative, uncooperative, and disobedient, and may engage in petty delinquent behaviors.

Conduct Disorder

When young people (again especially adolescents) become willfully and repeatedly disobedient and begin engaging in more serious crime and delinquency, they move from the category of Oppositional Defiant Disorder to a category called Conduct Disorder. Adolescents who are diagnosed as having Conduct Disorders almost always gain a police record and may eventually come into the criminal justice system.

The hallmark of conduct disorder is repetitive long-term criminal behavior which is done seemingly without much guilt, conscience, or feelings for the rights of others.

The Use of Power and Force Makes Stubborn and Defiant Behavior Worse

No matter which of the five types of stubborn behavior you are trying to handle, the power struggles that parents often find themselves in can result in unhappiness for both parent and child. Negative and oppositional children fuel the anger and resentment of parents, who in turn may resort to force and a show of strength to resolve the conflict. All children, and in particular very stubborn and oppositional children, dislike force and coercion, even if their behavior or attitude brings it about in the first place.

When handled in forceful or repressive ways, children usually feel mistreated, and they frequently become angrier and yet more obstinate.

Instead of resolving struggles and clashes, the use of coercion, force, or the parent's superior strength is almost always certain to solidify the position of a stubborn child. The end result is likely to be escalating resentment on both sides.

As parents become resentful toward their negative and stubbornly noncompliant children, they hold back love and affection. Their anger, meantime, increases. If they give in to that anger, they are likely to be abusive or harsh toward the child in word or action, only to suffer feelings of guilt about it later. If they stifle their anger, they may lack suitable ways of coping with it as it becomes bottled up and they may be unable to find or even think clearly about more appropriate means of discipline. Therefore, parents of defiant and stubborn children very often sense that they are caught in a desperate, no-win dilemma.

Parents Can Handle Stubborn Children Effectively

The message of this book is that there are effective methods of handling the stubborn and resistant youngster. The discipline methods presented here will help parents to avoid that repetitive and futile battle of wills and find calm, rational ways to deal with children. These strategies are both more effective and less risky than those disciplinary actions frustrated parents often take. They are designed to avoid forcing children into positions where their oppositional and stubborn behavior solidifies and leads to more serious noncompliance later. These disciplinary methods do not lead to abuse, criticism, or other emotional damage. Nor will using them make you feel guilty. You will, instead, find yourself viewing your child's stubbornness in a more positive light.

If you have a stubborn and oppositional child, be just as determined and persistent as he is. But don't expect that I will be advising you to be tough in a cold or uncaring way. That's not what oppositional children need. However, resolve that you will learn positive ways to handle your child to enable him to use his determination in ways that make him more—rather than less—successful.

CHAPTER 2

Why Are Children Stubborn?

Why do children have to be stubborn?

Well, there are a couple of answers. Some children are born that way and others are made to be that way.

But another answer is that children are just human beings trying to deal with life. As a result, sometimes they are oppositional or say no when someone else desperately wants them to say yes; these children are neither born nor made to be stubborn.

I remember a group therapy session I was conducting with about six teenage delinquents on probation to the juvenile court. I had an agenda for our sessions and there was a new boy in the group, Alex Black, age sixteen. Alex was charged with carrying a sawed-off shotgun, which he fully meant to use on another student who had wronged him in some way. Part of my agenda was to have all the group members work on identifying self-defeating behaviors. To assist them in identifying problem areas in their lives, I had a proposed worksheet which I asked all of them to work on.

Everyone, with more or less grumbling, got down to business on the worksheet except for Alex. So I moved into a seat by Alex in our circle, pointed to the page, and directed him to start by printing his name in the designated place.

Alex didn't say anything, but he dropped his pencil. I got firm: "Pick up the pencil and get busy," I said in my best authoritative voice.

Alex looked at me and looked down at the paper and mumbled, "I don't want to."

"I don't care," I replied in measured tones, "but do it anyway."

Alex said, "No!"

I looked around at the group hoping that they weren't listening—or maybe secretly hoping they would jump in and rescue the situation by supporting me. Cindy looked anxious, Rob had a bemused look on his face, and most of the others seemed to be thinking, "Why should we have to do this pukey work if Alex can get away without doing it?"

I was on the spot. I was not sure how far I could push Alex. I also wasn't sure that he didn't have a weapon on him. I couldn't let him get away with this. Yet, I also didn't want to resort to the ways most of these kids' parents would have handled this situation. I was angry that Alex was defying me, and my mind reeled with various possible ways of dealing with this affront to my authority.

"Alex," I finally said, "let's you and me leave the room for a couple of minutes." If I was going to blow this, I thought to myself, better in private rather than in front of the other kids.

How did I handle it?

I'll come back to that later. What's essential right now is that you see the difference between six-year-old Susan Chambers in Chapter 1 and Alex Black in this chapter.

Alex is a well-practiced stubborn boy. He has been diagnosed as having Oppositional Defiant Disorder. He says no to his parents, to teachers, policemen, and kindly group therapists. Going against authority and society is a way of life for him. He was made to be this way. If someone else in his therapy group is talking about being questioned by the police, Alex will jump in and say that if he were in that situation he would "play games" with them. What he means is that he would deny whatever he was accused of for as long as he could. He would also bait the police by being sarcastic and lying. He would recommend—and he has done this—that the police be goaded into hitting him or mistreating him in some way.

Susan Chambers, the contrary and defiant girl who made her mother so angry, is different. She's only six and has had no problems with the police or her teachers, and certainly not with the juvenile court. Nor is she ever likely to. She was born with a temperament featuring persistence and sensitivity. She will always be persistent and determined.

And if her parents learn to consistently use positive discipline methods with her, she will turn out all right.

Unfortunately for the Alexes of this world, many of them will go on to greater problems, and some will end up in prison.

In this chapter, I want to explain how children get to be teenagers like Alex and provide more information about the temperamental styles of children.

Every Child Goes Through Stubborn Stages

Everyone is capable of being stubborn and defiant at one time or another. Try to push anyone around too much and you'll get rebellion. Stubbornness is one of those very human reactions that all of us have resorted to.

It is particularly prevalent at certain ages. Take age two and a half or three, for instance. Stubbornness, defiance, and temper tantrums are part of the "terrible twos." Most new parents dread the fabled terrible twos and threes. That's when children are subject to more rules and regulations, but also have sufficient language skills and motor ability to truly assert themselves for the first time.

For a brief time, little kids put up with bigger and older people telling them what they should and shouldn't do. But as two- or three-year-olds, they have a way of dealing with their parents' rules and efforts to influence their behavior. That way of dealing with the world is achieved mostly through the use of one simple word: "No!"

With the word "no," they can control their lives and get others to react to them. They finally have acquired some power of their own!

And they use it—along with anger, crying, temper tantrums, and just plain stubborn refusals to do what an adult wants them to do. What power! What control! What confusion for parents! That sweet, easy-to-manage little tyke has, with the simple addition of a few words of vocabulary and a surprisingly rigid body and a will of her own, turned the tables on everyone. She can transform a calm parent into a raging maniac. She can frustrate an older sibling. A toddler can, in short, control more of her life. And all by acting stubborn.

Is this normal? Yes it is. Most kids come through the terrible twos and the "I've got a mind of my own" threes with a more tranquil personality at four or five. No one will suffer too much. And through this process, they become more socialized. They come to understand that they must obey some rules, they don't always get their own way, but they do have ways of making the world stop and pay attention to them.

If a child continues to act like an impudent two- or three-year-old after this age, she is usually said to be spoiled or to be a brat. No one will like her all that much and she will be difficult to get along with.

And the terrible twos tend to be repeated in early to mid-adolescence because young people have a need to exert their own opinions and needs as well as to define further who they are. When a teenager refuses to go to the family church or puts up a fuss about going on those visits to the relatives, or when she stubbornly refuses to support a parental position, she is letting others know that she has her own ideas about things. Again, this isn't abnormal. It's only a normal part of growing up and developing into an adult.

Some Children Are Temperamentally Stubborn

There's more to it, however, than just growing up and developing as an individual. Some children are born stubborn.

Of course, we don't call them stubborn. It's more appropriate to call them persistent. That's the accepted term for a trait of temperament that describes a child who is not likely to accept the word no easily or to stop something once started.

Because of the research of Chess and Thomas, who were mentioned in Chapter 1, temperament has assumed tremendous importance in increasing our understanding of children and teenagers.

A temperament is an inborn, enduring trait. Persistence is one of nine traits of temperament that Chess and Thomas identified, based on their studies. The others are Adaptability, Activity, Mood, Regularity, Distractibility, Intensity, Sensory Threshold, and Approach-Withdrawal.

Children, we now know, are born with greater or lesser degrees of persistence. A highly persistent child will continue an activity in the face of obstacles or difficulty. A child with low persistence gives up easily. Stanley Turecki, the author of *The Difficult Child,* has said that difficult children are a problem to manage because of negative persistence.

A negatively persistent youngster, writes Turecki, who studied with Chess and Thomas, is a "stubborn, strong-willed child with very definite preferences." Once such a child becomes used to things being a certain way, she doesn't want change. Turecki wrote: "She seems rigid and gets 'locked in'; . . . and when she wants something, she goes on nagging or whining if she doesn't get it."

There is a positive side to persistence, too. Young people like Susan Chambers stay with activities and interests for a long time. This can be a blessing for parents. But it's good for the child, too. Like my son Jason, they may keep practicing a sport or a hobby; they persist in the face of obstacles. They are not easily put off by detours and roadblocks. This can spell the difference between failure and success.

I was visiting a family recently and I saw a young, persistent child in action. Although my visit had been anticipated and announced, young Aaron Freeborn, age four, was not about to be interrupted. He was playing Nintendo in the living room.

The problem was that his mother had been playing with him before I arrived. She told him she would have to talk with me; he could go on playing by himself or do something else until I left and she could rejoin the game of Super Mario.

But Aaron couldn't deal with this. Although his mother was talking to me in the next room, Aaron constantly called to her and asked for some form of attention. "Ma, come and look what I did." "Ma, when are you coming back to play with me?" "Ma, come quick. Look what I did."

His mother quickly wearied of his frequent interruptions and said with increasing irritation, "I'm busy, Aaron" or "Just a minute, Aaron, I'm talking."

Aaron was not to be put off so easily. He was not going to give up his position at the TV to one of the other children, and he was persistent in trying to summon his mother away from the guest and back to the video game.

His mother finally began to talk about Aaron. "He's the most stubborn kid I ever saw," she said. "He won't give up for nothing."

And she was right. At four, Aaron was a master of the video game, which I found out as he came to the dining room to begin tugging on his mother's sleeve and I engaged him in conversation. His persistence made him good at the game. But his persistence was negative as he was locked—in this instance—in to getting his mother away from the guest and back to the video game.

How can you tell if your child has a stubborn, persistent temperament? By looking at the way she approaches life and asking questions about her and her behavior starting from infancy.

1. Does she have difficulty giving up or backing down?
2. Does she stick with things that would cause other children to give up in frustration?
3. Does she insist on her own way no matter how many times she's told no?
4. Has she always been a resistant or defiant child?
5. Has she always been a child who's had her own ideas about what she wants?

If you answer yes to all of these questions, there's a good chance your youngster has high persistence as a trait of temperament. Knowing this gives you the knowledge and ability to deal better with her.

How do you best handle a child or teen with persistence as a temperamental trait? This will be part of the discussion in each of the chapters in Part Two.

Some Children Are Made to Be Defiant

But first, let's see what causes children to become stubborn and defiant.

Joe Graham may have been born with a persistent temperament. Whether he was or not, he has been made into a stubborn teenager. His mother calls him hardheaded, and his junior high counselor referred to him as pigheaded. In fact, as I got to know Joe, who is fourteen, I thought of the humorous song Woody Herman sang in the 1940s, "Caldonia, Caldonia, what makes your big head so hard?"

If his mother left Joe a note before she went to work asking him to do some chores when he came home from school, Joe would decide not to do them. When his mother came home and asked him, "How come you didn't do the dishes like I asked?" Joe would reply, "Because I didn't feel like it" or "Because I didn't want to."

That was his standard answer at home and at school: "I didn't want to."

Once, when Joe had too many detentions and had walked out of his math class after sassing a teacher, the assistant principal told Joe that he would have to serve an in-school suspension. That meant that Joe would spend the next day sitting in a quiet room without talking to anyone else, with nothing but work from his classes to occupy his time.

Joe's response was, "I won't do it."

When he went home from school that night, he told his mother to call the assistant principal and "do something" because he would not serve an in-school suspension.

The next day, Mrs. Graham accompanied Joe to the school and went directly to the assistant principal's office. Mrs. Dutton and Mrs. Graham talked for a long time. When they came out of the office, they told Joe there was no choice. He had to serve the in-school suspension.

"I'm not going to," said Joe.

"Then you'll be in worse trouble," said Mrs. Dutton.

"I'll have to call your dad," said his mother.

"I don't care," said Joe.

His father was called and, a busy man at his office, was miffed at this interruption. He asked to talk to his son. "Joe, you know I'm busy at work and I can't be interrupted for this stuff. Stop being stubborn and serve the suspension. It's not that hard and it certainly won't kill you."

"No!" said Joe.

His father's blood boiled rather quickly. "You better do this or you'll have to deal with me," said his father sternly.

Joe hung up on him.

Later, Joe said that he was being hardheaded because he didn't want to be isolated in an in-school suspension. In situations when he doesn't want to do something, he says, "I just keep going until I get my way." He said he would never give in unless the consequences were too serious; then he might back down, but he would be very angry about it.

Although Joe may have started out in life with a somewhat persistent temperament, the difference between a youngster becoming oppositional and defiant and one who is able to channel his persistence into positive areas has to do with the quality of parenting.

In particular, it has to do with the consistency of parents in handling the difficult, demanding behaviors of persistent youngsters in positive ways, while avoiding excessive criticism, giving in to the child, or extreme and harsh punishment.

Joe Graham had an inconsistent mother who was not able to be firm and positive with Joe's persistence, a father who only interacted with Joe when punishment or sternness was to be meted out, and two parents who resorted to physical punishment and verbal abuse.

Harsh Discipline of a Difficult Temperament Creates Opposition

Stubborn and oppositional children are not a recent invention. The term "strong-willed child" may not have been used before the twentieth century, but there have always been children throughout history who irritated and frustrated their parents.

We know this because the Bible and the early Greek writers make references to stubborn children. It was no accident that "Honor thy father and thy mother" was among God's Ten Commandments. Clearly, there were disrespectful and defiant children and youth in biblical times.

Many methods have been proposed down through the years to handle the most recalcitrant of children. But there is no research that shows that spanking or harsh corporal punishment is a magical answer. Research, on the contrary, tends to show just the opposite. Harsh, punitive handling of difficult young children tends to increase stubborn behavior.

Rolf Loeber, Ph.D., is a psychological researcher with the Western Psychiatric Institute and Clinic of the School of Medicine at the University of Pittsburgh in Pennsylvania. He has been studying disruptive and delinquent young people for many years. Thanks to his pioneering research we have a new understanding of stubborn children. Disruptive children, Loeber writes in various research reports, show patterns of oppositional behavior and conduct problems. These behaviors can range from the defiance of young children to the more delinquent and violent behavior of disordered adolescents.

Over the last several years Loeber has considered how children get on pathways that take them to more serious misbehavior. Noting that other researchers had divided disruptive and delinquent youngsters into aggressive and nonaggressive types, Loeber and his associates built on this distinction to identify three pathways that lead to disruptive behavior problems of children and teens.

And interestingly, the starting point of one of his pathways is stubborn behavior. Loeber calls this the Authority Conflict Pathway. Stubborn behaviors, according to Loeber, often start by age three—although sometimes as late as age thirteen—and have a median starting age of nine. Loeber found an escalation pattern that begins with stubbornness, proceeds to defiance, and ends with avoiding authority. Stubborn children consolidate their position on the pathway to seriously disruptive behavior by being defiant (that is, by doing things their own way, refusing to do what their parents want them to do, and being generally disobedient), and avoiding authority (by coming home late and running way).

In adolescence, then, children who have previously exhibited stubbornness, defiance, and avoidance of authority often become difficult to handle and frequently are diagnosed as having Oppositional Defiant Disorder. This behavior can lead to conflict outside of the home with teachers and school authorities, the police, or the juvenile court authorities. Children on the Authority Conflict Pathway are usually not as disruptive or disordered as young people on Loeber's other two pathways (the Covert Pathway, which starts with lying and shoplifting and leads eventually to larceny, stealing, and breaking and entering, or the

Overt Pathway, which begins with aggression and leads ultimately to violence against others in the form of assaults, rape, or even murder). But these youngsters are still at considerable risk for crossing over onto one of the other pathways and ending up in more criminal behavior.

We don't have all the answers yet about how children are maintained on one of the pathways or how they get off a pathway and avoid serious behavior problems. The indications are, however, that stubborn children (children who are temperamentally difficult from birth) who receive positive parenting avoid becoming more stubborn and oppositional. Children who are subjected to inconsistent, negative, or harsh discipline become more disruptive and difficult to handle as they get older.

Pathways from Stubborn to Serious Behavior Disorders

Pathway #1. Authority Conflict Pathway: Stubbornness → Defiance → Avoiding Authority

Pathway #2. Covert Pathway: Lying and Shoplifting → Larceny, Stealing, Breaking and Entering

Pathway #3. Overt Pathway: Aggression → Violence Against Others → Assaultive Behaviors

---

Some Children Will Be Stubborn When Their Needs Aren't Met

Valerie Bergin, at eleven, was referred to the school psychologist for an evaluation because she was refusing to do her schoolwork and her teacher couldn't understand why a capable girl would refuse to do any work.

It didn't take the psychologist long to get an answer once she'd given Valerie an intelligence test. Valerie had a very high IQ, and obviously found the work too easy and well below her capabilities. Instead of just compliantly going along and doing the simple worksheets that all the other kids in her fifth-grade class were doing without protest, Valerie dug in her heels and in effect said, "No way! I'm not going to do this boring work anymore."

"Valerie belonged in a gifted class and should never have been given the uncreative worksheets," the psychologist concluded. "It was a crime to force her to sit in a dull class being treated like a robot."

Kids whose needs are not being met react by getting very stubborn and digging their heels in, as Valerie did, while giving the impression of acting in a very defiant way. It's the only way some children and teens can react to a school or home system that does not understand their needs.

Valerie Bergin and Joe Graham, the boy who refused to serve his in-school suspension, represent two very different kinds of young people. Both have been characterized as stubborn and defiant, but diverse circumstances brought about their behavior. For Joe, it was having one parent who was inconsistent and unable to react to him in the same way day after day, and another parent who most often used threats, force, and harsh punishments when he was growing up. Neither parent seemed—at least to Joe—to be truly responsive to how he felt about things.

For Valerie, defiant behavior came about because she was misplaced and misunderstood at school.

Both Joe Graham and Alex Black, the boy in my group who refused to do his worksheet, can be diagnosed as having an Oppositional Defiant Disorder. Children with this disorder commonly are argumentative with adults, frequently lose their temper and swear, and are angry, resentful, and easily annoyed by others. They will actively defy adults' requests or rules, deliberately annoy others, and blame others for their own mistakes or problems.

Some preschoolers and elementary school children may be diagnosed as having Oppositional Defiant Disorder. Such children are often referred to as "spoiled brats." They have frequent temper tantrums when they don't get their own way. Such children are likely to be verbally abusive ("You're mean!" "I hate you!" "I wish you were dead!") and to use screaming and anger as a veritable weapon to gain an advantage in power struggles with their parents or other authorities.

Family Patterns Common in Young People with Serious Defiant Behavior

Certain family patterns of interaction and parent discipline seem to be present in the backgrounds of children identified as having an Oppositional Defiant Disorder. They are also present in youngsters with a conduct disorder, a more serious diagnostic category given to children and teenagers who act out with more serious violations of rules, laws, and standards of behavior.

Some of the family interaction patterns that are typically seen with ODD types of kids are the following:

- Poor ability by the parents to provide appropriate consequences for both bad and good behavior.
- Poor ability by the parents to be consistent in responding to the behavior of children.
- Harsh and punitive discipline, often including physical punishment.
- Poor use of communication skills in responding to and being supportive of their children.

In addition to these factors, parents of oppositional and defiant youngsters often have considerable pressure and stress in their lives. Frequently they are depressed. These factors make it extremely difficult for them to respond in calm, patient, and consistently appropriate ways to the needs and the demands of their children.

The findings of research projects confirm these factors in the ways parents and society produce Oppositional Defiant Disorder children and teenagers. But I've seen them, too, in my direct contact with delinquent adolescents. One curious statement I have heard many times from young people in my therapy groups is that the way I (or my co-therapists) treat them seems fake. This puzzled me for a while, but I finally figured out what it meant.

I usually try to treat the kids I work with in a kind, patient, and responsive way. I try to understand how they feel and attempt to be nonjudgmental. However, this is usually so foreign to their experience that they just can't believe anyone could really respond to them in this way.

That was true of Alex Black. You recall from earlier in this chapter that Alex began to show his usual defiance and resistance to me in a group therapy session. How did I handle it when I took him in another room?

Alex was expecting strong-arm tactics. He was ready and he knew how to handle that sort of discipline. But that's not the approach I used. Instead, I asked him if he just didn't want to do the work on that day. He said yes, that was the case: he did not want to do the assigned work. I told him in my typically calm and controlled manner (which sometimes belies what I really feel) that that was okay. He didn't have to do the assignment.

"But you can't attend my group today and not do what everyone else is doing," I added. "So that means you have a choice. You can go home early and try again next week, or you can return to the group and do what everyone else is doing. It's up to you."

"But you'll tell my probation officer and I'll get in trouble," Alex said.

"No, I won't do that," I replied. "I'll give you a break on one condition."

"What's that?" he asked, looking at me suspiciously.

"That you take the work home and work on it this week and bring it back for the next group session."

He thought about it for a couple of seconds and agreed.

The upshot? That was the last instance of direct defiance from Alex in group therapy. I was very surprised that he became one of the better members of my group over the next few months! That didn't mean he stopped being stubborn, oppositional, and defiant in other areas of his life, however.

He still delighted in telling the group how he defied his parents and his teachers. He knew, though, that in my therapy group, he would have choices and I would be responsive to his needs. He didn't have to be resistant or defiant in that setting.

This will be one of the themes of this book. When youngsters deal with responsive adults who are concerned about their needs and feelings, when they are presented with choices, when they are allowed to make up their own minds, and when adults respond without force or coercion, then there is a much better chance that they will make reasoned and reasonable decisions.

Summary

Children display stubborn behavior for one of three reasons:

1. **The behavior is stage- or age-appropriate.**
2. **The behavior is related to a persistent or more difficult temperament.**
3. **The behavior is the result of inconsistent and harsh parenting.**

Factors in the family that lead to more stubborn and resistant behavior are:

- **Parents who fail to provide appropriate consequences for noncompliant behavior.**
- **Parents who do not provide appropriate feedback for compliant behavior.**
- **Parents who are not consistent in responding to the behavior of children.**
- **Parents who use harsh and punitive discipline methods.**
- **Parents who exhibit poor communication skills in responding to the behavior of their children.**

CHAPTER 3

How to Make Stubborn Children

In Mark Devlin's perceptive and evocative memoir called *Stubborn Child*, he details the events in his own life that led to his being labeled a stubborn child. The horrific experiences of Devlin's developing years, in which he was beaten by his father and stepfather, provide a classic first-person account of how a somewhat difficult child is made into a juvenile delinquent.

All along the way, Devlin encounters adults who provide little if any protection, very little support, and a great deal of punitive discipline, which literally creates a scared, insecure, oppositional, and defiant boy.

Devlin's autobiography indicts parental and adult mistreatment of children in a way that shows clearly how a bright, curious, innocent child can be transformed into a criminal by the age of thirteen.

While Devlin's life was extraordinary in that there was much drunken abuse by parents and brutal scapegoating and mistreatment by nearly every adult he encountered, other children who are subjected to much less can become stubborn, defiant, and resistant.

How can you make children stubborn? It's not all that difficult, as this chapter will show. Parents, teachers, and other authority figures can manufacture an oppositional and defiant child through improper discipline, harsh methods of control, and consistently nonresponsive ways of dealing with children.

Who are the adults who cause children to be stubborn, oppositional, and defiant? They are parents, for one, who manifest certain types of parental behavior. Two main kinds of parenting styles lead to stubborn children:

1. Parents who lack the understanding to respond adequately to children.
2. Parents who use ineffective responses when their children misbehave.

Parents Who Lack the Understanding to Respond Adequately to Children

I'll stress this again and again in this book: Children need responsive parents. When children feel parents and other adults are unresponsive to their needs and feelings, they become angry and resentful. And one of the primary ways children react to an unresponsive world is through stubborn, contrary, and oppositional behavior.

When parents have poor training or inadequate instincts to manage children effectively, they often resort to discipline methods that increase noncompliant and stubborn behavior.

Children, seemingly by nature, try to avoid the unpleasant, the boring, the banal, and the undesired. Parents must be ready for this and be able to respond in helpful, supportive, and appropriate ways. But parents who have poor aptitudes or poor training for parenting often respond in such a way that children become more noncompliant and stubborn.

Some examples of parental discipline that tend to increase stubbornness include nagging, arguing, yelling, and threatening; giving in to the unreasonable demands of children; and using reinforcement in the wrong way.

Gerald R. Patterson, a psychological researcher, has termed the negative interactions that go on between parents and their stubborn and often aggressive children as "coercive" behaviors. Coercive actions—threats, verbal criticism, nagging, and yelling—are both unpleasant and ineffective. They do not stop unwanted behaviors such as crying, whining, arguing, aggression, yelling, and throwing tantrums. Coercive actions by parents, in fact, frequently lead only to more noncompliant and aggressive behavior.

On the other hand, when such coercive methods are used by demanding and insistent youngsters against their parents, they are often "successful." That is, these behaviors often enable children to avoid doing what they're supposed to do.

One consequence of ineffective parenting is that children get rewarded for not following directions and requests, and for disobeying rules and commands. When they are able to do so without experiencing negative consequences, they are actually learning to be noncompliant.

Here's an example that illustrates what often happens in my office when parents bring in oppositional children for treatment:

Five-year-old Bradley Conners is brought to the psychologist because he doesn't mind, sasses his mother, and is aggressive toward his mother and his kindergarten teacher. He refuses to accompany me into the office, and says very loudly in the waiting room, "I won't go unless you do, Mommy."

Mrs. Conners agrees to come along, saying that she will only stay for a few minutes, at which time Bradley must stay and talk to the psychologist by himself.

Things go well in the office until it's time for his mother to leave. Then Bradley's face takes on a darker, different look and he asks his mother to stay. She says she must go because it's Bradley's turn to talk alone with the psychologist. Bradley doesn't listen to his mother's explanations, and begins to dig in his heels; arguing, whining, and cajoling. His mother begins to try her version of reasoning to convince him it will be all right. "Why don't you want me to leave?" she asks.

When her questions produces no reasonable answers, Mrs. Conners makes a stab at guessing the problem: "What are you afraid of?" she asks.

Bradley does not identify a fear and simply reiterates that he doesn't want her to leave. Mrs. Conners is persistent, though. Attempting to be a good, responsive mother, she asks him again, "What are you afraid of?" and then reassures him that she will be in the waiting room.

"You know I love you," she tells him. "I won't ever leave you."

Bradley just becomes more angry, defiant, and resistant. He tries to block the door and shouts that she cannot leave. When she tries to brush him aside, he hits her. She gets angry, her voice gets higher and shriller, and she tells him it's wrong to hit and he can't get his way by hitting. The next step is to threaten Bradley with dire consequences about what won't happen on the way home ("We're not going to stop and buy bagels now. You aren't acting nice. You're being very spiteful!"). None of her remarks have much effect on Bradley. He doesn't want his mother to leave.

While Bradley's mom is trying to be a supportive, loving, and responsive mother, it becomes clear in this interaction that Bradley has been through this kind of situation with her many times. Her attempts to persuade him to be reasonable are not effective ways to deal with Bradley. Nor are her threats. He has learned that his stubborn and resistant behavior leads his mother to respond in ways that accomplish something very important: He can waste lots of time by being the center of attention and all the while avoid what he doesn't want to have happen; that is, in this instance, for his mother to leave the room.

It may not look like a fun or rewarding way to interact with his mother, but in his eyes he is avoiding the unpleasant.

In the long run, the real problem is that parents like Mrs. Conners don't really understand children like Bradley. She doesn't understand his temperament, his need for firm and consistent directions, or his manipulation of her through his oppositional maneuvers. He may have fears, but it's the wrong time and place to drag out this possibility for discussion. In short, Mrs. Conners does not have a grasp of what leads to his stubborn and defiant behavior. Nor does she see that her inconsistent giving in to his coercive behaviors over and over again in the past has created this situation.

Parents Who Use Ineffective Responses to Noncompliance

Many parents are responsive and may even have a fairly good ability to understand children and relate well to them. Yet, when their children are stubborn, oppositional, rebellious, or assert their independence in negative ways, these parents may use ineffective or poor discipline methods.

Josh Pointer's parents provide an example of this problem. At fourteen years of age, Josh sometimes displays disrespectful, disobedient, and aggressive behavior. Not only are his parents' ways of dealing with him ineffective, they tend to reinforce Josh's worst behaviors.

On the other hand, when things are going well in the Pointer family, Josh will look after and protect his younger sister, he and his mother work together productively on his homework, and there is a great deal of good-natured kidding. However, this friendly atmosphere can change rapidly when Josh fails to follow a request or live up to a rule or standard. For example, when his father found that Josh was throwing cigarette butts out his bedroom window (in order to hide them from his parents), his parents went ballistic.

"We told you to stop smoking," his mother shouted. "Now what are you trying to do, burn the house down? What are we going to find out next? That you're smoking marijuana?"

"Maybe we should take you for a drug test," his father said. "We can't trust you so how do we know you don't smoke dope?"

As they continued to rail against Josh's behavior, their attempts to handle this situation led to an escalation. "We're warning you, Josh," his father shouted, "if I ever see another cigarette butt outside your window, I'm calling the police. As far as I'm concerned, you tried to burn down the house."

"You're incorrigible," his mother said, getting close to Josh and pointing a finger at him. "Incorrigible children belong in a juvenile home. Is that where you want to go? If it is, that's where we'll send you if you keep disobeying us."

Josh's parents ended the tirade by grounding him for two weeks "to teach you a lesson and let you know how it would be if you were locked up." At other times these kinds of angry interactions led to shoving and hitting. Josh once threatened his mother with a butcher knife and tried to hit his father with a baseball bat.

Usually, though, as Josh's parents began using warnings, threats, and punishment, they escalated their performance beyond the merely ineffective to downright reinforcing while displaying their own form of aggression.

Parents like Mr. and Mrs. Pointer who make repeated threats and warn of terrible consequences when "disciplining" ("If you don't start minding, we're calling the police"; "If you keep talking back to me, you can find another place to live"; "If you leave this house after I tell you you're grounded, you can just keep going because you're not welcome back here") are setting up their child for misbehavior. These coercive methods invite disobedience. That disobedience, in turn, increases parental frustration and the emotional intensity of subsequent parent-child interactions increases. In this escalation of intensity, the parents, out of frustration, impatience, and ignorance about what else to do, often resort to those threats, warnings, and predictions of dire consequences that have little meaning and often are not carried out.

These are among the coercive behaviors Patterson describes. Sometimes parents do follow through with such threats or warnings, or, perhaps worse, they back down and give in to the child. One way that parents give in is by allowing the child to conclude the interaction without fully complying with the original task or command. "Okay, just pick up your clothes for tonight. Tomorrow you can finish your room"; "Just read part of the chapter and then you can watch television" are typical outcomes.

This is how "spoiled brats" usually get their training.

Twelve-year-old Ashley, whom I mentioned in Chapter 1 and who was called "The Defiant One" by her mother, provides another example of a difficult and persistent child. Ashley has learned that if she keeps pushing, her parents will give in. When she wanted something as a preschooler, even if her mother or father had determined that she was not to have it, she kept asking, begging, and intimidating her parents for so long they would finally give in and let her have it. A favorite remark of her father's was, "Let her have it so she doesn't throw a temper tantrum again."

That's the intimidation factor of persistent and intense youngsters who employ their own coercive tactics. Their methods work and their parents often feel powerless to control them. Even if the parents of such children decide to use time-out, for example, as a consequence or punishment, they quickly conclude—as Ashley's parents did—that "Time-out won't work with Ashley" because she wouldn't stay in the time-out chair.

When children intimidate or terrorize parents to this extent, they have succeeded in calling the shots in the home. This means that they don't have to mind or obey rules. They can avoid being responsible and ignore requests or commands. Because they do not face effective consequences for their misbehaviors, they are not trained to do those things that are necessary but seem to them to be unpleasant.

What are the chances of this behavior being repeated many times in the future? Very high!

Parents who are raising temperamentally difficult children must have training and exposure in productive and constructive parenting methods specifically designed to reduce oppositional and defiant behavior.

The Temperament of Parents as a Complicating Factor

When a parent's own temperament is one that features impulsivity, intensity, persistence, or other traits similar to the difficult temperament of the child, the stage is set for a battle royal that can lead to some of the harmful and self-defeating behaviors parents resort to.

The parent who is impulsive, persistent, and distractible will often appear to a child as unresponsive. Such behavior suggests the parent does not understand a child's needs.

Parents with a difficult temperament themselves tend to be inconsistent, impulsive, and hostile with their difficult children. Such parental styles, especially in attempting to discipline a child, are the exact opposite of what difficult children need. Difficult and stubborn children require patience, firmness, consistency, and loving kindness. These disciplinary approaches are possible no matter what the temperament of a parent. It just requires more determination on the part of parents with such temperaments to keep their own personality and traits under control.

The Role of Stress as a Further Complicating Factor

The role of stress, which I will mention from time to time because of its importance in parenting, is a significant factor when it comes to adult and parental management of children, especially more persistently oppositional youngsters.

Frequent or chronic stress in the family may well lead to inconsistency in the discipline of children. Inconsistency is one of those things that make children more stubborn and noncompliant. When the stress level is high in the family, children are less calm, less able to obey or even hear rules and requests, and less likely to be able to concentrate on complying with their parents.

High stress is upsetting for both parents and children. It leads parents to be short on patience and unable to follow through on requests and commands. It also almost always means inconsistency. That is, parents are more likely to act in different ways on different days depending on what the level of stress is on that particular day. When the stress thermometer is high, parents may yell, criticize, and nag. They may also fail to punish or reprimand inappropriate behavior. On the other hand, when the stress reading is low, the same parents may act in more consistent, positive ways, and use appropriate discipline. For children, this can be highly confusing. The less predictable a child's world, the more anxious and unpredictable the child.

What Can Parents Do to Avoid Fostering Stubbornness?

There are several things parents can do to avoid encouraging stubbornness in children.

1. **Learn to understand what children need.**

   The better you understand child psychology and child development, the better prepared you will be to respond effectively to youngsters. The greater your understanding of what children need at every age and stage of development, the easier it will be to anticipate what your child requires and how he can best be handled.

2. **Learn effective discipline and child management techniques.**

   The more you know about how properly to discipline children, the less likely you will be to raise stubborn and resistant children. Several chapters in this book give you detailed recommendations and instructions for discipline that is effective. Also, the list of readings at the end of this book suggests other books you might want to consult for advice in the use of discipline.

3. **Do not reinforce children's defiant, stubborn, and noncompliant behavior.**

   That means using appropriate discipline methods when children behave in these ways. Make sure that you are not reinforcing their worst behavior under the guise of being loving, responsive, kind, or reassuring. The chapters on dealing with children in the age ranges from two through five will give more explicit information about how to avoid accidentally reinforcing stubborn and resistant behavior.

4. **Use commands and requests in appropriate ways and don't repeat them or nag.**

   Repeating requests and commands leads children to avoid an appropriate, compliant response. Chapter 13 discusses requests and commands that tend to produce more compliant, less stubborn behavior. (There is, however, one exception. That is the use of the broken record technique, discussed in Chapter 8, in which you repeat a request so that you are not pushed into nagging, arguing, or giving in.)

5. **Understand your child's temperament.**

   Once you understand that your child has a difficult temperament, you must then learn ways to handle such a child that will reduce the frequency of his difficult behavior rather than increase it. Each of the following chapters will discuss how to handle more difficult behavior at various ages.

6. Understand your own temperament.

If you yourself have traits of temperament that either are similar to your child's or lead you to be less patient and understanding than you should be, you are likely to respond according to your own temperament rather than according to what is best for your child. Once you understand your own temperament and recognize how it affects your interactions with your child, you will be able to change some of your less effective disciplinary strategies—especially those that are not in the best interests of your youngster.

7. Keep the stress level down in your family.

Because chronic and frequent stress leads to inconsistency on the part of parents and higher anxiety levels for children, you should do your best to learn to recognize when the stress level is high in the home. When the stress level is high, work at reducing it and keeping it under control. You will be a more effective parent and your children are more likely to be calmer and more compliant when stress is under control.

Summary

There are certain traits and behaviors of parents and other adults who care for children and young people which have a greater tendency to result in stubborn, noncompliant, and resistant behavior.

Two main types of parental behavior lead to stubborn and oppositional children. They are:

1. A lack of understanding about how to respond adequately to children.

2. The use of ineffective responses to noncompliance by children.

Parents who have poor training or inadequate instincts to understand what children need will often respond in inadequate ways. This will increase noncompliant and stubborn behavior.

Coercive, threatening, or punitive responses to children's oppositional or negative behaviors are ineffective. These responses tend to reinforce children's most oppositional behaviors.*

If parents learn more about the temperamental traits of their children and themselves, they will be more likely to handle their children in consistent and appropriate ways.

Parents can avoid fostering or exacerbating oppositional, defiant, and stubborn behavior by:

- Learning more about child psychology and the developmental needs of children.
- Learning effective discipline and child management techniques.
- Taking care not to reinforce children's defiant, stubborn, and noncompliant behavior.
- Using commands and requests in appropriate ways, without repeating them or nagging.
- Understanding your child's temperament.
- Keeping the stress level down in your home.

---

* Several discipline techniques will be mentioned or discussed in greater detail throughout this book. Readers are referred to Appendix A for more in-depth descriptions of these discipline methods.

PART II

Understanding and Disciplining Children

CHAPTER 4

Understanding and Disciplining the Infant

The Infant

At seven weeks of age, Emily Yeacker sleeps most of the time. When she awakens from a long nap, her diaper is wet and she's hungry. If she's not fed fairly quickly, she will begin fussing.

While being fed, she looks in her mother's eyes and there's a special kind of communication that takes place between them. At times when she is alert and not suckling, she smiles. And for the first time her parents think she is smiling because she recognizes their faces. In a couple more weeks, they will know this for sure.

For now, they are content to make sure she is fed when she's hungry, her diapers are changed when wet, and she gets lots of holding and rocking.

After her feeding is ended, Emily is held up to her mother's shoulder and gently patted until she burps. In a little while she starts to doze and then nods off for another nap.

At times when she's awake and alert she seems to be following movement. Her father says that she now sees things in her room beyond her crib—such as a bright picture of a clown on her wall.

Give Emily another month and she will be able to hold her head erect with more strength and be able to grasp objects, like a rattle, for more than a few seconds. She'll also make sounds when her mother talks to her or her father sings to her. By six months she will sit up when held, her hair will have grown in, and she'll be capable of rolling from one side over to the other.

When she's nine months of age, Emily will be on her way toward greater independence. She'll sit without support, be able to crawl comfortably around a room, and may even be able to pull herself up to a standing position—although she may not know quite how to get down again.

At birth the only sounds Emily could manage were her cries. By the time she is closing on her twelfth month, she will have mastered some basic steps in her language skills. Her vocabulary will be three very important words: "mama," "da," and "bye." She will be ready to communicate with her other people.

Not that she hasn't understood a lot for several months. After all, at seven weeks old she can already tell the difference between the emotions expressed by different tones of voices. When infancy comes to an end, when she's one, Emily will have learned to listen to people talking to her. She will have learned to make different sounds. And she will begin to connect meanings with words. With communication skills will come a greater ability to learn.

Handling the Opposition of the Infant

Can a child as young as a few months actually be stubborn and show her individuality?

If you ask this question, either you haven't had children yet or you haven't tried feeding baby food to an infant.

When my friend Mary's son Broc was about five months old, she began feeding him baby food. Broc liked bananas and peas, but not green beans.

"The first time he tasted green beans," Mary recalls, "he spit them back at me. There were green beans all over the tray of his high chair. By the time we were done he had green beans on me, on the floor, and in his hair." From that point on, whenever Mary tried to feed green beans to Broc, he'd scrunch up his face and turn his head away, refusing to open his mouth.

As Mary's experience illustrates, children around the fourth or fifth month are quite capable of displaying streaks of temper, negativism, and even a little stubbornness. Of course, no infant acts this way with malice. When infants fuss or show negativism, they are trying to communicate through the only means they have. They may, like Broc, twist away, go rigid, cry, or even scream.

Providing the Three Aspects of Love

There are three aspects of showing love as the parent of an infant that are important in establishing a close, trusting relationship with your baby. The first and most obvious aspect of love has to do with *comfort*. You can make sure your baby not only is healthy but also thrives and grows at an optimal pace by offering something that most mothers and fathers of infants do quite naturally. That is, you make the baby comfortable. You do this, in one way, when you take care of her physical needs and make sure she is properly fed, clothed, and bathed. But taking care of the baby's emotional needs is just as important. This means holding her when she cries, comforting her when she is frustrated or angry, and laughing, smiling, and talking with her.

The second aspect concerns *stimulation*. Healthy, alert infants respond to being held, talked to, and sung to. They thrive in an atmosphere rich in human contact and plenty of stimulation. Your role as a parent is to see to it that the infant's environment is stimulating, interesting, and appropriate for her developmental level. But there is more to do during the first year of life than just the teaching of new words, new activities, new tasks, and new play. You can stimulate growth by designing an environment that is not only safe but challenging. A challenging environment is one in which your baby has opportunities to move around and explore her world while getting acquainted with as much as possible.

Infants have greater ability to learn—starting from birth—than we ever thought. In the first few weeks of life, babies can memorize objects—certainly faces—and they have the ability to visually track movements. They check out their surroundings and in those early weeks of life gradually look for more complex stimulation.

One of the best ways to promote an infant's intellectual and emotional development is to provide appropriate, supervised toys, play, and activities in an atmosphere of loving acceptance and encouragement. Even the young infant, under three months of age, can benefit from an environment rich in color, sounds, smells, tastes, and things to touch.

And even though you may have a busy schedule or overwhelming demands coming from many directions, you need to take the time to make sure you are providing many opportunities to promote your baby's interest in learning during the first year. This is the age when everything is new and every experience involves some learning, whether it's her bath, being breast-fed, holding a bottle, reaching for a mobile, attempting to crawl, or just watching your face.

The best plaything an infant can have is loving, attentive parents. After that, toys that are safe and attractive can present a challenge at each stage of physical and sensory maturation during the first twelve months of life. Toys like mobiles and balls provide visual stimulation; bells, chimes, music boxes, and audiotapes stimulate auditory learning; teething toys made of hardwood, vinyl, or rubber stimulate oral development and help an infant explore the hardness, shape, and taste of things. Play and toys are not just to provide stimulation in the short run for infants. They encourage the urge to master the environment, they promote exploration, and they contribute to creative thinking skills that reach as far forward as adulthood.

The third aspect of love has to do with *authority*. In addition to providing comfort and stimulation, you have a responsibility to be an authority figure. An authority figure will offer help, behave consistently, and set limits gently.

Offering help means encouraging an infant to try things on her own, and when she accomplishes a task, expressing praise and excitement for her efforts. By about six months of age, infants begin to realize they can do things for themselves. Allowing and encouraging them to roll over, sit, or crawl facilitates the development of independence.

Being a consistent parent is crucial for children of any age, but it must begin with infancy. How well you establish your authority plays a role in your infant's sense of security. Consistency leads to trust when babies learn that their parents will meet their needs. Your consistency helps make an infant feel secure.

To be consistent requires parents to respond to the baby in a predictable way day after day. This could mean, for instance, that meals, baths, and play times occur at about the same time every day. It also means that your moods shouldn't vary markedly from one day to the next.

Furthermore, how well your child begins to learn about rules and limits depends on your establishing yourself as an authority figure even during the late stages of infancy. When her behavior goes beyond the limits you have set, you must let her know what you expect and what is acceptable behavior. At this age you will do this gently. For instance, you can let her know what is unacceptable by saying no when she's pulling at your glasses and by gently moving her hand away from the glasses.

And from these three aspects of love will come trust. You are providing love through bodily contact and by making yourself available so that your baby comes to rely on you for stimulation, comfort, and authority.

A baby learns to trust others gradually. But she must also learn to trust herself and through this gain the confidence she needs to move toward independence. With independence can come a positive sense of herself. This is one of the keys to a child's healthy emotional development.

Encouraging Independence

In our society, although this is not necessarily true in others, we place a lot of value on children becoming independent and asserting their individuality. Unfortunately, this is an area parents have difficulty with themselves. Naturally, during this first year of life, children are mostly dependent. And quite often parents enjoy the dependence of an infant so much that they accept a baby's early strivings for independence with reluctance or ambivalence. Often parents don't like to give up the feeling of being totally responsible for another human being— especially one who is so dependent and helpless.

But toward the end of a child's first year, you will see the first signs that she is learning how to do things for herself. This reflects her need and desire for independence. She wants to express her individuality. This is when she will start to feel the first stings of frustration as she recognizes her limited powers, and she will show her frustration in a crude, emotional way.

By nine months of age, a baby is well on her way to greater independence. She can sit without support, roll over from front to back, and crawl. Some babies can even pull themselves up to a standing position.

And she can do one other remarkable thing. She can express an important emotional state—distress. You'll no doubt have noticed this long before she's reached nine months of age!

How do babies do this? Through crying. In the first year, this is the main way babies let you know about discomfort and distress. In fact, parents often learn to distinguish what the infant needs—whether she's hungry, wet, or just wants to be held—based on how she's crying.

How the baby cries and how the parents respond influences how deep the attachment relationship is and how it will continue. By responding appropriately to the cry, parents let the baby know that they will be there and that other people can be trusted. Often, it's not necessarily what you do to try to comfort a crying baby that's important. What is important is that there is a response. Even a relatively ineffective response (something that often worries first-time parents) reassures the baby that someone cares about her and her needs. It's this message that reinforces the fledgling sense of trust.

Is It Possible to "Spoil" a Baby?

Some parents, perhaps many parents, are fearful of responding too quickly or too often to the cries of a baby. The fear is that they might end up "spoiling" her. Although not all experts agree on this subject, I think most of us believe that it is not possible to "spoil" an infant and that it is much better to try to soothe and comfort a baby than ignore her. Certainly, a baby is not trying to dominate her parents and keep their attention all to herself through excessive demands. Most often, she is simply expressing her needs in the only way she knows how.

It is just as certain that by ten or twelve months of age, a baby is able to sense that she can get attention by crying. By this age, too, the parent has probably figured out that it's not in anyone's best interest to give the baby everything she wants just because she is crying. Based on what we know of infant development, however, I would recommend that parents quickly respond to crying with loving comfort and soothing attention until the baby reaches twelve months. After twelve months, by slowly and very gradually delaying your responses, you begin to teach infants how to accept the temporary unavailability of a parent. It is not necessary to respond immediately to cries that do not indicate severe pain, acute discomfort, or more than momentary frustration.

Teaching Babies to be Independent

Parents "spoiling" are more likely to know how to feed, clothe, protect, stimulate, and comfort children than they are to know how to encourage independence. Even in the circumscribed world of infancy, there are many things you can do to encourage your child's independence. One is to begin to trust the baby's sense of what is right for her.

A baby's first expression of this sense often centers around food preferences. Babies have a sense of taste and smell. If something doesn't taste or smell good to them, they will let you know. Trust your child and don't force her to eat what she doesn't want. And don't try to force her to eat more than she wants to. Similarly, her efforts to be independent and feed herself should be encouraged. This should be done even if it takes longer and is messier for Mom or Dad.

As early as nine months, babies can begin to learn how to dress themselves. You can encourage this by asking your child to hold out her arms or straighten her leg when you're dressing her.

And even in play there are chances to encourage a baby's efforts to do things for herself. For instance, when she's holding a spoon, trying to catch a ball rolled to her, trying to reach for a toy, or struggling to accomplish something new, you can praise her efforts. Praise is an important form of encouragement.

All of these attempts to encourage a child's independence should be within a child's individual schedule of development. Each baby is unique.

Your child will grow at her own pace and her development should not be measured or compared closely to another child's. When giving or expecting a task, then, don't make it too difficult or too much of a struggle. That will often lead to needless frustration or anger.

As much as a child needs opportunities for freedom, her independence ultimately grows out of a sense of security. Independence cannot be forced. Babies are quite capable of choosing when and how they want to be independent. As with all matters of development, independence usually comes about slowly and in uneven spurts, but the secure infant will sooner or later start taking charge of her life.

Dealing with a Baby's Anger

Part of that taking charge relates to the expression of feelings, independence, and individuality. Babies show who they are by expressing feelings and emotions. Crying is obviously one of the primary ways a baby communicates wants and needs. Anger is one of the emotions babies express through crying, although they can do it in other ways as well.

Early in the first year, a baby's anger may be just another means of protecting herself. It can, for instance, be a way of letting her parents know the strength and urgency of her needs. Your baby probably shows she's angry in no uncertain terms if she isn't being fed on time! A delay in being fed is one of the most common reasons for outbursts of anger or rage in an infant. Later, babies will show anger at other annoyances—such as being restricted or being put down for a nap.

Giving Comfort Without Giving In

When your baby has a real need (such as acute pain or a wet diaper), and cries out in anger, you must try to deal with it. This doesn't necessarily mean that you always give in to a child expressing anger. Her health and safety come first. A baby might get very irritable at being strapped into a car seat, for example, but her safety requires it. In such instances, the best and perhaps only response is to comfort without giving in to the child's demands. Feelings, though, should never be ignored—even if you don't (or can't) give in to them. A responsive parent will remain calm and patient and will always acknowledge feelings with a smile and understanding ("I know this makes you angry, but Mommy has to strap you in so you'll be safe").

When safety and protection are not issues, then parents can respond to frustration and anger in other ways. Think about trying to encourage a baby to try a new food, to stand up, or to start drinking out of a cup. If she resists and seems frustrated or angry, consider that she's not ready for this activity. And then back off! Don't push new activities that lead to resistance or frustration. Allow her to take her time, but remain alert to her changing abilities and readiness for new advances.

Using Discipline

Parents often ask me when to start using discipline with a child. I usually respond that if you mean by discipline all those things that you do to guide and assist a child toward developing in a happy, wholesome way, you start the day the child arrives in your home.

But if by *discipline* a parent means using techniques to discourage behavior, correct it, and teach children right from wrong, this should begin by the end of the child's first year.

Infants are not yet conscious of what is "good" and what is "bad." They may cry or show anger for many reasons; it is certainly not to irritate their parents, although they may—toward the end of the first year—attempt to get attention through some behaviors. In general, babies touch the wrong things because they are curious and new things interest them. They put the wrong things in their mouths, not because they are naughty, but because they want to learn and because instinct leads them to investigate objects this way. And because they have no conception of consequences, trying to teach them about the results of their actions is useless.

When your baby is in her first year of life, you are the one who needs discipline. For you to be disciplined means that you have self-control and follow a consistent set of rules. If you are in control of yourself and stick to a small set of practical rules (such as not expecting an infant to handle temptation, removing items which present consistent problems, and attempting to prevent problems for the child), you will react to the baby in reasonable and appropriate ways when there is danger or when the child engages in troublesome behavior.

Controlling the Environment

You don't necessarily have to put up with everything a baby does, but you are the one who must act to stop inappropriate or dangerous behavior. More often than not this means changing the environment so the baby can't do anything dangerous or annoying. Your baby doesn't have the ability to stop herself. A big part of your job will be to anticipate the kinds of trouble she's likely to get into before she gets into it.

You must, of course, keep dangerous objects and toxic substances (such as cleaning supplies and insecticides) completely out of reach. You can also put away tempting but valuable objects. And you don't have to take the baby places she cannot yet handle—like restaurants.

Handling Your Child's and Your Own Frustration

You can also take your baby out of her playpen when she starts to be fussy or show that she's frustrated. You can pick her up from the crib even if her nap wasn't as long as you wanted it to be. You don't have to wait until she is wailing in anger or screaming from frustration. Making such changes is much more likely to result in an agreeable child than scolding or delivering an angry reprimand. Venting your own anger or frustration is never likely to achieve a positive outcome.

As I've mentioned, infants should be allowed flexibility. Babies need to be allowed to set the pace for naps, play, and quiet time, as well as for food preferences. It is important for you to be able to make a distinction between what you need and what the baby needs.

Once again, parental self-discipline is essential. Parental frustration and stress typically result when an infant is not meeting a mother's or father's needs. For instance, a fatigued parent may need sleep and it is easy to be upset, angry, or frustrated if the baby doesn't require a nap at the same time that the parent does. My point here—and throughout this book—is that the parent or the adult caregiver must take the child's needs into consideration. That often means putting your own needs and wishes second.

Consistency

Restrictions can be placed on an infant's behavior without anger or punishment. Consistency and a calm, serene response now will have a tremendous impact on a child's behavior in the future. If you react to the same situation with laughter sometimes and an angry voice or scowl the next time, the world begins to look very confusing to a baby.

It is during this first year that parent and child together begin a long journey toward independence and self-control. The journey gets off to an excellent start if you can be a sensitive, responsive individual who can gently and sensibly set consistent and appropriate limits.

Handling the More Difficult Infant

Are there really difficult infants? You bet there are. You need only ask the sleep-deprived parents with bags under their eyes about a colicky baby who has seemingly not slept and done little more than cry for the first six months of life. Or the parents of an infant who might be described as irritable.

Babies who are more fussy than most and less prone to easy soothing and management have "irritable infant syndrome." Many experts believe that the babies who are especially fussy during the first few months of life are the ones most likely to develop into hyperactive children.

So-called irritable babies are less cuddly and more resistant to loving touches and caresses from parents than are other infants. They are overly sensitive to almost all kinds of stimulation, and overreact to such things as loud sounds and the taste of certain foods. They are not as easy to console and soothe once they've begun crying or fussing. These "irritable infants" are this way by birth; it might be said that they have difficult temperaments.

Some of these fussy babies have Irritable Bowel Syndrome. Some children develop Irritable Bowel Syndrome as a result of stress in their lives in their first year. Such babies are going to act as miserable as they feel. The problem is that they can't tell you how and where they hurt.

Mothers, especially, are very good at perceiving and recognizing the temperaments of their babies at an early age. The particular way a mother becomes attached to her infant is often shaped by the difficulties the baby presents.

Children develop best and most securely when there is a secure attachment and special bonding between mother and child. Attachment is the word most psychologists and child development experts use to describe the relationship that develops between a baby and her primary caregiver. It is a long-lasting emotional relationship that begins at birth and takes much of the first year to form.

The quality of the attachment relationship is extremely important. From this early primary relationship the baby will learn about having her needs met. She will learn what kind of love and affection to expect, and begin to form ideas about the trustworthiness of her environment. If the attachment relationship is of high quality (a secure attachment), then the child and caregiver (usually mother) will have a close, meaningful, and intimate relationship that will allow for full development of affection, trust, and understanding between them.

If the relationship is of low quality (an insecure, ambivalent, or avoidance attachment), then the way the child develops will be affected. Children will not develop a sense of security in their environment or trust in their relationships if this attachment relationship is less secure.

An insecure or ambivalent attachment relationship develops when parents respond insensitively or awkwardly in their interactions with their babies. Children are not sure they can trust that parent. Such infants are likely to show more distress at separation from the parent and to look for affection when the parent returns. Such babies are not easily soothed or settled by the parent.

Infants in an avoidance attachment relationship have experienced angry or irritable rejection from their parent. In this case, the baby may show little or no distress when separated from the parent, and may ignore the parent when the parent returns.

Children who are secure in their attachments with their parents will feel wanted, loved, and worthwhile. Such children, in the years following infancy, are usually competent and have a good sense of who they are.

Forming a Secure Attachment with the Difficult Infant

Now the problem is that the temperament of the child will affect the way you as a parent attach to your child. It is much easier for a parent to become attached to a loving, serene, happy, cuddly infant than to a baby who cries a lot, is irritable and fussy, has a high activity level, and resists being held and touched.

The stakes are pretty high in this first year. How can you form a strong, secure attachment with that baby who's constantly screaming, rejects your attempts to comfort her, and is irritated by whatever you do for her? Try some of these things:

- Respond quickly to her cries for comfort and food. Even with a baby who cries a lot, you must be responsive. This won't always be fun for the fatigued parent, and you may not see immediate positive results, but you will be giving your child a valuable message for the future: "I'm here for you and I will try to comfort you whenever you feel bad."

- Find the best times to interact with your baby. When is she most willing to play or listen to what you have to say? Closely observe the baby so that you can determine her moods and her ability to tolerate cuddling, holding, and eye contact.

- Use the other parent (if willing), as well as relatives, friends, or baby-sitters, to give you a break from the rigors of an irritable child. You must learn early in such an infant's life that you can't be on duty twenty-four hours a day. You must be at your best to deal with the difficult baby. You must try to get enough sleep and exercise and find ways to nurture yourself in order to carry out what can be a very arduous and trying task.

- Watch for cues and signals that your baby has had enough play, holding, or interaction. When she begins to be fussy, give her quiet time and a chance to settle down.

- Be aware of your own feelings toward your baby and be honest with yourself about those feelings. Irritable and fussy infants are likely to evoke hostile and unloving feelings from parents. Accept such feelings and go from there.

- Where do you go from there? Recognize that an irritable, fussy baby needs a loving parent just as much as—and probably a good deal more than—a loving, serene, placid baby. Your attention, your ability to comfort, and all of your resources will be taxed. Doing everything you can to help the difficult infant grow and develop in the best possible way will decidedly reduce the risk of more difficult behavior in the future.

It is important that you look for the positive qualities and traits in your difficult infant. Even though she may remind you of a relative or someone else you never liked, you can't just dwell on the negatives of such an infant. Instead, look for the things you like, no matter how minute or insignificant. For instance, maybe she has cute ears, enjoys being stroked on the back, has a powerful kick, or possesses the energy to cry long and loud for what she wants. Remember that each child has many positives and you cannot choose all the traits that you want. What you can do is be thankful for the ones you got.

You won't feel as loving as you would if you were caring for an easy-to-raise infant, but your difficult infant actually needs you more than the less temperamental baby, and the long-term results can be very rewarding. A difficult infant requires a calm, patient parent who can provide all aspects of love in order to grow into a capable older child. The reward for you is your own sense of gratification that you have accomplished a most demanding job: coping successfully with a difficult infant.

Summary

Three aspects of love will influence your relationship with your infant:

1. *Comfort:* You can promote the health and growth of infants by making sure they are comfortable. This is done through caring for their physical needs and providing comfort when they are crying, frustrated, or angry.

2. *Stimulation:* Infants respond well to and thrive in an atmosphere rich in a variety of stimulation.

3. *Authority:* Babies also need an authority figure who, even at this early age, will offer assistance, be consistent, and set limits.

Training and encouragement toward independence begins during the first year. By nine months of age, babies are becoming more independent. Most of them can sit without support, roll over from front to back, and crawl. They can express discomfort and distress through crying and other signals.

You can begin to encourage independence during the first year of your baby's life by:

• Trusting the baby's sense of what is right for her.

• Supporting efforts to try things on her own.

• Giving praise at her accomplishments and efforts.

Many parents worry about "spoiling" an infant. This is not a concern until infants are around twelve months of age. Up to then, it is recommended that parents consistently respond to crying and other signs of distress with loving comfort and soothing attention.

Early in the first year of life, a baby's anger is one of the emotions expressed through crying. Parents can best deal with anger by offering comfort without giving in to the child's demands. Health and safety always come first, but parents can respond to anger with an acknowledgment of the angry feelings even when they can't give in to what the child wants.

Infants are not ready for "discipline," that is, attempts to correct behavior or discourage unwanted behavior, until near the end of the first year. Up to then, babies are not capable of understanding the concept of consequences. During the first year of an infant's life, it is parents who need discipline. Parents are disciplined when they have self-control, follow a consistent set of rules, and change the environment to help the baby avoid dangerous or annoying behaviors.

Parents must be aware of their own needs and feelings and distinguish these from a baby's needs. The baby's needs must be primary and the infant should not be expected to meet a parent's needs.

Some infants are more irritable and fussy or have "irritable infant syndrome." Irritable infants are usually very sensitive to all sorts of stimulation, are less responsive, and are not as easy to console or soothe when crying or fussy. Having an irritable infant may influence the quality of the attachment relationship between child and parent.

The quality of the attachment relationship is, however, very important as babies learn from it what kind of affection to expect and whether it is safe to trust others. Children who are secure in their attachment to their parents will feel wanted, loved, and worthwhile. In the long run, this leads to self-control, competence, and a positive self-image.

To form a secure, strong attachment to irritable infants, try these things:

- Respond quickly to cries for comfort and food.
- Find the best time to interact, which means when your baby is most willing to listen and play.
- Use the other parent, relatives, friends, and baby-sitters to give you a break from the rigors of dealing with an irritable infant.
- Watch for typical cues that your baby has had enough play, holding, or interaction; anticipate her fussiness and allow her to settle down before she gets too irritable.
- Be aware of your own feelings toward your baby and be honest with yourself about those feelings. Accept your feelings even if they are frequently negative.

CHAPTER 5

Understanding and Disciplining the One-Year-Old Toddler

The One-Year-Old Toddler

When Daniel Moultrup had his first birthday, he graduated to toddlerhood. Not only is Daniel better able to get around, he now is capable of demonstrating that he has a will of his own. So, while Daniel is at a delightful stage in his life, what with taking those first tentative, stiff steps and then suddenly zooming around with astonishing speed, he has discovered something very valuable.

He now has control over his environment. Sure, getting around better increases his control; but more importantly, he is able to communicate. The acquisition of language is the real key to control over his environment.

In only twelve months—by the time he is twenty-four months of age—Daniel will have developed from a fairly dependent young baby to a surprisingly sophisticated child. No longer does Daniel live in a safe, protected little world in which he requires almost complete assistance. As a one-year-old, Daniel has entered what some call the "runabout" age. Now he needs almost constant surveillance because he can be quick in his darting speed and impulsive in his change of direction or interest. And this can be as much a source of trouble as it is a source of pleasure.

Because of this change, Daniel—the toddler—is now fully engaged in a most important process: the one leading to independence and self-control. Add just one word—the word "no"—to his vocabulary and the mobile Daniel is now in a position to assert his wants and needs; or to put it another way, to ask for his independence and autonomy.

Most parents will find young toddlers like Daniel to be most delightful creatures. They're full of zest, mostly friendly, quite sociable, and usually agreeable. Most youngsters this age tend to adapt fairly well to whatever it is you have in mind.

Consider Daniel on the day he was celebrating his first birthday with a party attended by his doting parents, his three older siblings, and several aunts, uncles, and grandparents. On this day he is the picture of charm and poise. He enjoys the attention, delights in getting gifts (even though he needs help opening them), and appears thrilled at having a large colorful cake in his honor.

When his parents sit him at the dining room table by his cake, he goes along with it, trying to blow out the large candle in the shape of the numeral one. He is very proper in his blue slacks and plaid shirt, and only when he is directed to take a large bite of the heavily frosted cake is he anything but polite and correct.

During his first year of life Daniel has gone through some amazing developments. His vocabulary has gone from no words to several, his ability to handle objects has increased markedly, and he's beginning to venture away from his mother or whatever adult is watching him.

This one-year-old can be very sophisticated, but give him a few months and he will switch, often without much warning, into an oppositional young defiant. It's important to know that children during the toddler years can be quite defiant toward their parents and very inflexible about what they will do. They want what they want immediately and insist that everything be done in the same way each time. If you're sick to death of reading *Are You My Mother?* every night, they are not. Nor will they allow you to be creative or deviate from the original story!

Children's personalities emerge and take shape in the hothouse atmosphere of their constant testing and the nearly perpetual pressure they exert against parental authority. Their individual wills and personal initiative will first come to light during this second twelve months of life. Their struggles for independence and their attempts to be separate individuals will start in earnest around twelve months of age, and will continue well into adulthood.

Despite these first signs of defiance, a toddler's parents are still the most important people in his life. His fear of strangers or of separation from his parents may be even stronger now than it was during the first twelve months.

During the next few months after the first birthday, most children will not only learn to walk confidently but will figure out how to run— sometimes away from you. They will begin to be able to master the art of climbing stairs, reaching and getting into cupboards, into closets, into dressers and drawers. And they will become quite adept at turning the knobs on TVs, VCRs, compact disc players, and stereos.

And that's part of the wonder of these years. The twelve- to twenty-four-month-old is ready for new, independent experiences. He has more power than ever and wants to try it out. He seems to be straining at the leash.

Striving for independence, he often resents almost any form of control. He dislikes quick changes, and an unannounced change can spark defiance and a tantrum. He wants to reach what he never even seemed to notice before. He wants to dress himself. He wants to hold things or try things by himself, shaking off your efforts to help, which will generally meet resistance. You're most likely to hear "Daniel do it" or "Me do it."

With this striving for independence the toddler is likely to become demanding and oppositional in ways that will annoy or frustrate his parents.

With all the advances, independence, contrariness, and surprises between one year and two, you will have to be ingenious and resilient to keep up with your toddler. As Louise Bates Ames, Frances L. Ilg, and Carol Chase Haber point out in the Gesell Institute's *Your One-Year-Old,* this is a child who is at an in-between stage in the "process of becoming": not yet a preschooler, but no longer a baby.

Because of his newly discovered powers, the toddler at this stage is likely to be demanding and egocentric. Things are now "mine!" and he can be very grabby. He gets very set on one thing, such as having a toy, eating a certain food, or sitting in his favorite chair. He may, in a very stubborn way, insist on what he wants—no matter what the cost.

Kristy Summers, at fourteen months of age, had a screaming fit lasting twenty minutes one afternoon after she couldn't use the potty chair in the bathroom. It all started when Kristy announced she had to "Go potty." When she couldn't go after all and her mother removed her from the bathroom, Kristy started screaming, "Me go now!" But when Mrs. Summers offered to take her back to the potty chair, Kristy screamed louder.

On that afternoon, Mrs. Summers thought that she had a toddler who was two very different little people: one persistent and focused on one goal; the other flitting from one activity to another seemingly without rhyme nor reason.

Just as toddlers love to explore new areas, so too they love doing just the opposite of what you want. If you ask a toddler to "come here," he loves to dart off in the other direction. If you say, "Don't touch the electric cord," he is more attracted to it. If you say, "Eat this," he says, "No!" and pushes his dish away. If you ask him to put his toys in the box, he'll dump them all out on the floor. And if you leave him alone for just a few minutes, you may find that he is completely undressed when you return. This happened to me when my daughter was around twenty months old. I left her in the car in front of an office for just a few seconds, and when I returned she was naked as a jaybird.

But the toddler is never mean about these things and sometimes it appears that he's just playing and having a grand old time being oppositional. Even while opposing you, there may be a sense of playfulness, affection, and delight in what he's doing. However, don't be misled. As you'll find out soon enough, the toddler has emotions and rather strong feelings. He can show you—as Kristy Summers showed her mother—some Fourth of July fireworks when a tantrum erupts over a relatively minor issue.

Independence and Clinging

What often triggers these explosive episodes are the child's drive for independence and freedom on the one hand, and on the other his need to be close and involved with mother. This can drive some parents to the point of frustration.

Part of this frustration may be caused by the rapid mood swings these two impulses create: The toddler alternates between being totally independent and very clingy; in short, being quite unpredictable. Children between eighteen and twenty-four months often don't seem to know what they want.

Temper Tantrums

They can also have temper tantrums and display violent emotions. And indeed it's wise to remember that anger and aggression are universal in all young children. The whole idea of socialization is to help the child learn to control his feelings and emotions, especially the less pleasant ones.

Toddlers express their anger and aggression not so much through oppositional behavior as through such actions as holding their breath, kicking, biting, hitting, and screaming, to get their own way. Temper tantrums, in fact, are the ultimate way toddlers display their anger and aggression.

And what causes temper tantrums? Usually it's frustration— frustration at being unable to get what they want or at not being able to possess every toy they think belongs to them. It could be frustration at your attempts to help them dress or your insistence that they leave the potty chair or come in from play. Or it could be frustration at not being allowed to have the exact food they want. Frank and Theresa Caplan in their book *The Second Twelve Months of Life* cite research that shows that in the twelve- to twenty-four-month period, children are most likely to engage in temper tantrums when they are restricted in some way— whether they are not allowed to touch electric outlets or simply have been dressed in restrictive clothing. Being forced to remain on the potty chair, being harnessed in a car safety seat, or being put to bed are also likely to trigger outbursts from toddlers.

The Big No

No has now become all too common a word in the toddler's vocabulary, and mothers and fathers may take exception to this use of no when they would rather hear yes. What can ensue is the classic battle of wills between a parent and a toddler. This certainly happens when parents view the toddler's no as an act of stubbornness or rebellion.

If you regard his no's, his contrariness, his going in the opposite direction when he's called, or his persistent focus on touching something you specifically told him not to touch as disobedience, you will find yourself in a war between your will and his. Remember an important message of this book, particularly during the toddler stage: Much of children's negative behavior is not disobedience. Nor is it an attempt to undermine your authority. Stubborn, defiant, and oppositional behaviors are part of the growth process. Such behavior should not be taken personally, nor should you engage in power struggles. A toddler's behavior is not about power unless you make that the issue. Rather, it's about growth and development toward independence.

Handling the Opposition of the Twelve- to Twenty-Four-Month-Old Toddler

Perhaps the first rule of thumb in living with the one-year-old is to keep the right perspective. First, keep your expectations reasonable. *Expect* that twelve- to twenty-four-month-old children will be oppositional and stubborn at times. Understand that they will be independent one minute and clinging the next. Now that they have mastered the word "no," expect that they may use it indiscriminately—whether it actually fits the situation or not; or whether they actually mean it or not.

In other words, the parent who expects these behaviors from the one-year-old, and who is willing to keep things in perspective and to learn how to handle such behavior well, is the one who will do best. It is useless to think that because you are a loving parent your toddler won't say no, resist, or be persistently oppositional. He will, because that's the way all toddlers grow and develop.

Keeping the right perspective means that you will not see these oppositional and stubborn behaviors as disobedience, but rather as signposts on the way to more mature development. These developments are just as important as learning to walk and talk. They are necessary steps toward becoming the sophisticated preschooler the child will become in a couple of years.

Second, give the toddler as much leeway as you safely can. He needs you to give him as much freedom as he can manage. Let him take the lead and let him determine whether he needs to cling to you or be independent of you. In other words, do not push him into situations or try to force him to try out things he's not ready for.

Third, make sure you always give positive attention to obedience and compliance—even while you expect disobedience and noncompliance as part of the age.

If all goes well, you will find a general decline in negativism and oppositionalism, for a brief period at least, around the time of the child's second birthday. You'll never have to face this kind of challenge again! (Just kidding, but it is helpful to think that there is a light at the end of a dark tunnel.)

At the toddler stage, particularly in the early months of the second year, there is relatively little need for punishment or negative consequences. Early forms of independence and self-assertion should be seen as just that—a child's first attempts at independence and autonomy, which shouldn't be stamped out by repressive parental responses. Rather, they are to be allowed and handled in kind and gentle ways. A calm atmosphere in the home and in the relationship between parents and toddler is characterized by patience, occasional firmness, and lots of affection, praise, and positive attention for the behaviors that are desirable and laudatory.

Anger, Aggression, and Temper Tantrums

When the toddler is as young as twelve months of age, parents should be aware that they are modeling appropriate ways to deal with anger and aggression. That is, how you handle your own anger and your own hostile and aggressive feelings will greatly influence the way your child learns to handle his. He should be getting early lessons in understanding that anger is a normal emotion, but that it is best dealt with in verbal and nondestructive ways.

Teaching children substitute behavior—pounding clay, hitting a pillow, and saying how angry they feel—is the preferred way to handle frustration and anger.

When toddlers experience frustrations that result in temper tantrums, it is best to be ready for them and to face them with calm and confidence. Unless they are so out of control that they pose a danger to themselves or valuable possessions, the best course is to allow toddlers to tantrum themselves out. Trying to restrain them may simply escalate the intensity of their anger.

Do not, however, reinforce tantrums and angry behavior by trying to stop them with bribes or by giving in to the child's demands. This doesn't cure anything. In fact it nearly always ensures that the tantrums will continue and that you'll have a tougher time of it in the future. A bribe is giving the child what he wants in order to quiet him. Giving in does not curb the tyke's unreasonable demands; rather, it teaches him that the method is a successful one.

It is important to respond to angry outbursts or temper tantrums in a two-stage process.

1. Respond to the feelings. Do this by acknowledging what the child is feeling ("I know you're very angry right now") so that over time your child can learn to identify his own emotions.

2. Respond to the reasons for the tantrum. This isn't the same thing as giving the child what he wants, especially when this is contrary to his best interests or goes against rules. The idea is to respond to the reasons for the tantrum, not the tantrum itself.

Kristy Summers, the little girl who screamed when she couldn't go potty, reacted with a tantrum when she was frustrated. This happened one day with her grandmother, Barbara.

Barbara volunteered to take Kristy for the afternoon and had an entertaining agenda planned. But she was taking Kristy for the first time in several months and she was not aware that Kristy was now at a stage where she wanted to do things for herself. When Barbara scooped her up, took her to the car, and plopped her in the car seat, then pulled the padded bar down over Kristy's head, Kristy went ballistic. Barbara had innocently wandered into a new situation involving Kristy's growing need for independence. The little girl reacted to her frustration with a tantrum.

Not knowing why the tantrum was happening, Barbara did what she could. "I've got a very unhappy little girl on my hands," she said to Kristy. "I'm sorry you're so angry, sweetie."

This didn't stop the tantrum, and for a few minutes Kristy continued to wail angrily. At the same time, Kristy's grandmother went back over what happened, trying to figure out where she had gone wrong. She also observed that Kristy was straining to lift the bar holding her in the car seat. Barbara guessed that it was something to do with the car seat. "You don't like being in the car seat much, do you, honey?" she said soothingly. As she said this Kristy responded with her "Kristy do!" which her grandmother had not really understood before since it seemed to come out in one word that sounded like "Kwisty-due."

"You wanted to do that by yourself, didn't you, baby?" she said. Kristy began to nod her head and her crying lightened up.

Barbara decided to start over. She pushed the release button on the car seat, which allowed the bar to be brought back over Kristy's head. Then she offered to allow Kristy to do it herself. "You can do it, darling," she said and Kristy reached up and with some struggling pulled the bar and the straps down around her.

The crisis was over. Kristy still didn't much like being confined in the car seat, but she was less angry when she could do part of the job herself. Barbara didn't get angry, was able to acknowledge what the girl was feeling, and eventually responded to the problem, not the tantrum.

Using Substitution, Redirection, and Distractions

In most instances, parents and caretakers can handle negative, stubborn, and aggressive behavior through substitution, redirection, and patience.

By offering substitutes, parents can divert a child's attention to something more positive and desirable for both parent and child. For instance, when one-year-old Daniel Moultrup seems intent on playing with an electrical outlet, he can be diverted from this activity by being offered a bright red toy car to push along the floor.

Mary Pettit used redirection and distraction in the following way with her son, twenty-one-month-old Broc. It was a snowy January day, and Broc had been playing in the snow for the first time in his young life. Being a zestful toddler, Broc was enjoying himself. But Mary knew he had been outside long enough and brought him inside. Broc, of course, had no concern about the frigid temperature and knew nothing about the dangers of frostbite. All he knew was that he was having fun outside and wasn't ready to come indoors.

Which is why when he got inside, he stood in the hallway screaming and refusing to allow Mary to touch him or remove his coat and boots. Mary sized up the situation quickly and walked over to a window where she looked intently outside, waiting for his temper to subside.

After a couple of minutes, she began to comment about the squirrels that seemed to be playing tag with one another—darting back and forth in the snow between two trees.

"Look at those funny squirrels," she said quietly but with animation in her voice. "You want to see the squirrels playing, Broc?"

Broc couldn't resist something so obviously interesting. As Mary continued to describe the action which Broc was now observing, too, she gently removed his coat, boots, and leggings. Broc forgot all about his tantrum and his frustration at being brought inside. After the antics of the squirrels wore off, Mary offered Broc chocolate chip cookies and cocoa.

Mary's actions were simple and effective. She diverted Broc's attention without trying to stop his tantrum or engaging in a power struggle over the removal of his winter apparel. By redirecting his attention and distracting him with something he couldn't resist, she avoided a battle of wills that had an attendant risk of a prolonged tantrum, more unnecessary tears for Broc, and frustration for Mary.

Some toddlers are not easily diverted. They may be only temporarily intrigued by the diversion or may tire of it quickly. Those children need extra patience on your part when you are redirecting or offering a substitute. Make sure that the substitute is something that will catch his attention and offer it in such a way that he will have trouble resisting. Mary effectively did this, knowing that Broc likes animals and that he enjoyed watching the squirrels play in the yard. For the child who is doing something dangerous, like touching an electric outlet, use a prompt. A prompt is a more direct way of redirecting behavior. This could be done by taking the child's hand that is touching the outlet and moving it toward a toy car. Actually feeling the toy in his hand may prompt him to begin playing with it. Or a prompt could be taking the child by the hand and leading him to the more acceptable activity, perhaps even in another room.

Planning Ahead

Mary has also learned that she must plan ahead with Broc. As with most toddlers, Broc doesn't like to be moved quickly from one task to another. While she can't anticipate every situation that comes along, Mary tries to build some extra time into her plans so that she can devote a few minutes to helping Broc deal with disruptions in his life.

If Mary had been in a hurry and whisked Broc into the house, telling him they had to do something immediately because they were running late, she would have put herself in an untenable position. She wouldn't have been able to devote enough time to helping Broc get through his tantrum.

Avoiding Questions That Can Be Answered with No

It's a good idea for parents of toddlers to avoid questions that invite no answers. If Mary had asked Broc if he would like to come in the house and stop playing in the snow, or if she had asked, "Would you like to take your coat off now?" she would surely have gotten a big, fat "No!" Instead, it's better to say, "Time to get our boots off" or, "It's time to come in the house." Even trying to be tricky by asking, "Do you want to come in and have chocolate chip cookies?" might be inviting a no, even though the child may really want the cookies. Toddlers can't always say what they mean when they use words like "no" and as part of this phase of development the word frequently pops out of their mouths automatically.

Ignoring Misbehavior

Deal with toddler temper tantrums by ignoring the misbehavior. That is, don't make a big production out of what they're doing—which is usually screaming, being demanding, kicking, throwing themselves on the floor, or saying awful things to you. Don't respond with a tantrum yourself. If the youngster gets too frantic and out of control, you might remove him to a safe place, such as his room (if you're at home) or the car or a rest room (if you are away from home). This is done for the child's protection so that more severe misbehaviors, such as breaking valuables or aggression toward another person, are avoided. When a youngster goes ballistic, the trick is to be calm and not escalate the tantrum.

Modeling Appropriate Behavior

Giving a toddler his way only increases prospects for more tantrums in the future. When parents escalate a situation by having their own tantrum, it simply serves to decrease the child's self-control. The parent who reacts with calmness and serenity is giving the child one of the most potent lessons possible in terms of future self-control.

When children of this age show aggressive, hostile, and destructive behavior or feelings, they must be reassured that they are not aggressive or destructive individuals. The one best way to do this is by your self-control and your calm assessment and tolerance of the situation. If you react in an excited or hysterical way to the child's misbehavior, you will relay a most unfortunate message to your child: "You are an aggressive and destructive child and you have frightened me and you should be frightened of your own abilities to be aggressive."

Keeping Defiance in Perspective

Children at one and a half years of age often act defiantly. You tell them they can't touch the cake that is sitting out for the party, and they may stick their finger in the frosting anyway. It is almost always better to either ignore this sort of behavior or use a mild reprimand than to make a federal case out of it. Making a big fuss over it may only promote more contrary and defiant behavior. Usually one such gesture is enough for a child to prove his point: "I'm me and I'm autonomous." It may also be a good idea to give him something else good to eat (substitution) if it is hunger that led to the finger in the frosting.

Again, keep this sort of behavior in perspective. Contrariness on the part of one-and-a-half-year-olds is part of the age. In order to go on to more mature development they have to experience all stages of growth. Contrary and negative behavior at this age is growth promoting, not growth retarding. Even very good parents are going to be challenged at times by their toddlers between the ages of one and two. And there will be conflicts. The goal is not to avoid all conflicts or challenges. As a parent, your goal is to promote healthy development and growth. Growth is promoted by allowing some defiance and contrary behavior; it is stunted by trying to repress or punish each new instance of challenging behavior.

Overprotection Versus Permissiveness

Overprotective parents can afford to be permissive and protective when they have infants. However, overprotection doesn't work well with toddlers, as parents often become overly cautious and, as a result, too restrictive—especially when their children begin walking, running, and otherwise showing signs of independence. Such overprotective parents may try to "baby" their children by keeping them absolutely safe and protected, and thereby curb their children's independence and rob them of the chance to mature.

At around seventeen or eighteen months of age, it is inevitable that children will be contrary and negative. Your child may refuse your help or want to make his own choice or decision. If the matter is not of earthshaking importance, then you can allow him to try things on his own or choose his own way of doing something. While this will undoubtedly result in poor judgment, inevitable failure, and even frustrations, it is important for toddlers to learn that they are individuals who can make their own decisions, and that when they make mistakes those mistakes can be corrected.

More understanding and reasonably permissive parents allow moderate and more practical degrees of autonomy. This means that they allow their toddlers to do things necessary for proper development during this stage. Toddlers must be given the opportunity and freedom to explore, investigate, and manipulate. Given freedom and opportunities, children are likely to derive satisfaction from their discoveries, and thus develop self-confidence. They will feel zestful toward new and challenging situations, rather than fearful of them.

Handling the More Difficult Twelve- to Twenty-Four Month-Old Toddler

In the toddler years, children hear about rules and prohibitions for the very first time. The most basic purpose of our rules and restrictions is to protect toddlers from seriously harming themselves or others. Just as important, these rules are another way of letting them know that we love them.

A toddler needs firm and clearly stated rules about hitting others, touching the oven or electrical outlets, putting dangerous or toxic substances into his mouth, running out into the street, and so on. These rules are for his safety and well-being.

While all toddlers need these rules delivered in a calm, firm way, it is the difficult toddlers who need them the most. These children require as much patience, love, and consistency as any other youngsters, but they'll need more help with the rules, since they will be less apt to remember them and more likely to react in an impulsive, emotional, aggressive, or oppositional manner.

Difficult toddlers need more structure and firmness related to the routines of life. They need parents who are very consistent about bedtimes, getting dressed, bathing, eating, using the potty chair, and respecting other people and their possessions.

Setting Reasonable and Enforceable Rules

While they do need more supervision and strictness, difficult youngsters should not be overburdened with many rules. Too many rules will lead to more frequent rule violations. A child will feel unable to cope with rules when there are rules about his behavior, his speech, his toys, peer relationships, table manners, and so on. Obviously, toddlers will begin to learn some important rules (like not touching electric outlets, avoiding hot ovens, not running in the street, and holding on to a parent's hand in a parking lot), but introducing too many becomes unreasonable and toddlers won't be able to remember them. But once you've set a few reasonable rules, they must be reinforced absolutely consistently.

With the difficult youngster it is essential not to make rules that you won't be able to enforce. You don't want him to get the idea that by pushing you hard enough the rules will bend, break, or be abandoned. With easy-to-raise children, it's all right to bend the rules on occasion. However, it is a bigger problem with the toddler with a difficult temperament if you make "reasonable" exceptions to rules. If you are inclined to make frequent exceptions to some rule, maybe it shouldn't be a rule. When rules are unnecessary, too complicated, or not easily enforced, they don't work well with toddlers. For example, I know parents who have tried to enforce these rules with toddlers:

- Always stay by my side.
- No going into the kitchen.
- Don't ever tell me no.
- No talking back or sassiness.
- Don't bring out new toys to play with before the ones you're finished with are put away.
- You must always share with your brother.

These rules are usually neither enforceable nor reasonable for the toddler because most toddlers can't live up to them. Making such rules only invites inconsistency on your part.

Staying Calm but Firm

Handle the more frequent and more intense oppositional and defiant behavior of the difficult toddler with calmness, friendliness, and firmness. Sometimes the oppositional behavior can be ignored. At other times humor can work well for both of you. When neither is working well and your child continues to resist going to bed on his own, for example, you may have to pick him up and take him there yourself. While he will probably protest vigorously (and perhaps loudly) about this, if you can keep your sense of humor and be friendly, you can usually win him back over fairly quickly. If not, at least you are firm about your expectation.

Ignoring Tantrums

As with other toddlers, follow the four general rules given below in dealing with his tantrums:

1. Ignore as much of his tantrum as possible so that the temper outburst is not reinforced.
2. If the request or rule that sets off the tantrum is reasonable, don't give in. It is in his best interest to maintain a rule, command, or decision consistently.
3. Acknowledge the feelings he's expressing.
4. Deal with the cause of the tantrum, not the angry behavior itself.

For example, when Kristy Summers has a temper tantrum because she is not allowed to stay up past her usual bedtime, her mother can follow these four steps:

1. She will make sure that during the tantrum Kristy is safe, but she won't talk about the tantrum or make negative comments about Kristy's behavior. If Kristy tries to kick her mother or break something, Mrs. Summers will move her or restrain her.
2. Mrs. Summers will not back down and let her stay up longer just to stop the tantrum. To do so would teach Kristy that temper tantrums will get her what she wants.
3. Kristy's mother will acknowledge the girl's feelings. She will say, "I know you're mad because you don't want to go to bed right now, but this is your bedtime."

4. And Mrs. Summers will deal with the cause of the tantrum rather than with the behavior of the temper tantrum. She would say, for instance, "I'm sorry you're mad because I won't let you stay up later, but it is better for you to go to sleep and get your rest. You will feel better tomorrow and we can watch *The Lion King* video that you like so much. Right now, though, I want you to go to sleep. Goodnight."

As the difficult toddler's temper tantrum may be more intense and possibly more violent than other children's, make sure she is protected, and don't give in to demands that you consider unreasonable.

Summary

Toddlers between ages one and two are usually:

• Delightful because of their general zest, friendliness, and agreeableness.

• Able to exert greater control over their environment through the acquisition of language and especially with the addition of the word "no."

• Better able to control their motor skills and often quick in their ability to get around; as a result they are usually in need of almost constant supervision.

• Resentful of any form of control.

• Striving for independence, which will result in more demands and more oppositional behavior; insistent on getting what they want.

• Prone to throwing temper tantrums when their wishes aren't met.

• Likely to display mood swings as they alternate between being independent and clinging.

Parents can best deal with stubborn, negative, and oppositional behavior of toddlers by:

- Keeping expectations reasonable.
- Maintaining the right perspective, especially understanding that contrary and oppositional behavior is not disobedience.
- Giving a child as much leeway and freedom as he can manage; letting him take the lead and determine when he wants to be independent and when more dependent.
- Developing a consistent and secure relationship with the toddler.
- Viewing crude forms of self-assertion as just what they are—a child's early attempts to show his individuality.
- Not attempting to stamp out independence and autonomy.
- Handling temper tantrums with calm and confidence.
- Dealing with oppositionalism, stubbornness, and negative behaviors through substitution, redirection, patience, and planning ahead.

Parents can handle the more difficult twelve- to twenty-four-month-old toddler by:

- Being consistent about routines.
- Using clearly stated and firm rules.
- Setting reasonable and enforceable rules.
- Offering supervision and restrictions but not harshness.
- Not giving in to unreasonable demands.
- Handling temper tantrums by following four guidelines:
    1. Ignore as much of the tantrum as possible.
    2. Don't give in to stop a tantrum.
    3. Acknowledge the child's feelings.
    4. Deal with the cause of the tantrum, not the angry behavior.

CHAPTER 6

Understanding and Disciplining the Two-Year-Old Toddler

It's time for the terrible twos!

Quick, parents, batten down the hatches. Get ready for mayhem. That sweet infant, that adaptable toddler, now turns two and you know what will happen. She will be transformed into that scourge of parents everywhere: the Terrible Twos Monster!

But hold on. Maybe it's not so bad after all. Consider that you were able to deal with the negativism and the oppositionalism of the twelve-to twenty-four-month-old. Think of this new challenge as part of your growth and development as a parent—and part of the continuum of growth for children.

And honestly, folks, it's not that bad! Most of us parents survive. The "terrible twos," which really start at fifteen to eighteen months with the use of the word "no," never do get much worse than that. Well, okay, so at about two and a half it gets a little bit worse.

Anyway, try to relax and enjoy the two-year-old. She can be a pretty good kid—most of the time.

The Two-Year-Old Toddler

Marie is a typical two-year-old. She's gentle, friendly, and generally able to deal with her world. She's always curious, active, and eager to learn new things. She loves to play, enjoys looking at books, wants to know other children in the neighborhood, and loves watching the birds sitting on the bird feeder.

Marie's mother says that she seems more content and easier to get along with than she was just four or five months ago. One of the important reasons for the maturity and contentment of the average twenty-four-month-old child is that she has a greater vocabulary. Instead of just the five to ten words Marie possessed four months ago, she now has about two hundred words she can use. That allows her to express herself better. Her parents more often know what she wants, yet it seems as though her needs aren't so strong or vigorously expressed.

Marie doesn't get angry or frustrated quite as often as she used to. She's more stable and generally more friendly and better able to get along with everyone. She's warmer and more affectionate. And she will remain this way until about two and a half, when many children display the temper and emotions that give two-year-olds a bad rap.

Theresa and Frank Caplan, in *The Early Childhood Years: The Two-to Six-Year-Old,* refer to two-year-olds as "eager beavers." They are ready to take on the world, and as a result they lead an active life. Marie's mother can attest to this because, she points out, it's almost impossible to keep up with the child or keep the house looking neat and clean.

While children this age love routines, their own behavior is far from routine. Like the one-year-olds described in the last chapter, two-year-olds seem to be going faster than ever and sometimes in many different directions. But if their parents (or even an older sibling) change a routine or try to fence them in too much, look out for a battle or an outburst of emotion.

Again, like the one-year-old, toddlers at age two sometimes seem obsessed with exploring and learning about the house, the cupboards, closets, and the backyard. They wander, climb, touch, poke, and pick up things they shouldn't. They take things apart, but have no clue about putting them back together.

In stores they will wander away—and maybe hide. Take them to a museum and you may find them trying to explore on their own. They have a short attention span and if something new catches their eye they forget about what they were just holding, touching, or attending to.

In a restaurant, even if they are still constrained by a highchair, they tend to be very curious. Order them a glass of milk and a straw and you would think they're conducting a scientific experiment. Despite Dad telling her to stop playing with her milk and drink it, the two-year-old will spin the straw around the glass and try to find methods of actually getting some milk into her mouth other than the conventional way of sucking it through the straw. More than likely she will get more on herself and on the floor.

Marie often wants to be Mom's or Dad's helper. When Mom tries to put dishes into the dishwasher, she wants to help. When Dad is vacuuming, she wants to try it, too. The job Marie does is not much assistance to Mom or Dad, but she still insists on wanting to be a part of family activities.

While similar to the one-year-old in that she is more inclined to be independent, she has even more language on her side with which she can express herself. And like the one-year-old toddler, she will let you know what she wants by saying "I do it" or "I want to!" For Marie that means she wants to brush her teeth, get dressed, go to potty, put on her pajamas, try out the vacuum, and attempt to get a bottle of juice out of the refrigerator—all by herself. Obviously this can be a source of concern to parents, because two-year-olds drop things. They are often remarkably clumsy and inexpert at many of the things they wish to do to show their independence.

And then they hit the thirty-months-of-age marker. This is the two-and-a-half-year-old you've been warned about. While the characteristics of this age don't exactly appear right on schedule—some kids are ahead of others and some behind—most children show greater signs of negativism and oppositionalism at around thirty months, very much as they did at eighteen to twenty-four months.

Ames and Ilg, who also wrote a book for this age period called *Your Two-Year-Old: Terrible or Tender,* suggest that the two-and-a-half-year-old can become tense, explosive, and rigid. Such displays of emotion can make this an especially difficult age.

This is an age of extreme opposites, and toddlers at this stage have difficulty deciding what they want. If they choose chicken noodle soup, they may quickly change their minds and demand tomato soup. Nothing ever seems quite right. Offering a choice is a very sound philosophy at some times with youngsters, but it can also be a setup for an argument or an explosive display of temper.

Parents frequently see their once-friendly and tranquil two-year-old turn into a demon before their eyes. She becomes demanding, bossy, and temperamental. She may scream and throw a temper tantrum on the slightest provocation. The normal outlets for exhibiting tension—thumb sucking, bed wetting, and stuttering—may be exaggerated.

Two-and-a-half-year-olds don't handle frustration easily and they always feel as though their play is being interrupted by adults. They get told the rules more, experience more restrictions, and face frequent interruptions in their playtime.

If you thought your eighteen-month-old used the word "no" a lot, wait until the two-and-a-half-year-old gets going. It's usually at this age that parents remark that their child has developed "a mind of her own." Reasonable behavior is not her goal. Getting everyone—especially Mommy and Daddy—to do what she wants is much more the focus. Since she is so egocentric, her favorite word besides "no" is "mine." It's "My blankie" and "Do it for me" that are now very common. The world is supposed to revolve around the toddler at two and a half—at least that's what she thinks.

Tranquillity, decisiveness, and compromise are anything but the rule of the day for the thirty-month-old. She takes too long to make up her mind, and then immediately changes it. She doesn't compromise or give in. Instead she pitches a fierce fit. And it's no good trying to soothe her. She's too explosive and emotional.

The two-year-old will function best in a family that provides a warm, stable, affectionate, and consistent environment. This kind of environment will enhance the development of healthy growth in children, while an unhappy, restrictive, and inconsistent or unstable environment leads to a more insecure, dependent youngster.

Handling the Opposition of the Two-Year-Old Toddler

Children between twenty-four and thirty-six months need routines and consistency so that there is a regular tempo to their lives.

Keep in mind that parents cannot force growth. Growth comes from within a child. You can't force a plant to grow; that is something that comes from the molecular structure of a plant. Yet the kind of soil you're using and the water and sunlight you provide can definitely influence how well the plant thrives. So it is with a child. You can arrange a setting and an atmosphere that is congenial to and encourages optimum growth.

The atmosphere you provide has everything to do with how well children survive in a family and a home. You cannot turn curious, independent-minded two-year-olds into curious, independent, and self-disciplined preschoolers or elementary-age children by being too restrictive, punitive, or inhibiting. If they are always told no, they will either become resentful and stubborn or retreat from being curious, independent, and exploring children. The world of the toddler must support her efforts to move about, explore, and try out her needs to be independent.

Because two-and-a-half-year-olds will again assert their independence with the word "no," parents have to be prepared for this. As with the eighteen-month-old, it works a whole lot better when parents expect this and are prepared to deal with it comfortably. Don't overreact. Remember that negativism is an essential aspect of growth and development.

The healthy part of this fondness for no is that your child now has ideas of her own. She has a voice in how her world is run. Her ideas, however, may well run contrary to what her parents want.

Parents may envision and prefer compliant, easily malleable children. But young children grow into relatively well behaved older children by being allowed to grow through various stages of developing autonomy. In a sense, they are trying to control their environment when they make demands for equal status with adults. When one two-and-a-half-year-old I know tells his parents to "shut up" and "sit down" or

"Mommy, don't sit down," he is clearly trying to gain equal status with his parents, who clearly have a lot of control over the world he moves in.

Avoiding Power Struggles

How do you best handle the negativism and oppositionalism of the two- and two-and-a-half-year-old? Do not make a big deal of the child's negativism. Ignore her no's as much as possible, because she often doesn't really mean them anyway. Try leading her in the right direction rather than using force or engaging in a power struggle over her language, which is often riddled with words and phrases that indicate resistance.

This is a stage at which games and diversions can be used to particularly good effect. Make a game of what you want your toddler to do. If you want her to go in a certain direction, have a race ("I'll bet I can beat Marie to the door") or let her know that most children couldn't do what you want her to do ("This cantaloupe would be too heavy for most children. Think you could carry it over to the shopping cart?").

Another way to sidestep power struggles is to refrain from asking questions ("Do you want to eat now?") that can trigger an automatic no answer. Instead, ask questions that play into the child's developmental interests: "Who wants to help Mom vacuum?" or, "Who's big enough to put toys away?" Even better than questions are certain statements that avoid direct questions: "We're all going to work on picking up toys now" or, "I'm having fun folding clothes and putting them in dresser drawers."

Make commands and give orders as little as possible. Do so only when safety and protection issues are involved. Even then, you can often find alternative ways of getting what you want. A direct command such as "Hold my hand now" could be converted to "All the really smart boys are holding their parents' hands when they walk in the parking lot." And keep in mind that while you might want them to be compliant all the time, sometimes it doesn't matter if they assert their independence and autonomy by refusing to obey.

It's a little like training a tiger. You can't actually force a tiger to do what you want. Think of this when you're dealing with your toddler. We are constantly teaching children and guiding them in the right directions. But if they choose to be oppositional and defiant sometimes, there may be little you can do that's helpful or healthy. Everyone deserves to be independent sometimes. And toddlers are not trying to get rid of their parents or get their own way all the time. Parents can expect a full-scale rebellion only when they put too much pressure on their toddlers (for instance, by using too many no's or too many commands or too much forceful handling: "Do this now!" or, "If you don't do this, you're going to get a whipping!").

Handling Temper Tantrums

Often no matter what you do, you will have to deal with the two- or two-and-a-half-year-old's temper tantrum. Take away Marie's milk at the restaurant because she is playing with it and creating a sloppy mess, and she will scrunch up her face, arch her back, and reach for the glass. Then come the tears and the wail. She's feeling frustrated, but her limited vocabulary doesn't allow her to argue very successfully. Her only way of trying to make an impact on the world is through anger.

A two-year-old's outbursts of temper can be violent. They may involve not only tears and wails of outrage, but kicking, screaming, hitting, biting, and throwing herself about with incredible energy.

In the last chapter I gave you specific suggestions for handling the tantrums of the one-year-old. That advice still stands, but more needs to be added as the toddler at age two is bigger, stronger, and sometimes more violent. Handling the two-year-old's tantrum doesn't have to be difficult, however; often she can be distracted and even humored back into calmer behavior. If a two-year-old is really violently out of control, she can be picked up and placed in her room.

This may not stop a violent temper tantrum, but it offers you more control over the environment. Some two-year-olds can become so violent that they will kick, scream, and break things. They consequently need supervision and, because they may refuse to stay confined, need the protection of an adult who will restrain them or make sure they cannot act out their angriest and most destructive impulses. This will require physical restraint or barricading the child in a safe room.

An out-of-control youngster should be held or restrained only for her (and your property's) protection. She should be held gently but firmly, and only with your arms.

A barricade might be a thick board or piece of sturdy plywood that prevents a child from leaving a room but allows you to be able to monitor her actions and supervise her behaviors. Using such a device helps to establish that there are limits and that a parent is able to control the environment.

What you shouldn't do is argue, threaten, or use physical punishment. An angry outburst is not the time to employ more direct and controlling methods; they don't work. Better to understand what the youngster is going through—she feels frustrated and has too little ability to deal either with her feelings or the forces in her environment causing her frustration.

Understanding means letting her cry it out or allowing her to work through her frustration. When she is too aggressive or violent, and when she threatens or attempts to bite, kick, or hit you or others, then you might hold her so she cannot strike out at anyone.

In such a situation you will have to confront your own feelings, which may include frustration, anger, inadequacy, embarrassment, or the hurt of rejection. Keep in mind much of what I have said up to this point about why toddlers react with temper tantrums and the importance of their learning to control themselves. Also remember that this behavior represents a stage in life and has little or nothing to do with you. You will be in a much better position to follow my suggestions if you are not also battling your own emotions at the same time you're dealing with an angry toddler.

The most important part of this whole process is for you to remain calm, tranquil, and confident. That's where your understanding of the situation can pay dividends for you. If you keep in mind that the tantrum-throwing child is frustrated and feels unable to cope with her own emotions, then even if you're in public and even if you're feeling mortally embarrassed you will find the means to react in the ways I'm suggesting here.

Besides maintaining calmness, it is essential that you remain firm. Because usually the toddler's tantrum is caused by a restriction or a rule ("You must sit in the cart while we're in the grocery store" or, "You cannot touch the electric wires"), you must remain firm. While you are calm, tranquil, and reassuring, you will not give in and allow behavior contrary to the child's best interest.

Sometimes you can talk her down ("When you are sitting in the cart then you can help me pick out the best bananas") or you may just talk in a soothing, gentle way about what is next on the agenda ("We'll make cookies together and you can use the cookie cutter that looks like Santa Claus"). It's most important to remain calm while she takes her own time to run the course of her tantrum.

When necessary during this process, whether alone at home or in public, let her know what the rule or boundary is: "No. You must take Mommy's hand before we go any farther" or, "Sit down and then we can begin our fun."

As soon as the tantrum is over, you can show her love and let her participate with you in some way that shows you still care for her despite her behavior. This works very well in the grocery store where you can find tasks for her as you proceed: "You look around and see if you can spot the lemons; I just don't see them. Do you?" Or, "Can you reach over and grab that can of your favorite soup?"

Just as it is important to understand that all toddlers assert their independence and autonomy and all use the word "no" to be oppositional, it is well to keep in mind that all youngsters throw temper tantrums.

Handling Aggression

All toddlers are aggressive at times. That means that they will push, hit, spit, bite, kick, and take away toys from other children while shoving them aside. While not all of this is really intended as aggression, some is. But two-years-olds are small children who don't understand the social niceties or the best ways to cope with their own anger and frustration.

Because you understand all of this, does this mean that you let them hit, bite, and kick others? No, you don't. You have the job of teaching a child how to get along with others and how to respect the rights and the feelings of other people. Letting a toddler be aggressive is not very reassuring to the child. Remember that toddlers don't always know what they want. That means, too, that even when they are biting another child, they may not want to be doing so. It is reassuring to toddlers when their parents set limits and love them enough to stop them from hurting others.

There are two parts to teaching youngsters about aggression. The first is to teach the rules and the limits ("You cannot hit others"). The second part is to enforce those limits. When you don't permit them to hurt others, you are giving them a clear message that hurting is wrong and that you will not permit it.

It's at the toddler stage that parents can begin using reasoning. You will begin to tell your child in a very simple and direct way that hitting (or biting, pinching, scratching, poking, shoving, slapping) is not allowed and why ("When you hit, that hurts Sara").

That is not to say that reasoning is going to produce immediate and positive results with all toddlers. In many instances it won't. More important at this point is that you are explaining why certain behaviors are not allowed or approved and setting the stage for later years when your child will respond better to reasoning. At the toddler stage, you repeat the reasons frequently, but you try to prevent the aggressive behavior by supervising children closely and intervening before they are allowed to act in an aggressive way.

You should not resort to severe punishment for such behavior, because you don't want to call too much attention to it—and severe punishment sometimes actually reinforces such misbehaviors. Also, if you use spanking or hitting, you are modeling aggressive behavior yourself. Some parents think that one good way to teach toddlers about aggressive behavior is to show them how it feels: "That's how biting feels; it hurts!" But the two-year-old is at a stage when she's more likely to imitate your behavior and to see what you do as acceptable.

Parents usually worry when toddlers are too frequently aggressive. They believe their toddler, especially if he's a boy, will turn into an aggressive person with little regard for the feelings of others. They fear he could become a bully or a delinquent. But we know from studying children that aggressive bullies are likely to be created by parents who are highly punitive as well as by those who are overly permissive of aggressive behavior.

Instead parents who do not permit their children to be aggressive will teach them that aggression is not right through their own appropriate behavior as parents. By talking to their children and using reasoning instead of punishment, they will bring up children who solve problems rationally themselves, without resorting to aggression.

Beginning in the toddler years, if you are a warm and affectionate parent who sets clear and consistent rules about how people in your family treat other people, and if you consistently follow these rules yourself, you are in the best position to raise a child who can get along well with other people.

Establishing Rituals

Routines and rituals are very important to toddlers. They need things to be the same. And they don't like change. Typically parents begin to establish routines and rituals for starting the day, mealtimes, nap times, baths, preparing for bed, and bedtime. For instance, there may be a particular ritual for preparing for bed; a parent has to say the same thing ("Time to get our pajamas on"), proceed in the same way ("First our pajamas, then brush our teeth, and then the story"), and be sure not to leave out any part of the ritual.

Change can be as simple as a parent tidying up the toys a child left on the bedroom floor after play. Some children may need those toys left in disarray, rather than for a parent—bent on neatness—to put them away.

When parents forget about part of the usual routine, some children have difficulty getting through a task. And as they get older and it's time to change a ritual, children often give you some clues about that ("I can go upstairs by myself, Daddy"). In general, though, routines, procedures, and rituals need to be changed very gradually to avoid upsetting children. Any parent who has tried to change a favorite story knows how upset kids can be if you leave out a part of it.

Dealing with Dawdling

Two-year-olds tend to be dawdlers. This can be viewed as a type of negativism. However, it should also be expected at this stage. It's best not to try to rush two-year-olds as they pick at their food or take forever to get dressed. While most parents want to move forward with each task or chore, toddlers operate on their own time schedule. Toddlers need at least twice as much time to do things like pick up toys, brush their teeth, get dressed, or eat spaghetti. The reason is that they are new at these skills. To become expert at them takes practice; meanwhile they are more interested in the experience and the experiment than they are in getting the task done quickly.

To create as little upheaval as possible should be a primary goal of parents with little dawdlers at this age. Try not to take your child's dawdling personally. Instead, recognize her developmental limitations and take them into account. Attempt to lead her to new situations and through tasks while summoning up your greatest amount of patience. When a transition must be made with more dispatch than usual, give her as much forewarning or preparation as possible. For example, if you must leave the house very early the next morning, you might tell her well before bedtime, "We'll have to eat breakfast and get dressed very, very fast tomorrow morning." Remind her of this once or twice before she goes to bed. As Dr. Benjamin Spock has pointed out about this age, "Try to get things done without raising issues." And above all, encourage, don't criticize. You can do this, for instance, by saying, "Let's see those quick hands fly when you're putting on your shoes" instead of responding with, "Hurry up. You're such a slowpoke."

Providing Security

Security is important for the toddler. That means that she will have her favorite blanket, story, teddy bear, toy, towel, and so on. While this may create annoyances for you at times, these objects provide sources of security for children, especially when the adults are creating too many changes.

Using Face-Saving Techniques

Ames and Ilg in *Your Two-Year-Old* suggest using "face saving" techniques. Face saving means that the way you phrase a command or order allows both you and your child to avoid a conflict. Rather than issue an ultimatum ("Your hands must be clean before you can eat lunch"), it's better to suggest, "Let's wash up before lunch." If you have not given an ultimatum, you don't have to see that the order is followed to the letter. If she hears a suggestion ("Let's pick up some toys"), she doesn't feel forced to rebel or give in. It gives her a better chance to make her own decision.

Giving prompts is another way of using face-saving techniques with toddlers. Asking questions such as "What do we do before we put our pajamas on?" or, "Where do your toys go?" invites children to answer the questions or respond appropriately rather than to resist an actual command (such as "Put all your toys in the toy box now").

Using Diversions, Distraction, and Termination

Conversation tends to be a diversion with the two-and-a-half-year-old. You can dazzle a youngster of this age with a lot of talking, which they will find fascinating. While you have them diverted, you can lead or move them in the direction you want.

When Marie is demanding that you play with her, avoid saying something like, "No, not now. Maybe later." That may well initiate a further demand for "Now!" Instead say, "Okay, but let's first get this over with." This serves as a diversion, avoids starting an oppositional demand ("No! Now!"), and often distracts children from their original demand. Distracting and terminating may be two of your best approaches to the two-and-a-half-year-old. At this age, a toddler can be easily distracted. Just ask a question or make a statement that will divert her attention.

Asking "Can you guess who's coming over tonight?" when a child is in the middle of rejecting all choices offered to her can result in taking her mind off the impossible posture she's taken.

Termination is a similar technique. As kids in this stage frequently can't make up their minds, and giving them choices only makes things worse, try terminating the situation. You can do this by picking the child up and moving her to a new location, room, or distraction.

Terence, a lively and active two-year-old boy, wanted the doll his four-year-old sister was playing with. He tried to grab it from Cindy, but she refused to give it up. Terence quickly flew at Cindy, pushing her down. But Cindy still refused to give up the doll. Terence began scream-ing in rage.

Their mother, Rosemary, asked Cindy if she would let Terence play with the doll. Cindy easily gave it up because she needed reassurance and sympathy from her mother after being pushed down. When Rosemary handed the doll to Terence, he pushed it away and cried louder.

"Do you want the doll?" Rosemary asked Terence. He kicked his feet in a rage.

"Get up or take the doll," his mother said. Terence continued his tantrum.

"Sister is giving you the doll," Rosemary said, trying to talk him out of his angry outburst. Terence's only response was more angry wailing.

Rosemary could see that neither handing him the doll nor telling him to get up was going to work. She picked him up off the floor and walked outside with him. She sat him down on the grass where he could see their dog on a leash not too far away. In a few minutes, Terence had forgotten about the doll and his anger and was walking over to pet the dog.

By changing the scenery and taking Terence to the backyard, Rosemary avoided giving him more choices (which he would only refuse anyway), avoided an argument, and most of all avoided an impossible to resolve power struggle.

Programming

You can program a two-year-old by going over in detail what is going to happen. Don't ask her if she wants to go to Grandma's. Tell her what will happen: "In a few minutes, you're going to put on your new red shirt and then we're going to get in the car and drive to Grandma's house. When we get there, she said you could use the swimming pool. First you need to go to your dresser and get your bathing suit. Can you remember all that? How much can you remember?"

Programming children by telling them what will happen is one kind of structure that works well. Almost always the best way of handling an argument or a tantrum is to avoid it in the first place. When you find through experience that your child is overwhelmed by choices, never likes the ones you give her, or can't make up her mind, don't give choices. It's better to program and give direction.

Handling the More Difficult Two-Year-Old Toddler

Terence is a good example of the difficult two-year-old. He is a child with a stubborn temperament. He doesn't learn from his mistakes, his mother's scoldings, or the time-outs she gives him by making him sit in a special "time-out chair."

Difficult toddlers like Terence may cry more, be extra whiny, respond in stubborn and oppositional ways, and use no more often and more forcefully than other tots. They tend to resist longer than other children and are likely to throw more pitched fits and have more violent temper tantrums. Discipline breaks down when they won't go to their room or stay in a time-out chair.

Are such children beyond hope? Is your only recourse to spank or spank harder?

No to both. Studies have shown that when difficult, oppositional, stubborn, and aggressive toddlers are dealt with by calm, patient parents with some specific training, these youngsters do become more compliant. But it does take training and a great deal of understanding on the parents' part.

At this age it is absolutely critical—for the future development of the child and the relationship between parent and child—that parents have a thorough understanding of child development. In addition, parents need to develop skills in sensitive discipline in order to help the difficult child learn to live within the rules of the family. Sensitive discipline is a way of handling children that takes into account a youngster's temperament and does not attempt to harshly coerce children into conforming to parental expectations. It is important, when disciplining in this way, to refrain from losing your cool and resorting to physical punishment. When you're aggressive, impatient, or unreasonable in your demands, your child is likely to feel alienated and rejected and to respond with greater opposition as a result.

Aggressive, oppositional, and stubborn toddlers can be given a congenial atmosphere in which to learn to control their stubborn and aggressive traits. Or they can be turned into overly aggressive, more stubborn, and more oppositional individuals. The latter result is all too easy to achieve when parents unwittingly reinforce the child's use of coercive tactics or respond with repressive, harsh approaches. The frustrated parent commonly makes both of these mistakes.

Difficult toddlers often engender negative and aggressive methods, unfair labeling, and forceful, coercive approaches from adults. Unfortunately such methods can set up lifelong patterns of misbehavior, including oppositional and defiant interaction with authority figures.

Neglect, rejection, and even abuse are frequently the lot of the very difficult child. But it's these very kids who most need affection, acceptance, approval, and calm, loving, reasonable discipline from parents. They are the children most at risk for future problems and are in need of special treatment.

Responding with Firmness

It is essential to handle the toddler's persistent demands, intense requests, and opposition to rules with firm and reasonable limits. Despite the youngster's intense objections or determined nagging, it's very important that you stick to what is necessary or right.

Taking your hand when crossing a street, staying with you (or sitting in the grocery cart) in a crowded store, or riding in the car seat are examples of situations in which a toddler may marshal considerable resistance toward what you want and know to be in her (or everyone else's) best interest.

Firmness in these situations requires that you be as determined and firm as the child may be headstrong and stubborn. While the child may get angry, throw a temper tantrum, or resist by kicking and screaming, your best defense is to stay firm in a calm, controlled, and (for the child) reassuring manner. You might say, for instance, that the car doesn't move until she is firmly belted in the car seat ("Sorry, but that's the rule").

Giving Limited Choices

When it is possible, you might give such children limited choices. But when the child decides, you accept her choice, so the choices you offer must be acceptable to you. They must also be limited to no more than two or three so that the child is not overwhelmed. And the child cannot reject all choices and select her own.

For example, there are choices she might make about which of two pairs of pajamas she will wear for bedtime, or which of three stories she would like to have read to her when she's in bed. But there is no choice about what time she goes to bed or whether she goes to bed at all.

If difficult children are to grow up feeling they have control over their environment, it's essential to teach them at a young age that they have choices. This will not only help them feel somewhat more independent and autonomous, but sometimes get you what you want on some important issues.

Programming

I've already advised that toddlers be programmed. This is especially true for difficult toddlers who frequently have trouble making transitions. Make sure that you give warnings and advance notice about changes and new situations. Children who do not deal well with abrupt changes need to have a parent who prepares them ahead of time with warnings, and also leaves enough time for them to get used to making the change. Unless you want a battle of wills, don't spring anything on difficult children at the last minute.

Again, as I've said before, avoid statements, requests, and questions that can be answered with the favorite word ("No!"). Instead of asking, "Would you like to have a baby-sitter tonight?" it's always better to state directly, "The baby-sitter is coming after dinner." Rather than ask,

"Would you like to get your pajamas on now?" it is more effective to ask, "Would you like to wear your Superman pajamas or the green ones Grandma gave you?"

Of course, nearly every toddler, but especially difficult tykes, can get to the point of rejecting all reasonable choices and options. In this case, it's past time for discussion and rationality; it's better to take action by picking her up and putting her pajamas on her.

Playing "No" Games

If you have an oppositional and resistant toddler, not only should you expect her to say no frequently, but you must make it safe to do so. You may find it helpful to build into daily life plenty of opportunities for her to use The Word. Playing silly little games, perhaps while reading a story ("I think the cow says 'bow-wow,' don't you?"), can help children use the word "no" in safe situations. You can also ask questions that have no particular importance attached to them. For example, "Would you like to go to the store with me?" or, "Would you like to share my Pepsi?" or, "Would you like to wear your purple shorts?"

When my son Jason was younger, I liked to use drama when he said no and it didn't really matter. For example, if I asked him if he wanted to play on the swings at a nearby school's playground and he said "No," I made a big deal out of it in a playful way.

"Did you say no? I think I heard you say a big fat no! All right, the kid doesn't want to play on the swings at the school! Okay! That's fine. Let's see if we can find something he will say yes about. How about going fishing? Would he like that?"

All of this was done in a loud voice and as if I were announcing it to the neighborhood. He got a kick out of it and he could go on saying no as long as he wanted because it really didn't matter.

As silly as these examples might sound—suggesting the cow says bow-wow or being overly dramatic because Jason said no to playing on the swings at the school—they give toddlers chances to say no without anyone getting exasperated with them. These "no" games also free up children to say yes when they're ready. They may even help children to get bored with saying no.

Think about those instances in which you might prefer the child to say yes, but you can tolerate a no (for example, "Would you like to tell me what you and Danny were playing?"). You might be curious and you may want to communicate, but it's really okay if she answers, "No." Then you can be gracious in giving in: "Okay, maybe next time you'll tell me."

Difficult children may sometimes be able to give in on the big issues themselves if they begin to realize that they frequently have choices and it's okay to say no once in a while. For such kids, it's important that no not become a major weapon in their arsenal of ways to deal with anger and frustration. When children are actually given lots of opportunities to safely say no, it's not as important to look for chances to use a negative approach.

Finally, consider that difficult children are just as likely as other toddlers to say no when they mean yes. So, don't always take their no as a final answer but give them a way to change their mind. If you ask your child if she would like some Kool-Aid and she vehemently refuses, accept this and make a face-saving suggestion: "Well, maybe you're not thirsty now, but if you get thirsty you can have some Kool-Aid whenever you're ready."

Summary

Some of the characteristics of the two-year-old toddler are:

- She is gentle, friendly, curious, active, and a real "eager beaver."
- She has many more words at her command.
- At times she seems to be going in many different directions, so that her activity seems out of control.
- She is often clumsy and inexpert at many things she tries.
- She shows greater signs of negativism and oppositionalism at around age thirty months.

- She may act indecisively at about two and a half and change her mind often.

Parents can best handle the negativism and oppositionalism of the two-year-old by:

- Creating an environment that is not too restrictive, punitive, or inhibiting.
- Supporting her efforts to move about, explore, and try out new ways to show her independence.
- Trying to lead her in the right direction rather than trying to force change or engaging in power struggles.
- Using diversionary tactics and making games out of situations to assist her to be compliant.
- Avoiding an overreliance on offering choices.
- Not arguing, threatening, or using physical punishment to deal with temper tantrums.
- Responding to temper tantrums with calmness and firmness, and refusing to allow behavior that is not in a child's best interest.
- Reacting to aggression by teaching the limits and rules and enforcing the limits.
- Setting up routines and rituals to organize a toddler's life.
- Handling dawdling by providing extra time and not taking the dawdling personally.
- Using face-saving methods, distractions, prompts, and termination rather than ultimatums with two-year-olds.

Parents can better deal with the difficult two-year-old by:

- Recognizing that difficult toddlers, because of their temperament, may be more likely to cry or whine, may be more stubborn and oppositional, and may use the word "no" more frequently and more forcefully than their more compliant peers.

- Developing skills in sensitive discipline.
- Using firm and reasonable limits.
- Giving choices within limits.
- Programming; that is, giving considerable details about forthcoming situations or events, to help to provide a structure.
- Playing "no" games that give toddlers opportunities to safely say no.
- Giving children chances to change their mind and say yes.

Understanding and Disciplining the Three-Year-Old Child

The Three-Year-Old

When his father gets down on the floor with him and plays, three-year-old Jesse Thurman is in seventh heaven. He loves to show his father how he puts plastic blocks together to make buildings and cars.

He also likes to play with toy cars and enjoys constructing ramps so his metal cars race against each other. His play with cars can go on for an half hour before he thinks of something else he'd like to do.

As he's playing, Jesse talks. And what a talker he is. He uses the word "telecommunication" and his father has no idea where he heard such a big word. In fact, Jesse comes up with other words, in his burgeoning vocabulary, that amaze his father.

Jesse, while still a young child in many ways, now has better speech, a better ability to walk and balance, an increased understanding of what others mean, and much more control over his body than when he was two. He knows about sharing and taking turns. He can play simple games and follow simple rules. However, when his father tries to teach him the "right way" to play checkers, Jesse quickly loses interest and just likes to move red checkers around the board—following no particular rules at all.

Jesse, more now than when he was two, is ready for greater independence. As a toddler, he needed to be negative and oppositional to find a sense of autonomy and competence. Out of that frequently negative two-and-a-half-year-old grew a more self-confident and exuberant three-year-old boy, one who is less oppositional and more fun. At three, Jesse can afford to be compliant more often—although he may surprise himself when he discovers himself saying yes whereas a few weeks or months ago it would have been an automatic no!

Like many three-year-olds Jesse wants to please both his mother and father. He wants to have approval and he knows the way to get it is to listen and obey.

Unlike the two-and-a-half-year-old, the three-year-old is challenged more by the forces outside himself than by his internal struggles. With increased motor skills and language ability, he's ready to deal with his peers, his parents, and other adults—well, almost ready.

Now it's his peers and other adults who provide the great challenges. He feels ready to do almost anything, but it's those other guys who get in his way. Parents, recognizing his greater ability to communicate, really try to communicate things like rules, restrictions, and values. And because he's more mature, he can handle this better than he could at two and a half and with fewer tantrums.

He would rather imitate his parents than oppose them. Therefore, he is easier to manage and much more conforming. He will tend to be more loving and affectionate and in general more on the delightful side than not.

He can play by himself, engage in fantasy play, ride a tricycle, or talk to you. The parents of a talkative tyke will have little difficulty noticing he has a vocabulary of a thousand words and is able to talk in sentences. This is not to suggest that he's forgotten how to annoy and infuriate you. He is able to use many more words than "no" to bother you now! He is more than willing to express all his desires, his problems, and even his fears.

Sarah Downey, age three, provides a good example of how a greater ability to use imagination and fantasy leads to more fears. When she spends the day with her grandmother, things go well until it's time to go to bed. "Can I sleep with you, Grandma?" she asks.

"It's better that children sleep in their own beds, darling," her grandmother says.

"But I'm afraid, Grandma," Sarah says, and the look on her face suggests she's being truthful. "Mommy lets me sleep with her when I'm afraid."

When Sarah's grandmother explores the reasons for her fears, she learns that Sarah thinks there could be monsters in her bedroom when the light is out and she's also afraid of bugs getting in her bed. Her active imagination brings on fears that were never present before. Like her mother, her grandmother on some occasions may permit Sarah to sleep with her.

Fears aside, three-year-olds are also very interested in friendships and social relationships. They can even have an imaginary friend—not uncommon for children beginning at about three years of age.

By the age of three and a half, however, most youngsters will experience another change. According to Theresa and Frank Caplan in *The Early Childhood Years: The Two- to Six-Year-Old,* ambivalence is one of the watchwords for the three-and-a-half-year-old. The once outgoing and friendly child can become more withdrawn and unpredictable. He can have sudden outbursts of anger, temper, or whining. If your child goes through a particularly whiny stage, age three and a half is the time he's most likely to do it.

At this age children may also turn bossy, become insistent on attention, and at times be unbelievably demanding. Only a few months ago you may have been delighted that the toddler was finally really growing up. Now you're not so sure.

The delightful three is likely to become a no monster again, in a few more months. It's almost a replay of the change that occurs between two and two-and-a-half. Some mothers complain that the chief preoccupation of three-and-a-half-year-olds is their interest in disobeying.

They show themselves to be strong-willed, and while they admire their parents they're not afraid of opposing them. Violent disagreements may come about because you say it's time for dinner, a bath, church, or bedtime.

Also characteristic of this age is the use of bad words and offensive terms or language. Potty talk springs forth from the child's mouth unexpectedly and parents often say, "I don't know where he gets it because we don't talk like that at home." Words like poop, poopy-head, stupid, jerk, and so on enter the three-and-a-half-year-old's vocabulary. Also, aggressive language is not uncommon. Three-and-a-half-year olds sometimes threaten to shoot their teachers and cut off Mommy's head.

Why does this strange new behavior come about? Perhaps in part because this is when children try to control others. A three-and-a-half-year-old may say, as the parents in one of my parenting classes reported about their son Jerry, "We were at the zoo having a great time. All of a sudden, when we were going to sit on a bench to eat, he shouted to his dad, 'Don't sit down!' "

Later, Jerry told his mother not to stand up. His parents didn't expect this and were understandably confused over what was going on. Three-year-olds, frustrated by the control being exerted over them, sometimes like to feel in control, too. The orders and directives they give to adults are their way of attempting to exercise a little control also.

Typically today, this is about the age children start going to a nursery school or preschool. This entails new adventures, transitions, and challenges. The child's innate personality traits and temperament are usually recognizable and relatively stable at this stage of development. That doesn't mean that the three-and-a-half-year-old won't be bossy, demanding, whiny, or determined. Once again, this is a natural phase of development. The basic temperament and personality of a child will still be evident throughout the difficult phases that ordinarily occur at eighteen months, two and a half, and three and a half.

If the temperament of the child is such that transitions and new situations are difficult, these new challenges and adventures will make his temperament readily apparent to everyone.

What may look like oppositional behavior is sometimes just the child's inability to make a smooth transition. Or it could be a negative attitude about going into a new situation. And sometimes it's the sensitive temperament which leads to conflicts between parent and child over dress, temperature, flavors, textures, or styles.

It's especially important that parents become aware of the temperament of their child so that clashes can be handled skillfully.

Handling the Opposition of the Three-Year-Old

The three-year-old, as Louise Bates Ames and Frances L. Ilg point out in *Your Three Year Old: Friend or Enemy*, is a conformer who likes to please. But as the Gesell Institute followers (like Ames and Ilg) suggest, after every smooth period of conforming there will be a turnaround. Just as two and a half is a tailspin age, so is three and a half. The aware parent can expect some oppositional behavior and rebellion at this mid-year marker.

Refusing to obey may be the most frequent form of opposition for the next few months. Maybe your child's main concern is to strengthen his will. He will know by now that one certain way to do this is to oppose Mom or Dad.

So, while handling the three-year-old is easy, dealing with the three-and-a-half-year-old is not. Your best weapon, as always, is preparation. If you expect this stage of rebellion and if you understand that it is part of the developmental process, then you won't take it personally.

His "No! Poopy-head!" doesn't have to be seen as a direct assault on you because you're a bad parent or because you're doing something wrong. In fact, most of the time when this rebellion occurs it's because you have asked him to do something relatively routine or simple, like "Please put your G.I. Joe's away." This is also usually something that just a few weeks ago would have been met with, "Okay, Mommy."

One of the most useful things to bear in mind—and this will be a constant theme throughout this book—is that it's up to you as a parent to find ways of avoiding battles of will and the head-to-head combat that can result when two strong wills collide. With the three-and-a-half-year-old, there are a couple of ways of avoiding these titanic clashes.

Using Commands and Requests Well

One way is by phrasing requests and commands in such a way that they are not ultimatums in the first place. This allows you to back down without losing face, and you don't have to make it a life-and-death struggle for your child either. For instance, you could say, "I'd like to see you put away your toys." This avoids the ultimatum that sometimes sets up an unnecessary clash.

A common situation leading to rebellion at this age has to do with going to bed. While you can give plenty of warnings that bedtime is approaching, you can also have a routine about what has to be accomplished first, second, and so on. However, some part of this routine is now likely to engender opposition. It may be over what he wears to bed or who comes to tuck him in and kiss him good night.

He may insist that he sleep in the T-shirt he's been wearing all day. Saying, "Let's put our pajamas on, okay?" can be one way of letting him know what you want him to wear. He may rebel with, "I sleep in my T-shirt, Daddy."

Since no ultimatum has been used, it's easy to back down and be agreeable. "Okay, go get your teeth brushed and you can sleep in your T-shirt tonight." Whether he sleeps in his T-shirt or not is not a big deal and you need not make a federal case of it.

Another way of handling these minor skirmishes with opposition is by making sure you are giving directions in a positive way. "Your bedroom is going to look so clean and neat when your toys are picked up, right?" is much preferable and more easily tolerated by children than the more negative approach: "What a messy bedroom! How many times have I told you not to leave your toys scattered all over the floor."

Using Distraction

Also, be ready to wave the magic wand of distraction. Throughout these younger years, your ability to use language to distract children will be invaluable. While you're talking about what fun it will be tomorrow when he gets to help you bake cookies, the two of you will have managed to pick up the toys and put his pajamas on and be walking to the bathroom for the toothbrushing ritual.

Instead of engaging in the battle of wills ("Yes, you will pick up your toys" "No!" "Pick up your toys now!" "No!") or what often happens when the battle escalates ("I don't like you, Daddy! I'm going to shoot you with my gun!"), distraction can avoid this frequently unnecessary rebellious scene.

Recently when I was meeting with several mothers and their preschool children for a discussion group, the children played with two boxes of toys. When the discussion was over, it was time for the children to pick up their toys. We couldn't believe how many plastic toys, cars, and blocks had been scattered around the room. I suggested distraction and we all began talking to the children.

"Who knows what goes in this box?" one mother asked.

"Somebody show me how these blocks go together," another parent said.

"What shall we do outside when these toys are all put back in the boxes?" yet another mother asked.

The children responded to the questions and sometimes mothers and children continued to talk and play while the toys were being picked up. The beauty of the situation was that no parent ever ordered the children to pick up the toys. Nevertheless they were all picked up in a few minutes and the room looked neat once again.

Establishing Rules and Setting Limits

In situations in which limits have to be set and rules have to be followed, make sure (and this applies at every age and stage) that the limits and rules are appropriate for the developmental stage and maturity level of the child.

Obviously there are some major requirements related to order and hygiene. Your child must get up each day, get dressed, eat meals, play, and go to bed. There will be some additional rules and expectations that go along with these "musts." Still, within these basic requirements there can be great flexibility.

While a child has to get dressed, he can choose what clothes or socks or shoes he will wear. He can refuse one food, but not all foods. Rules that apply to safety and protection, of course, will not be very flexible. But kids can live with some rigidity if there is also enough flexibility, reasoned permissiveness, and room to be oppositional and rebellious in areas that are of lesser consequence.

Responding to Anxiety and Fears

At three and a half, children commonly display more anxieties and fears. They have fears related to bedtime and the dark, wake up with nightmares or night terrors, and may display more anxiety when parents leave than at other ages.

You may want to keep your absences to a minimum for a few months. Nevertheless it's important for you to get away from your child for periods of time whenever you are experiencing a particularly rebellious and oppositional stage. This helps beleaguered parents to recoup their strength and keep their own feelings in perspective.

Handling the More Difficult Three-Year-Old

Henry Johnson is a difficult three-year-old. While he seems very bright and is often very affectionate, there is another side to him as well. At his day care center he bit another little boy. He spit at his teacher when she asked Henry to come up from under a table at lunchtime. At nap time, when the other children quickly fall asleep, Henry is active and attempts to awaken them. If a teacher tries to isolate him at this time, he resorts to threats. "I'll break all the windows at the school," he threatened one day.

Another time, when a staff member asked him to wash his hands after a painting project, he refused, shouting, "Shut up, asshole! I hate you!"

When playing with other children, Henry may push them down, grab their toys, or call them "butthead."

Even at home, when his mother tells him it's time to go to bed, Henry may react with sudden violence. "Shut up, bitch!" he snarled once. On another occasion he told his mother he would cut her legs off if she kept telling him to put his toys away.

While all three- and three-and-a-half-year-olds will be negative and oppositional at times as they strive for more independence and a little more control over their lives, the truly difficult three-something child will be hard to handle.

In most cases, difficult behavior will be a carryover from infancy. The biggest surprise you may face with your three-year-old is that you're having the same problems with him that you had when he was one and two. If the difficulties of your child are related to temperament, the traits are not going to magically melt away. They will remain in one form or another.

Your task, as parent, is to help your child channel his more challenging characteristics, behavior, and traits into positive areas of life—without making these traits actually worse.

Like the difficult child at age two, the difficult three-year-old will be more demanding, more stubborn and oppositional, and more intense than other children of the same age. However, the difficult three-year-old will be different from the way he was a year earlier because he has better language skills, his motor skills have improved, and his aggressiveness may be more blatant. "I hate you!" "My dad is going to come here and shoot you!" "I'll kill you!" and "I'll do what I want!" are not unusual statements for angry young children to make. They suggest the difficult time parents (and day care workers) have when dealing with a youngster who uses threats to try to get what he wants.

These early oppositional and stubborn behaviors must not be reinforced or ignored. Instead they are to be recognized, first for what they often are: the signs of a youngster with a difficult and demanding temperament who lacks the self-control that other children of the same age may have. This does not mean that the child can't be handled or that he is destined to become an out-of-control teenager. It does, however, signal the task confronting you, and other adults who spend time with the child: to find and use the appropriate means for helping the child learn better self-control, and, above all, to avoid reinforcing the child's aggressive, angry, and violent behaviors.

Understanding Your Child's Temperament

To be able to manage such a difficult child adequately, you must be aware of your child's temperament. You must see him as an individual who has personality traits that are uniquely his and that give him the special qualities that make him an individual. By getting to know his temperament, you can begin to accept the traits you didn't cause and you can't change. Once you begin to see these traits as uniquely his, you can learn to adapt to them and avoid seeing those traits and your child as troubled, abnormal, or impossible to live with.

It's essential to avoid labeling the child in a negative way or damaging his self-image. Do not use negative and critical names, comments, or statements about him within his hearing, and do not allow anyone else to brand him as angry, aggressive, violent, or unmanageable. Once a child begins to see himself in this way, he will be psychologically obligated to continue to live up to the label.

Managing Stress

You won't be able to handle a difficult child unless you work on your own stress level. This will require parental time-out from the child to replenish your energy level. The more positive social and emotional support you can get, the better.

Mrs. Johnson, Henry's mother, attended an eight-week parenting class on Tuesday nights. When the class began and she told other parents about how difficult Henry was, she got lots of sympathy. As the class went on, it usually started with someone asking Mrs. Johnson how Henry was that week. Mrs. Johnson found it helpful to talk about Henry's behavior and to receive support.

While some of Henry's behavior made parents laugh, Mrs. Johnson had found some understanding friends. Often she and other parents would stretch out their Tuesday nights by going out for coffee after the meeting was over. At the end of eight weeks, she thanked everyone for being so kind to her and several exchanged phone numbers with her so they could keep in touch.

One mother of a difficult three-year-old said she never drank during her pregnancy but when her child turned two she began having a glass of wine at night. Other parents of difficult children I know use the time at day care to relax, pamper themselves, or talk to friends. Some start regular exercise programs or return to work. Still others begin to dream about the future when their child will be old enough to go to camp during the summer. When difficult children are older, their parents can enroll them in camp, sports, Scouts, or other social activities that, although they may well be good for the children, are more important for the respite they give to stressed parents.

Handling Aggression

It is important not to model aggressive, hostile, or out-of-control anger. When you spank and use other physical punishments, your methods contradict what you're attempting to teach. You teach your child to continue acting in a violent or aggressive way. Modeling and teaching ways to control angry behavior and solve problems without resorting to force will be one of your biggest challenges.

Children who tend to react to everyday situations with aggressiveness and hostility should not be exposed to aggression. They should not be allowed to watch TV shows, videos, movies, or cartoons with aggressive themes. These children will be less able to adequately handle aggressive content in stories and TV shows, and are more likely to imitate such material or act it out in play and in day-to-day dealings with family, pets, and friends.

After forty or more years of research, studies conclude that children are definitely more inclined to accept violence as a way of resolving problems if they are exposed to aggressive and violent behavior on television and in the movies. Parents must screen whatever children will be exposed to in order to make sure that those who are already prone to acting in violent ways aren't reinforced in their aggressive attitudes.

Similarly, when at-risk young children see violent behavior in their homes, the chances of acting in hostile or violent ways are significantly increased. Parents of difficult young children must make sure their own actions do not suggest that aggressive behavior is acceptable behavior.

Giving Directives Effectively

Use requests, instructions, and commands that do not lend themselves to opposition, defiance, or angry stubbornness. All requests and commands should be simple, clear, and direct. Instructions to such children must be given with direct eye contact and in an authoritative voice and posture. They should be given one at a time, and the child should be given a few seconds to respond appropriately. If he fails to respond in the appropriate way, the parent must then respond with a consequence.

Using Negative Consequences

Consequences for three-year-olds may include a reprimand (a statement of disapproval such as "I don't like it when you don't do what I ask"), but should consist of at least a time-out. This procedure involves removing the child to a dull, nonstimulating area for a period of time not to exceed five to ten minutes. The accepted standard is about one minute for every year of age.

Difficult young children often attempt to avoid time-out, and frequently actively resist it. They usually don't like the negative consequence, the restriction of having to stay in one place, and the control placed on them. Therefore, they may cry, pitch a fit, throw themselves on the floor, run away, hit, kick, bite, or threaten you. This often leads parents to conclude that time-out won't work with the child, is the wrong punishment, or is making his behavior worse.

Disruptive children who avoid time-out, or delay serving it, should not be let off the hook. Difficult, stubborn, and disruptive children can be taught to abide by the consequence of time-out. If the child is engaged in a tantrum, he is to be told his time-out doesn't begin until he's quiet and sitting in the time-out chair. The same response is given if he refuses to go to the time-out place.

You can lead him to the spot or the chair. If he leaves or refuses to quiet down, he should be picked up and taken to a "quiet room" in the house. This could be his room, but wherever it is he is to be placed and barricaded there. This does not have to be a harsh or forbidding experience. Yet, it is important that you establish that this is serious business, you are in control, and he will serve the consequences of his original behavior. A barricade should be some sort of gate or half door (a three- to four-foot piece of half-inch plywood would work just fine) placed in such a way that the child cannot leave the room, but he can see out and you can see in.

He is kept in this quiet room for just a few minutes (again no more than five to ten minutes once he has quieted down) and then released.

Following the release from time-out or the quiet room, the child is expected to comply with the instruction, command, or request that caused the problem in the first place. If he complies, you are to respond with generous praise and attention. If he still does not comply, you can give a simple warning ("If you do not put your toys away, you will have to go to time-out again").

If he does not comply within a few seconds, there is no second warning and he must go to time-out. If necessary, repeat the procedure with the barricaded quiet room as well.

Using Positive Consequences

Be sure that you use praise and attention and positive consequences (extra playtime or a special treat, for instance) when your child is compliant. Just as oppositional behavior must be consistently disciplined, nonoppositional and obedient behavior must be frequently reinforced.

With Henry, Mrs. Johnson has learned to be generous in her praise and positive attention. If he comes in for dinner when his mother calls him or puts his pajamas on when he is told that it's bedtime, she says, "Henry, you got ready for bed so quickly tonight that I have time to read you an extra story. What two stories should we read tonight?"

Staying Firm

Do not give in to threats, demands, stubborn persistence, and attempts to wear you down. Difficult children are good at this.

When Henry wants something—like an action hero figure from the store—he becomes very persistent. He doesn't ask once and drop it when he gets a no. He keeps it up. If an ordinary request for the toy doesn't work, he will become demanding ("You better get a Batman for me!"). That turns into threats such as "If you don't buy me a new Batman, I'll cut your face off!"

His mother has found that if she gives in to his persistence, he is not easier to get along with the next time he wants something—he's more difficult.

This will be true for all parents of difficult children. Every time you are worn down and give in, you are demonstrating that negative tactics are successful. You might buy yourself a few minutes of peace now, but you will surely pay for it in the future.

Summary

Some important characteristics of the three-year-old to remember are:

- They are generally less oppositional and more fun at thirty-six months than at thirty months.
- They are more compliant because they want to please their parents.
- They now have a vocabulary of about a thousand words and can talk in sentences; thus, they are better able to express desires, problems, and fears.
- They tend to have active imaginations.
- At three and a half (forty-two months), they may be more withdrawn and unpredictable, with outbursts of anger, temper, and whining.
- Three-and-a-half-year-olds are more strong-willed and disobedient than three-year-olds.

Parents can cope better with the oppositional and negative behavior of the three-year-old if they:

- Expect some rebellion between three and a half and four years of age.
- Realize Threes may be engaged in the process of strengthening their willpower through negative behavior.
- Avoid clashes by phrasing requests and commands in ways that do not reflect ultimatums.
- Give directions in a positive rather than a negative way.
- Use distractions in dealing with a three-year-old by talking and keeping him busy listening to you.

- Get to know his temperament so that you are well aware of the special qualities that make him an individual.

You can better handle the difficult three-year-old when you:

- Remain aware that more difficult three-year-olds can be very demanding, intense, and volatile. Temper tantrums are likely when they don't get their own way.

- Avoid reinforcing aggressive, angry, and violent behaviors. Use disciplinary methods that will help your child learn better self-discipline.

- Avoid labeling the difficult child as angry, bratty, selfish, aggressive, unmanageable, or "bad."

- Give requests and directions in simple, clear, and direct ways.

- Use time-out to teach difficult children that they must comply; always use time-out in firm but appropriate ways.

- Do not give in to threats, demands, stubborn persistence, or attempts to wear you down.

CHAPTER 8

Understanding and Disciplining the Four-Year-Old Child

The Four-Year-Old

Four-year-old Leslie Brigolin knows how to push her mother's buttons—at least that's what Denise, her mother, thinks. Leslie gets stubborn about "little things," which then escalate into bigger issues.

Like wearing shorts in the winter. There may be snow on the ground and the temperature may be in the frigid range, but Leslie insists on wearing shorts to play outside. Denise has tried reasoning by telling Leslie that it is very cold out, she will get chilled, and everyone dresses warmly in such weather.

"I don't care!" Leslie replies with a determined look on her face. "I want to wear shorts." No amount of explanation will change her mind.

Denise goes through the reasons over and over, pointing out that Leslie could catch a cold or get sick. Leslie was not to be swayed. Next comes the clash of the titans as young Miss Leslie stonewalls while her equally stubborn mother takes her own very definite position.

Tears turn to anger and these are followed by some nasty words hurled back and forth. And no matter what the outcome, Denise always ends up feeling guilty and as if no one has won this battle.

However, one snowy day, Denise didn't feel up to an argument and let Leslie go out to play in shorts.

"I hope the neighbors didn't see her," she said in recounting the incident. "They'd probably think I made her dress like that."

Leslie didn't stay out long and came in shivering, complaining about the cold. Denise couldn't help saying, "I told you so." Denise realized the moment the words came out of her mouth that this was probably a tactical error.

"I should have just kept my mouth shut," Denise said, "then it would have been easier for her to make a decision on her own and not have to be stubborn."

Although Denise didn't have to rub it in about being right, Leslie learned a lesson. She didn't ask to wear shorts on cold days after that.

Four-year-olds like Leslie have a lot of drive, enthusiasm, and a great sense of adventure. Four is a wonderful age of confidence and exuberance, of passions and a need to know. Four-year-olds can bully you with questions and wear you down with their seemingly endless gusto for life. They love to try new things, but if they don't like them, they will passionately resist trying them again.

If you have a determined, persistent four-year-old like Leslie, then you frequently wonder how to handle her. While the three-and-a-half-year-old could be resistant because she wanted to oppose the all-powerful authority figure, the four-year-old wants to try out things on her own just to see what it's like. She has begun to discover that her parents are not infallible and that she, therefore, has some of the answers. If she wishes to wear shorts in the snow and knows instinctively that broccoli tastes yucky, then there's no talking her out of it. Whereas you might convince a three-year-old child through persuasion, the four-year-old is not so easily swayed.

But overall, the four-year-old is a funny, energetic, curious youngster. Nancy, the mother of two children—Sean, age four, and Paige, age seven—says it's one of the best, most interesting ages. "They grasp a lot of things now," Nancy says. "They understand more, they have better motor skills, and they're more independent. Basically you can trust them more."

Fours typically ask a million questions because they are curious and interested in everything. They want to go more places, do more things, and try out new skills. And if they do something wrong, they will lie about it. Nancy told about one of four-year-old Sean's lies.

"I went into the basement to check on him when he was playing," Nancy said, "and the laundry I had folded was lying all over the floor. Maybe I shouldn't have handled it in this way, but I asked him who did it. He looked at me and said, 'The wall did it.'" Nancy responded in an appropriate way: "I hope the wall never does that again."

That's typical of the four-year-old, who isn't above telling lies, nor is she beyond cussing and using bad words. She can be bossy, possessive, and even threatening if she doesn't get her own way. It's just fortunate she knows most of the rules now and will usually follow them. Boundaries, rules, and roles assume a greater importance at this age. Telling a four-year-old what the structure is and what her role is ("You are the guest at the birthday party. A guest is polite and obeys the mommy in charge at the party") will help her conform her behavior to the situation. But she needs that structure from you to know what to do.

The fact is that at age four children are much better prepared developmentally to delay gratification. Certainly they are more advanced than are two- and three-year-olds, who respond more impulsively. But even at age four, with their greater skill in understanding instructions and inhibiting actions, children need assistance from adults. Rules and clearly defined boundaries not only satisfy the four-year-old's thirst for new knowledge, but give her assistance with her self-control. Rules and boundaries, when clearly spelled out, will seem new to a four-year-old. She will regard any such information—even when it concerns rules—as evidence that she is learning something new about her world.

Handling the Opposition of the Four-Year-Old

Ignoring Opposition

"I want to go with Paige to Gloria's house," four-year-old Sean said one summer day.

"Nope. That's too far to go," said his mother, Nancy. "Besides, your sister wants to play with her friends."

"Yes! I want to go," persisted Sean, who began to whimper.

"There's no one to watch you there. Why don't you go to Gary's house and play with him?" Nancy suggested.

"No, I don't want to!" retorted the now wailing Sean.

"Then you'll have to find something interesting in our yard," answered his mother evenly.

Sean began twisting his cap and pulling on the ends of his hair. "I'll mess my hair up," he said to his mother.

Ignoring his threat, Nancy replied, "Think about what you want to do and let me know."

"No!" Sean growled and sulked off in search of something to do.

In a few minutes, Sean was done crying and had found a puzzle to play with.

Four-year-olds will have their oppositional and stubborn moments. They are usually brief, however. Because of their interest and curiosity they will find something else fairly soon to occupy their time.

This was evident in an incident with another four-year-old named Christopher. He was playing in the yard with his squirt gun. His mother stepped out on the porch to check on him. When Christopher noticed her, he said, "I can squirt these shoes," and he pointed his yellow squirt gun at his white sneakers.

"I'd prefer that you don't squirt them," Kathy, his mother, said.

"I can if I want to," said Christopher. "I'm the boss of my shoes and I can if I want to."

Kathy didn't say anything. She just arched her eyebrows. Christopher didn't say anything either, but he glanced across the yard and saw his friend Jeff walking toward him. Christopher tossed his squirt gun on the grass and said, "Hi, Jeff."

Things can be very transitory and fast-paced with four-year-olds. They're crying one minute and playing with a puzzle the next. If they're defying you now, give them a minute and they'll be off playing with a friend. By four and a half, you might even say that they are definitely unpredictable.

One of the best ways of dealing with the oppositional or seemingly stubborn behavior of the four-year-old is to ignore it. That's basically what Kathy did when Christopher said he was going to squirt his shoes. She avoided a big scene and eliminated a problem by not saying anything.

With Fours, you know something else will grab their interest before too long. You can wait them out.

Joining In

Another way to deal with these exuberant kids is to join in and have fun along with them. If they lie (or, to put it in a more positive light, exaggerate), then you might respond by telling an even bigger story. They'll enjoy it and no harm is done. If they're boasting about how big and strong they are, tell some exaggerations about your own strength.

If Christopher says, "I could throw this ball so hard I could break the window in the house across the street," his father might reply, "You could? That's nothing! I could throw a ball so high, it would knock airplanes out of the sky." Christopher would get a tremendous kick out of it. All of this is far better, and more enjoyable for you, than telling him he's lying or that he's not supposed to stretch the truth —which he knows anyway.

Fours love adventure and new things. You can almost always hook them with a story, trip, or any new experience that seems like an adventure. When they won't do something you want them to do, make it seem like something unique or exciting and see what happens.

You want your daughter to walk to the grocery store with you, but she doesn't want to go? Tell her she can skip there or jump over all the cracks in the sidewalk on the way and she's off on a new adventure. Or talk about how exciting or how much fun a new task or direction will be, and she's likely to share your enthusiasm.

Is she calling you a name or attacking you with cuss words? Try getting back at her with your own made-up "insult." If you call her a plaid, pokey porcupine or a yucky zucchini, she will likely dissolve in laughter rather than become angry or stubborn.

Setting Limits

Four-year-olds need boundaries and these have to be spelled out for them. When Nancy told Sean that Gloria's house was too far, she could have said that he could only go to the corner and Gloria's house was farther than the corner. Fours need to know the limits and have physical ways of determining where those limits are. So they need to be told that they can't go farther than the corner, or that the rule is "No crossing streets," or that they must stay in the yard. While they might not always like these boundaries, they're likely to respect the limits.

But if the four-year-old doesn't respect them or follow them, or if she needs a reminder, telling her "It's the rule that you can't go farther than the corner" will get some attention. Stating "the rule is . . ." is helpful to four-year-olds, because they are now old enough to know the importance of rules and to understand that they are to be obeyed.

Using Reasoning

Fours are also smarter and have better reasoning abilities than Threes. You can reason with a Four at her level. Give her a reason for something and she's much more likely to follow the instruction or rule than if you just tell her to do something. Saying to her "The reason why I can't let you play at her house is because there is no adult home and that can be dangerous to children" will be more satisfying than telling her "No, you just can't play at her house."

Using the Broken-Record Technique

When a child is not listening to you and you know you have to stand firm, one way to do so is by using the broken-record technique.

If Brandon is demanding to watch a program on television that he's not allowed to see, he may try to wear his mother down or engage her in an argument. A way for his mother to avoid this is through repetition: being a broken record about what is not allowed, what Brandon can do, and what the limits are. Repetition helps her to stay out of a meaningless discussion or argument. She could say, "I'm sorry, but you are not allowed to watch violent shows." She can repeat, "The rule is no violent shows." If he tries to escalate the situation by threatening her, she should calmly but firmly say, "You can watch *Sesame Street* but no violent shows."

The broken-record method helps keep parents on track and helps prevent them from being worn down by an insistent child.

Using Language Creatively

Because the four-year-old tends to get interested in new and exciting things, you may find it effective to phrase your commands and instructions in clever new ways. Instead of just saying, "Don't try to ride your bike down the steps," be dramatic: "Sarah, listen up, good buddy. Don't ever, and I repeat ever, ever, ever, try to ride your bike down the steps. You could take an awful—did you hear me, gal?—I mean an awful, terrible crash. Then I would be very, very, very sad! Got that?" As always with the Four, your use of new, exciting, and exaggerated words will capture her attention.

The four-year-old loves to ask questions, and you can make use of her hunger for learning new things by asking her questions when you need to give an instruction or teach a rule. For interest, refer to a story character or a TV character she knows well. When she says she can't find something, try referring to a familiar story: "Do you remember the beaver in *Just a Mess*? Remember how he couldn't find his baseball mitt? Where did he find it?"

When your child replies, "He found it behind his bed," you can say, "That's right. Maybe if you look hard enough in your room you'll find your summer hat just like he did."

There are plenty of favorite children's stories with a moral, like *The Little Train That Could*. If a child is frustrated and looks as though she's giving up, try saying: "Remember when we read that story about the little train that had to keep trying?" She'll get the point.

When you need to distract her attention from a squabble with her brother or get her attention when she's not listening, try saying something nonsensical. Children at four are highly amused by "Hey, look at those monkeys kissing!" or, "There's an elephant standing on our front porch!"

Since she loves to talk and to learn, use this when you're trying to convey new information, review a rule, or let her know what the limits are. Sit down and talk with her. Let her ask questions. Look and act interested. She will, too. You'll find that you get farther and she will respond in a rather mature way.

Giving Praise and Positive Attention

The four-year-old loves praise and attention. Don't spare your praise just because she's older and should know the rules. She is becoming more comfortable with rules and is better equipped to remember and follow them. But she still needs encouragement and reinforcement. Using praise and positive attention is the best way to let her know that you like the person she has become.

Giving Reprimands

What happens when your Four needs punishment because praise and positive attention by themselves are not sufficient to stop all bad behaviors? Try the punishments that are most likely to work with this age: reprimands, time-outs, and the removal of privileges.

Use a reprimand when you express disapproval ("You are never, ever to cross the street without asking me first and I don't want this to ever happen again") and then use some form of encouragement. An example would be, "You've been doing so well by asking me for permission, I really appreciate that. I think you're getting so big that I can trust you almost all the time. I know you will come and ask me for permission the next time you want to go across the street to play. Right?"

Using Time-Out

Place a four-year-old in time-out for about five minutes. Young children do not have sufficient memory to remember why they got in trouble for a long time. A time-out, which means removing a child from the source of fun or enjoyment, should be relatively short. An appropriate time for a four-year-old is four to five minutes.

After the time-out is over, make sure she knows what the rule was. "The rule was that you cannot hit people. That hurts them. When you hit other people, that makes them unhappy and you'll have to sit in time-out whenever you hit someone."

Effective Discipline Techniques to Use with Four-Year-Olds

Ignore It: Ignore some misbehavior and opposition; their interests change fast and they will find something else to do rather quickly.

Join In: To handle exaggerations and lies, join in and tell an even bigger or more nonsensical tale.

Set Limits: Fours need boundaries—make sure you set limits and give reminders as needed.

Reason: Fours have improved reasoning ability and like new information; satisfy their natural traits and increased capabilities through reasoning.

Use the Broken-Record Technique: One way to stand firm is to repeat—in broken-record style—what the limit or rule is.

Be Creative with Language: Play up to their interests with drama, references to storybook characters, and silly statements or questions.

Give Praise: Since Fours love praise and attention, don't forget to keep giving praise to reinforce their following the rules.

Give Reprimands: When a punishment or consequence is called for, use a reprimand in which you express disapproval.

Use Time-Out: As another type of consequence for misbehavior, use a short time-out.

Remove Privileges: One other negative consequence appropriate for the four-year-old is removing privileges.

Removing Privileges

Take away a privilege by stating the infraction and the consequences: "You left the yard when I told you to stay here. Now you will have to play in the house for the rest of the afternoon. The rule is you have to stay in the yard when I ask you to do that. Understand?" Let the punishment fit the offense; do not remove a privilege unrelated to the misbehavior. Also, make sure that the length of time involved or the severity of the consequence is moderate and appropriate to the seriousness of the infraction.

Handling the More Difficult Four-Year-Old

Jeremiah Sullivan doesn't listen or follow directions. "He's mean," says his mother, Becky. "He fights and hits constantly."

When Jeremiah gets angry with his mother, he threatens her. "He tells me he's the boss and I can't tell him what to do. Then he says he'll chop my head off. That scares me because he acts so mean."

Jeremiah is also destructive. When Becky wouldn't let him watch his favorite video, he got angry and smashed a video his mother liked.

Becky feels powerless with Jeremiah and fears he will be a violent, out-of-control teenager one day. "He's scary right now," she says. "I can't imagine what he'll be like in ten years."

Jeremiah's mother is desperately in need of practical strategies for dealing with a stubborn child. More difficult and persistent by temperament, Jeremiah was becoming even more stubborn and strong-willed by getting his way far too often. In other words, his mother gave him too much power.

Many tots with some of the traits of difficult children—being more demanding, more persistent, and more intense—are overindulged by parents who have allowed them too much freedom, given them too much power over their own lives, and failed to stand firm with rules.

Such children tell parents what they are or are not going to do: "I'm not going to get dressed and you can't make me!" Or they may loudly and stubbornly announce their power: "I will do what I want and you can't tell me what to do!" They assume a lot of power and responsibility that rightly belongs to a mother or father, and parents frequently feel helpless in taking it back.

Several steps must be taken to reclaim power and deal with such a belligerent young tyrant.

Step 1. Define and reiterate the limits in everyday situations.

For instance, if a child, in a demanding and stubborn way, says she wants an omelet and only a cheese omelet for breakfast, the parent may say, "Here are your choices. You can have French toast or cereal. Those are the only choices."

Limits may also be defined by letting kids know what the rules and expectations are. By saying, "You can play outside, but only if you do not ride your bike farther than the corner," you are establishing a limit. Or when your neighbor complains that your four-year-old "beat up my little girl," the limits can be emphasized: "When you're angry at someone else, you don't hit. Hitting is the wrong way to solve problems."

Step 2. Do not overreact or panic at the child's protests, complaints, or insistent demands.

This requires patience and a willingness to stand firm. It helps to remind yourself that this is an important issue (which it is if a child has become a despot in the home!) and that this approach will work. It also helps if you expect some complaints: some children need to push all limits or test all expectations or rules.

An example is Molly. Even though she may be told that she cannot hit other children and even if her mother is watching, Molly will hit other children when they make her angry. From the time she was one, if her mother told her not to touch something—whether an electric cord or the knobs on the stove—Molly would look at her while she touched the forbidden object. When Molly's mother set limits and remained firm and calm, she was no longer as bothered by this kind of misbehavior. Molly's insistent demands decreased.

Step 3. While reasoning is helpful with young children, it should not be used when a child is angry, throwing a temper tantrum, or misbehaving.

It is better not to become involved in reasoning, explaining, or justifying your behavior in this situation. Nor do you have to castigate or criticize your child's behavior. It is enough to repeat (in broken-record fashion) what the limits or choices are ("I will only allow you to have cereal or French toast" or, "I said no farther than the corner"). However, you can be sympathetic or even sound sorry that the choices are so limited: "I'm sorry, but that's all I can offer you today."

Step 4. Set a time limit for the child to obey or make a decision within the guidelines set by you.

You could say: "You have just five more minutes to tell which choice you have selected. After that no more breakfast will be served." In all these cases, it is essential that you stick with your pronouncement in a kind but resolute way.

Step 5. If the child fails to live up to the rule or expectation within a reasonable time, or neglects her choice, then there must be consequences.

Parents must use consequences that they are willing to enforce with firmness and that are proportionate to the offense. For example, to the child who rides her bike beyond the corner, a parent could say, "I told you that you could go no farther than the corner. Now you have lost the use of your bike for the rest of the day." Or, with the child who has hit another youngster in a dispute ("She said she was going to take my bike and never give it back"): "I have told you that hitting is not the right way to solve problems. Now you must come in the house for an hour."

When Jeremiah gets mad at a playmate and hits him, his mother reacts in a kind but firm way: "Jeremiah, you know I cannot allow you to hit other children when you get mad at them. I feel bad that this had to happen, but you'll be staying in the house for the rest of the afternoon."

Step 6. Consistently use this approach until the child understands that you have reclaimed the power you had previously abdicated to her.

This does not mean that you rail at the child or blame her. Remember that you are the one who relinquished power and your child's increasing stubbornness is the result. It's all too easy to fall into this trap. It is much more difficult to take back the power and retrain your child to be a more respectful and less stubbornly insistent or demanding youngster.

Summary

Four-year-old preschool children will exhibit these characteristics:

- They have a lot of drive, enthusiasm, and a great sense of adventure; they like to try new things.
- They can bully you with questions and wear you down with a seemingly endless gusto for life.
- They are often funny, exuberant, energetic, and curious.
- They tend to understand more, have better motor skills, and are more independent.
- They can be trusted more, but may lie to cover up misdeeds.
- They can be bossy, possessive, and even threatening if they don't get their way.

Parents can best handle the negative and stubborn behavior of four-year-olds by:

- Remembering that things can be very transitory and fast-paced for Fours; since they change quickly, often you can wait them out.
- Ignoring oppositional or stubborn behavior.
- Joining in and having fun along with them; telling an even bigger story if they are lying, for example.

- Making things they don't want to do into an exciting adventure and "hooking" them.
- Making up your own "insults" if they swear or use "bad" language.
- Letting them know specifically what the limits and rules are; they always need to know what the structure and boundaries are.
- Reasoning with them more.
- Remembering that Fours love to talk and keeping in mind that it is useful to exaggerate or describe things in exciting, new ways.
- Using such punishments as reprimands, time-outs, and removal of privileges.

Parents can best handle the difficult four-year-old when they reclaim lost power and authority by following these specific steps:

1. Define the limits.
2. Do not overreact or panic at the child's protests, complaints, or insistent demands.
3. Do not become involved in explaining or justifying your discipline when your child is angry or throwing a temper tantrum.
4. Set a time-limit for the child to make a decision within guidelines given by you.
5. When your child fails to live up to your expectations, or neglects her responsibilities, provide consequences.
6. Consistently use this approach until the youngster understands that you will provide the authority. Continue to use firm, consistent discipline as she begins to comply with limits, rules, and expectations.

CHAPTER 9

Understanding and Disciplining the Five-Year-Old Child

The Five-Year-Old

"I'm really strong," said five-year-old Jeremy to his father in the supermarket.

It was fun for him to go shopping, and Jeremy especially enjoyed showing how big he was by accompanying his father to the market. In the produce department he proudly carried a five-pound sack of potatoes to the grocery cart while he exclaimed again about his strength.

"See how big and strong I am," he said, loud enough for several older shoppers to hear and smile over it, while his father smiled himself and gave him verbal encouragement.

"You sure are," said his father. "You're a big help today." Jeremy beamed and asked what else he could carry for his daddy.

Jeremy is a typical five-year-old. He is an upbeat, cooperative talker who exudes self-confidence as he shows off how much more accomplished he is than he was just a year ago.

In general, Fives have a much broader vocabulary than they did only a year ago. They enjoy showing themselves to be independent, and are always ready to display their increasing self-confidence. After all, they can go to kindergarten—and do it all by themselves.

Although the five-year-old will want to do many things for himself, you may also find him constantly at your side—and, you may think, in the way—insisting that he "help" you do things like vacuuming or mowing the lawn. More than anything right now he seems to want to do all the grown-up things his parents do.

You may become very frustrated by this child, clingy one minute, fiercely independent the next. But the Five's sense of self-worth comes from the significant adults in his life. When he is treated as a competent, independent child (just as Jeremy was by his father), he will be more likely to see himself that way.

A five-year-old has a vocabulary of around two thousand words. And he likes using them. Long gone are the days when "no" was his favorite word. In fact, at five he usually has a sunny, sociable disposition and is typically easy to get along with. But he also likes routine and an orderly world. So he might not be so easy to get along with if you upset his need for routine and order, and his idea that things are supposed to be a certain way—and only that way.

He's pulled in his boundaries a bit; is no longer as adventuresome as he was at four and would prefer staying around home or with his mother. He knows the boundaries of his world and he wants to live within them. He will tend to follow the rules automatically or rein himself in with a reminder from someone he loves and respects.

Like Jeremy, who enjoys going shopping and helping Dad out with putting food in the grocery cart, Fives like to take on responsibilities and imitate grown-ups. Therefore, they are usually quite cooperative and will help with household chores. This is a good time for children to begin picking up the toys in their rooms, emptying wastebaskets, and taking garbage out.

The Five is learning to relate to other people, and he likes to play with other children his own age. This is facilitated by his greater vocabulary and increased ability to take turns and consider others. He has a sense of what fairness is, and he is not as likely to create big problems by being bossy. And because he understands the concept of fairness, he is better able to accept consequences imposed by adults.

He shows a somewhat greater range of emotions and thankfully he doesn't have the wild temper tantrums and the loss of control of a couple of years ago. That's usually because he thinks more before reacting or speaking. However, he can still be intense in his reactions and violence is still very much on the minds of children this age.

Even though he has most likely been in a nursery school or pre-school, now he goes to kindergarten. That makes him a big boy and he's proud of this. And most Fives have the maturity to do well in kindergarten. That means that he can separate from his mother, and can tolerate being in a classroom where he's one of many children and doesn't always get immediate attention.

Kindergartners will usually love their teacher, think she's wonderful, and try to please her. They'll enjoy the many things they learn and do in kindergarten every day—even though they may not tell you much about it.

In addition to trying to please his teacher, the Five wants to please his mother and father. Mother, though, is really the center of the five-year-old's universe. He may enjoy doing some things with his daddy, but Mother is the most important person in his young world. Mothers should enjoy this while it lasts—it changes at age six when there are disagreements with moms.

Handling the Opposition of the Five-Year-Old

Though the five-year-old finally seems to be at a fairly mature age when he remembers rules and tries very hard to please, he is still a youngster and his growth and development still have their ups and downs.

At times five-year-olds seem mature and wise beyond their years. Five-year-old Anne knew exactly what clothes she liked or disliked. Chris, at five, responded this way when a clerk in a department store asked him one December what Santa Claus was bringing him for Christmas: "Don't you know what Christmas is all about? It's not about gifts and Santa—it's about the Baby Jesus."

Yet this same five-year-old who has been showing off how big and strong he is and innocently displaying his wisdom suddenly can't tie his shoes, remember what letter of the alphabet comes after D, or put his bike in the garage. He may ask you for help to tie his shoes, tell him the next letter, or put the bike away. What should you do?

If this is an occasional setback, don't fret and do give him some of the needed assistance. But if this happens too frequently, then be gentle but definite in drawing the line: "Jeremy, I think you can walk your bike into the garage all by yourself" or, "I think you know what letter comes after D; just start from the beginning of the alphabet."

It is important to keep in mind that five-year-olds will slip back into less mature behavior from time to time—being, for instance, whiny, clingy, or helpless. And this should be permitted when it is needed.

Smoothing the Transition to School

One of the central issues at five is the beginning of formal schooling with entrance into kindergarten. Being separated from parents for finite periods of time is usually not a problem for the five-year-old, but still some children have difficulties. To help them cope better with the longer separations required for school, before they start kindergarten give them practice in being separated with short stays at day care, with a sitter, at their grandparents', or with a friend.

Despite such "trial runs" your child's fears about separation may come flooding back anyway when he actually starts school. So plan to give him time to ease into it. That might mean you will spend time with him at school on the first few days. You can plan to be present at school for an hour or more on the first day, and gradually reduce that time over the course of the week. This usually is enough to make the transition to a new school or new environment fairly smooth.

Although I said earlier that most Fives are mature enough for kindergarten, some are not. Some children need to spend more time maturing while others are not comfortable separating from their parents. When a child clings too much or cannot mingle comfortably with other children at kindergarten, it is not necessarily a sign of stubborn, oppositional, or defiant behavior. It could be the child's indication that he is not ready for even a half-day of school away from you or his regular caregiver.

If the battles of getting your five-year-old dressed, into the car, and into the building on school days are too frequent, it may mean he is not ready for school, and entrance into kindergarten might best be delayed a few more months or another year. Other indications that a child may not be ready for kindergarten include a young age. Some experts say that a child younger than five and a half at the beginning of the kindergarten year is at risk of experiencing problems. Also, children who have had health problems, were late talkers (or have significant speech problems), had low birthweight, or have had to deal with important family turmoil or change (such as a move to a new house or a divorce) may be better off waiting up to a year to start school.

Understanding the Need for Routine

Since children of this age like order and routine, you may encounter opposition and a negative attitude if you or other adults try to change the order of things. Don't try to give a youngster juice in a "milk glass" or ask him to put "school clothes" on to play in the yard. That disrupts his sense of the orderliness of the world.

This doesn't mean you can't sometimes deviate from the routines. Just be prepared for a protest when you do, and try to handle that protest in a fairly sensitive way ("I know I usually read you a story, but Daddy has to talk to a man about business so I can't read to you tonight. I'll read two stories tomorrow night. Okay?").

Five-year-olds tend to be more cooperative and content if there is a regular time for getting up, meals, outdoor play, chores, and bedtime. It is generally wise to have a schedule and stick to it without being overly strict or rigid about it.

Supervising Responsibility

Fives, although less adventuresome than Fours, still want to take on new responsibilities—often more than they can handle. This causes problems for parents and caregivers when the things they want to do aren't safe—things like crossing busy streets, using a knife to cut cardboard boxes, playing video games that they see older children play, or going to the store by themselves.

Five-year-old Mikey, a friend's son, thinks he's matured enough to drive the family car and shave—although he hasn't tried either yet. Melinda, another five-year-old I know, thinks she's big enough to take care of her baby brother—which means that she should be able to push him in his stroller on the side of an unpaved street near his house. Many five-year-olds want to help wash dishes or make meals; you'll frequently find them standing on chairs by sinks, countertops, or cupboards.

So, while you're doing everything you can to encourage autonomy and independence, remain alert to what could be too much responsibility for a youngster. This means that you let a child try new things only under strict supervision or in a practice situation. This may be the first time that you will hear the time-honored child's lament, "Why can't I do it? Mazy's parents let her do it." But don't be pressured into giving in for this reason. Preparing a child to take on greater responsibilities takes place over a period of time. There may have to be many "practice tries" before you're willing to let a child try it on his own without close supervision.

It's especially important at this stage to keep in mind the importance of modeling. If the parents and older siblings in the family display good common sense and caution in order to reduce the risks of accidents, then a younger child is likely to act in the same responsible way.

Using the Five's Desire to Please

The single most important way to influence a five-year-old is by virtue of his desire to please his parents or teacher. It is this desire that will motivate him to respect the limits you set on his behavior while you help him learn to be self-disciplined. You can take advantage of this typical trait of the five-year-old by asking for his cooperation and telling him what will please you.

Fives will accept rules and limits because they want to win parental approval. Using lots of praise, positive attention, and encouraging feedback will work well with children at this age.

Accepting Consequences

Fives are also in a better position than Fours to understand the consequences of their actions. Now you can let a child accept the consequences of many of his behaviors. If he went against your suggestion or advice to wait until you got a glass for him out of a high cupboard, then broke the glass while reaching for it, he is old enough to understand that he will have to sweep up the broken glass (under adult supervision) and may be deprived of the drink he wanted.

Two consequences are most effective with five-year-olds:

- **Removing Privileges**. Depriving children of privileges or activities becomes a useful way to help them learn to follow the rules. It is both effective and likely to be seen as fair. Certainly Fives will see losing a privilege or desired activity as more fair than a spanking or other physical punishments.

- **Time-Out**. Time-out is also an effective consequence or punishment for not following established rules and expectations. Five minutes in a special time-out place or a time-out chair can be another "fair" consequence that is easily administered and quickly served.

Lying or Exaggerating

One of the times when five-year-olds appear stubborn is when they have misbehaved. Perhaps because they want to please so much, they have difficulty telling the truth when they've done something wrong. It may be best for parents and caregivers to understand this about Fives, and not expect them always to tell the truth about misbehaviors. It doesn't mean they are compulsive liars if they don't accept responsibility for a misbehavior. Adding the issue of truth telling may overcomplicate things: you'll probably have an easier time dealing with the initial misbehavior if you allow the Five to save face.

This means finding a gentle way to help them explain what has happened. Ask them what happened rather than insist they admit wrongdoing. Saying "Tell me how the glass got smashed" will probably get you a lot further than asking "How did you break the glass?"

When a five-year-old youngster gives you his explanation, which often will shift the blame to someone or something else ("I was standing on the stool and reaching in the cupboard and the glass just fell by itself"), respond in a nonaccusatory manner: "Maybe next time it would work better if you waited until I could get things out of high cupboards for you, then glasses wouldn't be falling down by themselves."

Handling the More Difficult Five-Year-Old

While many Fives enter a remarkably amiable stage, the five-year-old with a difficult temperament will be less easy to handle. Some children don't seem to learn by experience. To concerned parents and teachers, it appears that they keep making the same mistakes over and over again.

There are also Fives who are very oppositional and defiant. Jonathan is one. When his grandfather asked him to wash his hands before coming to the dinner table, Jonathan responded with, "No, poopy-head!" When his kindergarten teacher asked him to put a book back on the shelf so he could listen, he said, "I don't have to!" and ripped the pages out of the book.

Jonathan stays awake late at night and walks around the house when everyone else is asleep. Once he took a knife out of a kitchen drawer and cut his pillow and mattress. Another time he found matches and lit paper in the kitchen sink. His temper tantrums are furious and have gone on for an hour or longer.

Five-year-olds like Jonathan have already been difficult for several years, and as they've grown bigger and stronger they've become more stubborn and oppositional.

Randall is another such child. When he is not allowed to do what he wants to do, Randall responds with his fiery temper. When his mother or father then tries to take charge, Randall becomes very resistant. For instance, if they try to use time-out as a consequence for his failure to follow requests, directions, or rules, he has a violent temper tantrum and refuses to go to the time-out corner.

"No, you can't make me!" cries Randall. Or he may shout, "I'm not going to do that!" If a parent advances on him, he may throw himself down on the floor, run away, or defiantly cross his arms. If the parent insists he go to time-out, he gets louder, screams out, "You're hurting me!" even before his parents have touched him, and attempts to avoid the punishment.

Even if his parents carry him to the time-out corner, he refuses to stay there, runs away, or throws himself on the floor, flailing his arms and legs. His violent and prolonged reactions greatly concern his parents and they always feel that they are mishandling the child, that time-outs "won't work" with him, and that he will be totally out of control when he's older.

Most parents worry about youngsters like Randall or Jonathan for several reasons. One is that parents recognize this behavior to be immature. A child should have outgrown it before age five. With the approach of kindergarten and first grade, moreover, comes the worry that he'll use the same behavior in school, and if he does perhaps special services in school will have to be considered.

No doubt about it, it is going to be somewhat more difficult to deal with an obstinate five-year-old than it was to deal with a stubborn two-, three-, or four-year-old. However, it is my experience that children like Randall and Jonathan can be taught to be more compliant and agreeable.

A gentle but definite response to the oppositionalism and defiance of Fives is best. Remember that Fives tend to want to please and they do imitate adult behavior. Therefore, keeping calm and using both your authority and the five-year-old's wish to please are in his best interest.

With children like Randall and Jonathan, it is usually best to respond with: "Playing with matches is very dangerous and you could be hurt. That would make me very sad if you got hurt." Or, "I would like it very much if you put the book back on the shelf." Parents tend to overreact to dangerous behavior, such as playing with matches. Taking severe measures, such as imposing harsh punishments, spanking, or angrily shouting at a child, is not likely to alter the behavior of a difficult five-year-old. Indeed, the extreme measures parents frequently think are needed can have more detrimental than positive results. Even if children repeat dangerous misbehaviors, the advice I've given remains: Be calm, firm, and authoritative. If you must change the environment of the home (by getting rid of matches, for instance), do that, and by all means supervise this child more closely.

Dealing with Temper Tantrums

Temper tantrum–throwing five-year-olds I've worked with seem to recognize the power of their active resistance and they tend to know—even when they seem to be out-of-control—what they can get away with and what they can't. If they have been allowed to be violent and destructive during an explosion of anger, they will continue to do so and will escalate that violence in an attempt to force their own way.

Once again you must remain calm and in control. Use a reprimand as soon as the tantrum begins, in order to let the child know that his behavior has no approval from you. You could say, for instance, "I expect you to put your bike away when I ask you and I do not like it when you throw a temper tantrum."

You cannot stop a temper outburst directly and you should not try to do so with threats, anger, or bribes. Instead allow the outburst to play out while you remain firm about the reason it started. If, for example, it started because the child wanted to ride his bike outside longer than you were willing to permit, do not rescind this decision in order to buy a peaceful evening. Instead, the decision should stand no matter how loud or violent his outburst. You should, however, set some limits for what is and what isn't allowed during tantrums and extreme oppositional behavior. This is important because the five-year-old is so much bigger and stronger and could do more damage to others or to himself.

You may decide that he cannot throw himself on the kitchen floor and stay there for an hour. You may say, after ten minutes, "If you want to stay on the floor, you're going to have do it in your bedroom." Also, you may set some limits on his behavior while in a temper tantrum. Children who are too much out of control or are violent can be told that they cannot kick walls, cannot hit you (or anyone else), and cannot throw objects. If your child is kicking a wall, for example, he can be told directly and firmly to stop ("You can be angry but you are not allowed to kick walls"). If he doesn't desist within five to ten seconds, move him away from the wall, or take away the object he is about to grab or throw.

While the tantrum is going on, keep one eye on the child to ensure that his safety is not endangered and be prepared to intervene when limits have to be set on his actions. Intervention in the form of a physical restraint (hugging from behind or holding his wrists so that he can't throw an object) may be necessary at times to reinforce a limit. Physical restraint should not be used to stop the tantrum, however. Generally it's best to ignore the child and to engage in some other activity, such as reading a magazine or writing a letter.

It's important, also, not to talk to him, natter about his behavior ("I'm sick and tired of the way you're acting," etc.), or tell him to change his behavior. Better that you appear to ignore his behavior by looking away, although whenever an angry child is out of control, you should keep one eye on the situation to make sure he doesn't hurt himself or others, or break valuable objects.

At times, you may ask if the child would like to end the tantrum, or if he would like to know how he can get what he wants ("Do you want to know how you can ride your bike outside?"). If he replies that he would in fact like to know, you can tell him in a direct and straight-forward way: "You can get to ride your bike outside when you ask me politely and when you can accept me telling you no sometimes." However, if the decision has already been made that he may not ride outside that day, this cannot be an option—although the next day can be a new beginning. If you are asking if he would like to know how he can leave the room and rejoin the human race, the question should be phrased like this: "Would you like to know how you can leave your bedroom and come downstairs and play?"

If a temper tantrum came about because the child resisted serving time-out, the answer must be: "Okay, it's simple. You have to stop crying and sit in the time-out place for five minutes. Then you'll be able to play again."

If the child is not able to stop the tantrum, you are to say nothing more, continue to keep an eye on him without direct eye contact or interaction, and wait it out. Of course, you do not allow a child—no matter how much running around he does, screaming, crying, kicking, or flailing—to play or do anything else he would like to do until he has complied with the original request, whether it was to put his bike away, put on his pajamas, or serve his time-out sentence.

For you as a parent, the hardest part is to be patient and firm as you wait out the tantrum and explosive behavior. Many parents become impatient or frightened at the intensity or the violence of the angry outburst. Some parents worry that the youngster will carry this tantrum on for hours (although this is possible, I have never personally supervised a child who has carried it on for more than two hours). Parents may also fear that the child will somehow experience some emotional trauma from crying or screaming, or that the youngster will feel rejected, abandoned, or unloved.

Such fears, however, are usually unfounded. In most cases what is most important with a five-year-old is that you be firm and consistent, making it clear to him that you will not be manipulated or coerced, and that you'll protect him, yourself, and your property from the tantrum.

Most youngsters will give up trying to coerce you with regular temper outbursts when they come to realize some important things:

1. You will not give in or allow them to manipulate you.
2. You will not reinforce their explosive behavior by responding to it.
3. No matter how they carry on, they still must do what you originally required of them.
4. You will calmly and patiently wait out their tantrum.

Dealing with Other Disruptive Behavior

Aside from temper tantrums, Fives may show other kinds of disruptive behavior both at home and at school, including aggression toward other children, an inability to share with others, disobedience to rules, and outright defiance toward adult requests and commands.

If a child has a difficult temperament that causes him to be more active, more distractible, more impulsive, and more emotional than other children, he may well be considered a problem in the classroom. Often it is in kindergarten that children with difficult temperaments or attention deficit hyperactivity disorder are identified for the first time.

To deal with more oppositional and seemingly stubborn Fives, it is important that both parents and teachers recognize the value of frequent, immediate, and consistent feedback of both a positive and negative nature.

Obviously if you are concerned about a youngster's self-image, then the feedback has to be positive more often than it is negative and critical. Yet, both are important for the more difficult youngster who doesn't easily learn the rules and procedures.

A good place to start is to make sure that you (and the child's teacher) are giving frequent verbal feedback in the form of praise, encouragement, attention, and support. Whenever the child is following rules and established procedures, or doing an acceptable job of handling some form of behavior that's usually difficult, you need to give him positive feedback. For example, a teacher could say, "I liked the way you listened when I read the story to the class today." Or, a parent could comment, "You were such a big help in the store today by helping me find the just the right gift for Uncle Claude."

In addition to verbal praise and encouragement, though, such children also require tangible rewards. For the five-year-old, brightly colored stickers and small, inexpensive gifts or certificates can be useful in reinforcing specific, targeted behavior. For example, if Suzanne is having difficulty listening to the teacher's instructions or raising her hand to speak, when she does either of these things, she can be rewarded with a sticker or certificate.

All the children in the family or classroom can be given such rewards for good behavior, and a larger, more exciting group award can be given when everyone has collected a certain number of stickers. For example, if all of the children have collected ten stickers, they might be rewarded with a trip to the playground or the park.

More difficult children will require more frequent praise—perhaps as often as every five to fifteen minutes—and the feedback may have to be given from close by. That is, a parent or teacher may need to move closer to a youngster to say such things as, "I see Suzanne is listening to the story today" or, "Jeremy is playing so nicely with his friend this afternoon."

But don't think that difficult children only need praise and positive attention. They also need feedback regarding their negative behavior. If Justin is pushing other children at the Halloween party in order to get to the candy treats first, his behavior must be addressed immediately. Justin's behavior can be stopped or he can be told that "We don't push others because we might hurt them and make them feel bad."

But it is not just verbal feedback that's necessary. There are other ways of letting Justin and other young children know that their behavior is wrong and that there will be consequences. If Justin hits others or bullies them by taking their toys, he should be told that his behavior is wrong and why it is wrong. A more tangible system of negative feedback may also need to be used. For instance, you might have a chart or a sheet of paper on the refrigerator and when Justin misbehaves in aggressive or other serious ways, his name goes on the chart. When his name is on the chart three times, there is a penalty—for example, Justin might have to give up something, like an hour of TV or video game time.

When serious or dangerous, negative behavior should definitely result in a loss of privileges or other consequences. Time-out continues to be a useful consequence or punishment for aggressive behavior in five-year-olds. This should not be overdone, but can be used when there is repeated noncompliance or defiance, or when the child is aggressive.

Another consequence, suitable at home or in the classroom, is giving a child extra chores such as cleaning out a dresser drawer or a toy box, or extra work, such as copying numbers or letters. When children attempt to hurry through these extra chores, they are required to do the work over or get more work tacked on. But don't overdo this or they'll develop aversion to work and a hatred of the punisher.

Dealing with Aggression

A very important consideration with difficult children, particularly those children acting in hostile, aggressive, or bullying ways, is to make sure you are teaching them appropriate social skills. Children who act in aggressive ways often do not know how to get along better with others.

If Jonathan grabs crayons away from other children at school, or hits his younger brother when he makes him angry, it's clear he needs to learn how to deal with other people who frustrate him. Parents and teachers can instruct children in social skills by telling them how they can handle a situation in other ways.

For instance, Jonathan could be told, "First try asking Amanda nicely for a crayon. Say, 'Amanda, could I have a green crayon please?' Okay, now you try it." This social training can take place in the natural situation, at home or at school.

Or Jonathan can also be taught by verbal instruction and by role play when no one else is around. With role playing, Jonathan can practice dealing with a child who won't share crayons with him. In this way he can learn to cope with this situation the next time it occurs.

Finally both parents and teachers should constantly model appropriate behavior as well as problem-solving skills in front of difficult children. By demonstrating how you handle problematic situations, you are giving a powerful message to young children about how to deal with them.

You can exhibit problem-solving behavior by talking aloud about how you are solving problems that come up. For example, if you're a teacher with a difficult child, you can say aloud how you will deal with a problem or conflict. "I would like to finish reading this story, but there isn't enough time before lunch. That frustrates me. Doesn't it frustrate you? I wonder how we could solve this. . . . Let's see. . . . I could stop the story now and finish it after lunch, or I could read faster. I know what I'll do. Let's stop now and then take our time and read it after lunch. Then we won't have to hurry. Okay?"

Summary

Five-year-old children usually have the following characteristics:

- They are upbeat, cooperative talkers who exude self-confidence, have sunny, sociable dispositions, and are generally easy to get along with.

- They have a greater vocabulary and enjoy showing themselves to be independent and ready to display their proud senses of self-esteem.

- They are still very dependent on the important adults in their world, the most important of whom is their mother.

- They stick close to home and parents and are less adventuresome than four-year-olds.

- They like to take on responsibilities and imitate grown-ups; they want to be helpful—especially with chores.

- They don't have the wild temper tantrums and the loss of control of three-year-olds and early four-year-olds.

- They are proud of being big and able to go to kindergarten; most have the maturity to attend kindergarten, which means longer separations from Mother and being in a class where they are not the center of attention.

Parents can best handle the oppositional and negative behavior of the five-year-old by:

- Permitting him to slip back into less mature behavior when he needs to do this and remembering that all growth and development still has its ups and downs.

- Giving him needed assistance when he regresses and says he can't do something he was able to do before; and if drawing the line on that assistance, doing it with a gentle nudge.

- Remembering that oppositional or defiant behavior about going to school may be a sign that he is not ready to attend kindergarten and needs more time before beginning school.

- Making sure to follow a schedule, because Fives function best with order and routines in their lives; expecting negative behavior when that order and routine is upset.

- Trying to handle negative and oppositional behavior caused by deviations in the routine in a sensitive way.

- Allowing him to try new and mature (but not unwise or unsafe) behaviors only under strict supervision or in a practice situation.

- Modeling cautious and appropriate behavior.

- Using plenty of positive feedback to provide encouragement.

- Letting him begin to experience the consequences of his actions.

- Removing privileges or activities to teach him to follow rules or expectations.

- Using time-out as a consequence for misbehavior.

- Trying to be nonaccusatory so he doesn't have to shift blame or lie, and finding a gentle, face-saving way to help him explain what happened when he does tend to lie about an event.

The difficult five-year-old can be handled best by:

- Remembering that Fives want to please and they do imitate adult behavior.

- Reacting with calmness.

- Using physical restraint if need be with a five-year-old who still has violent temper tantrums.

- Establishing limits for acceptable and unacceptable behavior during a temper tantrum.

- Not resorting to threats, anger, or bribes to try to stop a temper tantrum.

- Not giving in to temper tantrums or the child's unreasonable demands in order to buy temporary peace.

- Taking a firm, consistent stand indicating that he must follow the rules and comply with what you want when he throws a temper tantrum.

- Giving both positive and negative feedback about behavior.

- Addressing disruptive or aggressive behavior immediately.

- Making sure that aggressive or excessive negative behaviors result in a loss of privilege or other appropriate consequences.

- Teaching social skills as a part of your handling of behavior problems.

- Modeling a problem-solving approach as a parent or a teacher.

CHAPTER 10

Understanding and Disciplining the School-Age Child: Ages Six to Nine

The School-Age Child

Years six through nine are usually referred to as the school-age years. These are the elementary school years, marked by growing independence. During this time children find it much easier to be away from home through the school day than kindergartners do, and they usually want to play with their friends after school.

Sometimes this period is referred to as the golden years. They're the years of Cub Scouts, best friends, Brownies, Little League, dance lessons, soccer leagues, music lessons, secret clubs, family vacations, and wishes to be a grown-up.

Think of the movies that evoke such wonderfully nostalgic memories of these years: *Stand By Me, Radio Flier,* and *To Kill a Mockingbird* are three that come quickly to mind. Childhood from age six to nine or ten is seen as a relatively quiet and stable time. Absent are the dramatic changes that highlighted the infant and toddler years—and that will come around again in adolescence.

Instead, school-age children tend to build on the rapid growth and development of the early years and dream of what they will become in the future. These years are filled with mystery, magic, and seemingly endless explorations of the fascinations of their immediate world and its secrets.

While the youngster between six and nine years is gaining new skills and greater knowledge, playing new sports, or learning to play the piano, she is more than anything else figuring out who she is and how she must act to get along with other people. The early school years, then, are a time for peer relationships and going to school; one cannot be separated from the other. That interaction with her culture helps to define the school-age child more than anything else. By going out into the world, she meets people and makes friends. These interactions help her to learn to relate to others, and in turn these relationships help to shape her attitudes and behavior, her self-esteem and success.

It is at this stage of development that children begin to view themselves in terms of the traits they usually display in their dealings with others. Preschoolers might tell who they are by giving their names and ages. The elementary-age child will describe herself as someone who is kind, friendly, shy, or tough.

Gender differences are more apparent at this stage as well. Most elementary school children play with a relatively stable group of friends. For girls, though, this is commonly a small group with one or two best friends, while for boys it is a larger group with an emphasis on loyalty and shared activities.

The differences between boys and girls during the elementary years show up in another way—in the way they are raised and prompted by their parents. Typically, boys are allowed more freedom to explore and do more on their own. Girls, in contrast, tend to be encouraged to stay closer to home, be more involved in domestic activities, and be more docile and dependent. While parental expectations play a part in the gender roles and the personality characteristics of children, the personal adjustment of each child is a complex process that relies only in part on the expectations parents have for that child and the quality of the relationship each parent has with a particular child.

The Six-Year-Old

Six-year-old Michael sits in front of his father's computer and looks through the encyclopedia on the CD-ROM. "Dad," he exclaims in an excited voice, "did you know that some dinosaurs were as big as a six-story building?"

His father comes over to the computer to look at the great graphic on the screen of a *Tyrannosaurus rex* and talk for a few minutes about dinosaurs. He cherishes these times with Michael, who is now in the first grade.

Other times, however, are not such cherished moments. That's when Michael is defiant, immature, or completely unable to make a simple decision. His father remembers an incident a few days earlier when Michael sat on the floor of his bedroom, staring into the closet trying to figure out what shoes to wear. After fifteen minutes, he insisted that Michael make a choice—which Michael finally did.

Six-year-olds like Michael are very different from preschoolers and even five-year-olds. They are grown up enough to confidently take a bus to school. At school, they're learning to read and beginning to do math. Like Michael, many of them have been playing with computers for three years.

Their parents have seen them getting taller, becoming more coordinated, and gaining self-confidence. While life is exciting and six-year-olds are able to do much more than ever before, life is also hard for them. It's full of opposites and difficult choices. They can play with the computer or go outside and ride a bike. They can visit a friend or stay home with Dad.

Life is full of those kinds of difficult choices, and because Sixes don't always want to make them, they may often feel completely overwhelmed. To some parents, this looks like a stubborn refusal to make a decision.

For Sixes, life—which involves decision making—is complex. After they've made a decision, they reconsider and sometimes change their minds. One day Kristen, age six, asked a friend to play dolls. After her friend Samantha came over, Kristen changed her mind and said she wanted to play a game on the computer. When Samantha protested, Kristen changed her mind again and said, "Oh, I guess dolls is okay, but why don't we see if my mom will take us to the mall."

Sixes sometimes just don't seem to be able to handle things well. With all their new challenges, even simple tasks may become overwhelming.

Take Cassandra, for instance. While she loves and adores her mother most of the time, when things go wrong, guess who gets blamed?

"Why did you let me spill the soup?" Cassandra whined at her mother one day. "It's your fault that I can't ever do anything right! I hate you!"

Her mother, Lillian, was perplexed. "Just a short time ago she was saying how much she loved me and how much fun we were having," Lillian said to her neighbor. "I wonder what I'm doing wrong," she added.

Lillian wasn't doing anything wrong. The world has just shifted a bit for Cassandra. Her mother is no longer the center of her universe. Cassandra, like most Sixes, is the center of her own universe. Unlike most five-year-olds, she's more concerned about herself and things that go on in her little world than she is about what her parents think and do. She definitely wants everything to go her way. But when it doesn't, Mom or Dad is likely to get the blame.

It isn't always noticeable, but both Cassandra and Michael are beginning to separate much more from their parents. There is less dependence on and closeness with their mothers and fathers. As much as they love them, there are times when the love seems to turn to hate or some other intensely negative feeling. Sometimes they can't even make up their minds about what exactly they do feel. There is, however, one thing both Michael and Cassandra know—they often wish they weren't so close to or so dependent on their parents.

It's not just children who experience this sort of ambivalence. Parents of six-year-olds do, too. Seeing their child loving and carefree one minute and stubborn and independent the next may lead parents to look inside themselves and make steadfast promises to act in more loving ways toward their first-grader. Yet by the end of the day those promises may have evaporated and been replaced by anger. When a child is so changeable, it's no wonder parents feel perplexed.

It is certainly not uncommon for Cassandra or Michael to come to their parents late in the day and ask for reassurance. "You still love me, don't you, Mom?" Cassandra will ask.

"Are you still mad about what I said, Dad?" Michael says.

Six-year-olds have fragile egos, and parents need to be able to feed these egos when they're hungry for reassurance—and to do so in spite of their own ambivalence in the wake of a child's hateful outburst.

Sixes show their insecurity in another way—by bragging, boasting, or stubbornly insisting that they can do something because it's really easy. Michael bragged he could hit a baseball "really far." But after joining a T-ball team, he cried after games when he struck out.

Sixes are enthusiastic, particularly in regard to their newly discovered intellectual abilities. They love learning and are very proud of their achievements in reading, writing, and solving arithmetic problems. And while they may act stubborn or intensely negative at home, parents will be relieved to learn that this doesn't generally happen at school. Most six-year-olds like their teachers and are typically well behaved in class.

The Seven-Year-Old

At six, Cindi was enthusiastic and upbeat most of the time. Now at seven she seems surprisingly subdued. Her mother worries that she's withdrawn.

"Cindi seems sad, almost depressed," her mother lamented. "I don't know what's wrong with her."

It's almost as if Cindi can't stop this withdrawal once she starts. Inevitably she seems to turn into what her mother calls a "I-can-get-along-without-you-very-well kid." This is especially true if there are guests in the house or if the family is at church. Cindi just isn't her old self, her mother thinks, when she's around others.

Socially more withdrawn, seven-year-olds often complain that others don't like them, are unfair, or are picking on them. One day Cindi came home from school and told her mother, "My teacher doesn't like me."

Cindi's mother found this strange because just a week earlier, in a parent-teacher conference, Cindi's second-grade teacher had told her how much she enjoyed having Cindi in her class.

All of this is typical for the seven-year-old. She worries about many things. People won't like her. She might be late for school. Kids will make fun of her because she can't read well. Her father likes her brother better than her, or maybe her mother doesn't love her anymore. And so on. To Cindi and other Sevens, the world is suddenly full of things to be concerned about and afraid of.

There is a reason for this. Up through age six, children are unable to make use of social comparison information (how others do versus how well they do) in judging themselves. As Sevens become better able to incorporate information from the environment regarding their performance, self-esteem adjusts to a more realistic level. Usually this means a dropping-off from the previous overly favorable estimation of self-worth. With this increased sensitivity to the people around them, Sevens are much more self-critical and aware of what others think about them. This results in a more reflective, pensive, hyper-critical child.

With all of this weighing down the seven-year-old, it's no wonder she goes around with a frown on her face. But forget about the brooding worry, the ominous feelings about things going wrong, and the fears that nobody likes her, and the seven-year-old is actually a rather delightful child.

She still likes to learn and enjoys intellectual challenges. She's becoming even more independent, which can be seen in her interest in joining a dance class or participating in sports. She's even better at reasoning, and she seems to understand when her parents explain why certain things are right or wrong. And now at seven, she is willing to listen to someone else's side of a story. When her mother intervenes in an argument between the seven-year-old and a sibling, she is able to listen to her brother's version of the problem. There is still the side of her that is worried and fearful and this keeps her from being too adventuresome or to display the keen sense of humor she may have shown before—or will again in the future.

Ben's mother found this out that when she tried to make a joke about his teacher not liking him. "What a relief," his mother teased, "now you can stop taking an apple for her every day." Ben, thinking his mother was making fun of him, burst into tears.

With all her worry and her fears comes a certain sense of perfectionism. The seven-year-old worries she won't get her schoolwork right, so she keeps working at it until it is perfect—only to begin to feel that it's just never going to be good enough. Pity the poor second-grade teacher!

Many parents worry that their seven-year-old has become too withdrawn or gloomy, or is crying too much. It's good for parents of seven-year-olds to remember what Louise Bates Ames and Carol Chase Huber write in *Your Seven-Year-Old: Life in a Minor Key*: "Seven tends to be a quiet, withdrawn, pensive, and in some even a rather gloomy age."

The Eight-Year-Old

Eight-year-old Brad is busy. Constantly on the go, he can't wait to get home from school in order to go outside and play. If his usual friends aren't around to play with him, he's riding his bike or trying to hit game-winning shots with the basketball in the driveway.

When he gets up in the morning, he wants to watch television or work on a puzzle he started the night before—or maybe he'll try to do both. His mother says she gets tired out just watching him. "I don't know where he gets his energy," she sighs.

That energy is translated into speed and liveliness. It's action, action, and more action for most eight-year-olds like Brad. Everything has to be done fast.

This is the way Brad often handles school as well. Consequently he makes mistakes or gets careless in his work. At home, his chores may be half completed before he shifts gears and goes on to something else he would rather do. The problem is that when he reflects on his own performance, he can be hard on himself.

"I hate myself," the mother of eight-year-old Melinda has heard her say. "I wish I was dead," Elizabeth mutters when she is called to task for not doing a chore she said she would do.

Eight is a sensitive age, a time when both Elizabeth and Brad are sensitive to criticism and concerned about how others will feel about them. Their feelings get hurt easily, and that's when they can blame themselves and show a strong self-critical streak. "Why don't I ever do anything right!" Elizabeth says in self-condemnation.

Not only are they hard on themselves, they're also tough critics of others. People just don't act the way they ought to, they think. It's

Brad's mother and father who are frequently the target of his high expectations and criticism. "My dad never talks to me," he tells his mother. "Mom, you talk too much on the phone," he said to his mother another day.

But Eights love to talk, too. They often come home from school with talk about the events of the day. And they'll be rather dramatic about what's going on in their lives. They like to hear others, particularly adults, talk. They listen closely (unless they're being assigned a chore, of course) and seem to have an intense curiosity about what people are talking about—especially when this has to do with relationships.

Brad's mother becomes annoyed with Brad because whenever she's telling him about a chore she wants him to do, he says, "What?" "How can he not hear me?" his mother asks. "He hears everything else said in our house."

Most of the time—when he's not playing Pogs with his friends or trying to be the neighborhood champ at the latest video game—Brad demands his mother's attention. "It's like sometimes he can't get enough of it," his mother complains.

Elizabeth's mother, on the other hand, likes her closeness with her daughter. "I see her growing up and spending more time with her friends," she says. "So I value the closeness we have. I know it's not going to be this way long."

The Nine-Year-Old

Valerie, age nine, says she knows she "growing up."

"I don't fight as much with my brother and I don't argue as much with my mother." She stops and thinks for a few seconds.

"Also," she says after pondering this idea of growing up, "I'm not around my mom and dad as much as I used to be. So, I can just tell I'm growing up because I go to a new school . . . but when I thought about my old school today, I almost cried. But I didn't."

Valerie is perhaps too busy to cry. She goes to dance class and belongs to the Brownies. She plays soccer, goes to the Boys and Girls Club after school, and has an apparently endless schedule of birthday parties and sleep-overs to attend. There are, of course, frequent camping trips with the Brownies. "It's fun," she concludes, "doing all sorts of things."

Shane, another nine-year-old, is also involved in important activities. He plays on a baseball team and has a group of friends he pals around with. Sometimes his mother gets calls from his teacher about his activities in school.

"Shane squirted juice on a girl's hair in the lunchroom," Shane's teacher reported to his mother one day. "And when I asked him to apologize to her he was sarcastic and insincere."

"I didn't mean to do it, Mom," Shane said when he got home, "so why should I apologize?"

Shane and Valerie, like most nine-year-olds, are more independent and more self-motivated than ever before. Less dependent on either parent, they move off in their own direction at their own pace. They want to do things in their own way—without any interference. They like the idea of having lots of freedom and the ability to plan events and carry them out.

Nine-year-olds like Valerie and Shane have many interests and plenty to do. They want to do everything and sometimes there's a real crunch to get it all in. And they take all of their activities very seriously. If you ask Valerie, she will demonstrate exactly what she's been learning at dance class or a new way to kick a soccer ball. Give Shane a chance and he will show you how to beat a video game or how to shoot free throws. These activities are front and center in their lives right now, and they will practice their moves over and over until they get them just right.

Yet nine-year-olds can be unpredictable with fairly wide mood swings. Grumpy and acting out of sorts one minute, the next they are enthusiastic and rattling away about their next activity. Arun, for example, carries his skateboard with him so he can practice at any given moment. But at times he's down in the dumps over his younger brother not having to do as many chores as he does.

Arun is very responsible sometimes; at other times he makes excuses and passes the buck. He'll complain about things when his father asks him to finish his schoolwork or help rake the yard. He can't because he has a headache or stomachache or because something else isn't right.

Like other nine-year-olds, Arun loves to collect things—right now it's Pogs—and loves to arrange the round pieces in categories. He keeps a list of baseball players he likes and the amusement rides he'd like to go on next summer. Organization is important to him.

But so is fairness. He gets angry when he feels that his father is treating him unjustly. He gets very cantankerous when things aren't equitable in his mind. But he is more likely to accept responsibility, or even a punishment, if it is fair.

In order to evaluate whether something is fair, he needs reasons. "Why can't I go camping?" Arun asks, and he expects a clear, impartial reason. While he wants things to go the way he's planned them, he is more willing to accept changes and alterations in his organized planning if the reasons seem right and consistent with established rules. This is partly because he is able to stop and think about things and reason them through.

Handling the Opposition of the School-Age Child

Parents frequently greet the growing independence of the school-age child with a certain degree of ambivalence. It can be said that all parents want their children to become capable, competent individuals who can take care of themselves. But it's the wise parent who understands—and accepts—that the path to independence is anything but smooth and direct. And the process of letting go, after six years of protecting and holding a child close, is not easy.

As youngsters strive for more and greater independence, mothers and fathers will often worry about safety and welfare issues. Independence is necessary and important, but parental guidance is still needed. Along with guidance—in the form of giving affection, enforcing rules and family standards, and supervising the whereabouts of their children—should come positive feedback. This assists children in maintaining an adequate sense of their own worth and capabilities. Supportive parents, who encourage their kids in positive ways, help them maintain a good sense of who they are and make it easier for school-age children to weather the temporary setbacks they may encounter with school and friends. While parents can't prevent those setbacks, they can be there to listen to their problems and help them find ways of solving their conflicts.

Reviewing the Rules

Along the way, children will be seeking more freedom. Yet, parents cannot afford to allow children to have more freedom than they are ready to handle. Children, of course, differ widely in this regard. That is, some youngsters want more freedom and insist on greater independence than others. Parents, therefore, have to test out how much freedom a child may need and how much she can be trusted with. By the time a child is nine, parents worried about issues of independence should no longer be troubled by (or buy into) arguments like "Everyone else gets to stay out until after dark." By now you will know better, but you do need to keep in mind that during the elementary school years, rules need to be reviewed and changed from time to time as children become more competent and trustworthy. Parents must always be trying to strike a happy balance between allowing a child to be as independent as she needs to be while still protecting her. To gain the cooperation of school-age children in this process of learning to trust and granting freedom and independence, expectations and rules need to be reasonable, fair, and clearly stated.

When children ask for more freedom ("Can I go to Sherry's house to watch a video until eight o'clock?"), their rules can be reviewed in a reasonable way. A parent could say, "Well, let's see. The rule is that you can't go out after dinner on school nights. Right? We all agreed that that was a fair rule. Now you want to make an exception. Okay, there's nothing wrong with asking, but your mother and I need to talk about this so we can decide if we want to let you go for just tonight or whether we should change this rule. I think it's a good rule and I'm not in favor of changing it. But you've got all of your schoolwork done tonight and maybe we could relax the rule for one night."

Communicating Effectively

If there are frequent arguments about independence, you need to take time to talk about the problem. Communicating about freedom and independence should help both of you to understand each other and improve the relationship. There is no doubt that from the school-age years into adolescence, communication assumes greater importance.

But communication about a problem like independence works better if it takes place in an atmosphere of relative calm and tranquillity—not when either parent or child or both are angry. When you are angry, you may be too restrictive, fail to understand your child's point of view, or shut off communication with negative or critical comments. When your child is angry, she may fail to listen to what you have to say, fail to understand your point of view, or simply assume you're just trying to be mean or controlling.

A way to start such a discussion is to say, "It seems we yell a lot about things I won't let you do. For instance, you want to stay out and play until after dark and I won't let you."

Then tell her the reasons for your decision. You could say, "I know you want to play outside later in the evening, but I need to think about your safety. Not only that but on school nights I have to see to it that you come in early enough to finish your schoolwork and be in bed in time to get plenty of rest for school."

After explaining your reasons, listen to her and let her know you're paying attention. One way to let her know you're listening is to use a method of communication called reflective listening. You can reflect back to her what you hear her saying. For example, you could say in a reflective way: "It sounds as if you think it's unfair for me to say you can't hang out with teenagers." Then you give her a chance to respond back to you.

In this kind of discussion, it is most important that you communicate to your child that you are really listening and that you understand her point of view. By giving calm and rational reasons for your decisions you also let her know that you respect that she is growing up, but that you still have her best interests to consider. Finally, it may be important to solicit her suggestions for solving the problem and coming to an agreement.

The agreement may or may not represent a compromise on your part. As the parent you must make sure that your child is being protected from her own need for freedom. At the same time you need to let her know, through your encouragement and support, that you believe she is better able to take care of herself and able to participate more in decisions affecting her.

By age nine, youngsters are more responsible, but they tend to be caught up in their need for friendships and involvement in activities outside the home. Between ages six and nine they are more likely to simply tune you out and not listen than to behave in ways that are directly oppositional. If you talk, listen, give feedback, and solicit your child's ideas and opinions, you will stand a better chance that she'll hear you when you want her to listen.

Monitoring Diet

Besides issues related to independence and freedom, clashes with school-age children can occur over food and eating. If there's one thing that Sixes, Sevens, and Eights have in common it's that they don't like to experiment with unfamiliar food. Given a choice, they would probably be satisfied with a steady diet of hamburgers and french fries. But seeing that they have a healthy diet is part of your job of protecting their health.

Again this might mean that you need to review rules and expectations. Both at home and when you're eating out, there should be limits set on what foods are ordered and eaten. Limits can be stated ("You can have a hamburger only if you eat a salad, too") and rules explained. You'll have a little more control at home in this regard, of course, than you will in a fast-food restaurant.

Instilling Manners

One other area related to eating that causes problems during these years is the elementary school child's table manners and eating behavior. Some parents may be inclined to think of this period as the "gross-out years" rather than the golden years.

If there's one thing kids in this "stable and quiet time of life" like to do, it is shock (especially parents and other adults) and entertain (especially younger siblings) with noises, body sounds, gross jokes, talk about bodily functions, and loud belches. This goes for girls as well as boys. While such behavior deserves a review of the rules and expectations, especially when eating in public, generally the less attention afforded their temporary interest in grossing you out, the better.

Handling the More Difficult Six- to Nine-Year-Old

At eight, Sean has become adept at detecting loopholes in the rules given him by his parents.

"You said I couldn't go to John's house," Sean will argue. "You didn't say anything about not going in his front yard."

When they sense a loophole, difficult school-age children will try to exploit the situation. This can lead to frustration on the part of parents and often useless arguing.

"That's not fair that I'm going to get punished," Sean protests. "I didn't sock my sister like you said . . . I pushed her."

Difficult school-age youngsters tend to debate everything. For instance, when Shane got in trouble at school for squirting juice on a girl, he debated with his mother about whether it was intentional or not. "I just was pretending to zap her with a ray gun," Shane contended. "It wasn't my fault the juice squirted out of the box."

And they may try to keep the argument going so that they can avoid doing the responsible thing. If they can wear you down, they have won and they will find ways to get away with more.

While all children need to have rules clearly stated, it is even more essential for the difficult school-age child, for this is a child capable of fairly complex reasoning and able to remember whatever contradictory things you may have told her "before."

It is equally important to be certain in your own mind what rules and expectations are reasonable. With the difficult child, you cannot appear to be unsure or insecure.

S.M.I.L.E.

Eight-year-old Robby often acts out of control. He is aggressive to other children, swears, steals from classmates at school, and lies to his mother. When Vicki, his mother, tries to handle these behavior problems, she gets lies and excuses from Robby.

"This girl gave me this watch," he'll say when his mother discovers a watch that doesn't belong to him in his room.

Vicki tends to snap at him in impatient annoyance and anger. "How can you do this?" she asks angrily. "You know it isn't right to steal!"

"But," Vicki told me in exasperation, "no matter what I do, he keeps doing bad things."

For Vicki and other parents of the more difficult school-age child, I have developed an acronym that might help. It's called S.M.I.L.E. Because consistency and firmness are so critical in dealing effectively with the difficult child during this period, S.M.I.L.E. may help save some days.

The *S* in S.M.I.L.E. stands for: "*S*ay what you mean." That indicates that you have to be very clear in indicating the rules, limits, and expectations. Don't provide children with any loopholes that can be used to avoid meeting their responsibilities.

Shane's mother, who recognized many years ago that Shane was a difficult child, has become adept at saying what she means to her son. "I want you to behave at the birthday party today," she told him one day. "That means you don't swear at anyone, don't hit or shove anyone, and act politely from the beginning to the end of the party, even if someone else tries to start something. Okay?"

M stands for: "*M*ean what you say." You have to be very sure that when you set a rule or lay out your expectations, you mean it. You have thought it through and have decided that this is an important expectation and you mean to stick with it. You will also monitor the child's behavior to make sure he lives up to it.

When Robby's mother sets a limit she means it: "I will let you work on your model car. But if you get angry or frustrated or stop following the directions, then you'll have to stop for today. Understand?"

If Robby gets angry or frustrated, or starts to improvise by not following the directions—which his mother has learned inevitably leads to too much frustration for him—she will in fact suspend his working on the model for that day.

I stands for: "*I*nsure that you're the same every day." It's not enough to be clear, reasonable, and firm on your good days. You have to be firm and consistent about what you say and what you mean every day. As Shane's mother says, "He always remembers when you once let a rule slide."

L stands for: "*L*et your child experience the consequences." In other words, it's not just a matter of saying what you mean and believing you mean what you say. You only mean it if you are willing to back it up. For a difficult kid, that often means letting her experience the consequences of not living up to a standard or rule.

When eight-year-old Shawna had extra money that she wasn't supposed to have, her father suspected that she stole it. He contacted Shawna's teacher and found out that a girl in Shawna's class had "lost" a five-dollar bill. Shawna's father made her take the money back to school, apologize to the teacher and the other student, and perform extra chores at home for four days.

Finally, *E* stands for: "*E*mpower yourself to be a consistent and firm parent." Give yourself the permission and power to be a parent who believes in the limits, rules, and expectations you provide for your children. You will be a more effective and more self-confident parent.

Consistency, firmness, and monitoring are very important in order to deal with the demanding, exploitive, argumentative, and persistent youngster. Children who know that their parents will stand firm and will enforce rules are less likely to even try to talk them into making an exception "just this once."

Children by nine are able to understand the concept of fairness, and if punishments or consequences are invoked in a fair, evenhanded manner, difficult children will often be able to accept them. When rules are broken, if you handle things in a calm, reasonable, and fair way, difficult children will be much less resentful about accepting consequences than they will be with more angry or unfair handling. Even difficult children can accept that they have a consequence coming when the rules are broken.

With the more challenging school-age youngster, particularly the one who says that certain consequences are "not fair," rather than argue about it sometimes it helps to turn a situation around by asking, "What do you think your consequence should be?"

On the other hand, with youngsters like Robby, Shane, and Shawna, there have to be firm rules and firm consequences. No matter what a child's excuse about a misbehavior, she must know that if she breaks a rule, a consequence will surely follow. For example, when a teacher calls home and says Robby has been disrespectful to her, there has to be consequences. And it doesn't matter that his excuse is that she said something that made him mad. His parent should say: "I'm sorry, our rule is that children in this family treat all teachers with respect. If you have a problem with a teacher, you can discuss it with us and we'll find a way of handling it. But you can't be disrespectful just because a teacher made you mad. Because of what you did, you're going to have to stay in the house for three days without being able to play with your friends."

Children of this age need firm rules along with consequences for disobeying those rules whether they are difficult or relatively easy to raise. That assists them to feel that the world is an orderly place in which they will receive fair, just, and relatively predictable treatment from others. It's your job to make sure that their world is a predictable and fair one.

Summary

The school-age years in general are:

- **A period in which children develop growing independence.**

- **The so-called golden years of childhood, as they are a relatively happy and stable time filled with seemingly endless explorations of the fascinations of their immediate world and its secrets.**

- Years in which children develop peer relationships and begin to view themselves in terms of social traits.

- A stage when gender differences are more apparent; girls have a small group of friends with one or two best friends, while boys have a larger group of friends built around loyalty and shared activities.

- A time when parents typically raise and prompt boys and girls in different ways: boys are generally given more freedom and independence and girls are usually encouraged to stay closer to home and be more dependent.

- The time when parents must learn to let go and allow the child to grow up and away from Mother and Father.

The school-age child will display the following characteristics at certain ages:

At six, she is . . .

- Often excited about going into first grade and learning new things.

- More self-centered and more likely to want everything to go her way; as a result she may appear defiant and immature at times.

- Faced with conflicting options and often confronted by difficult choices; once having made a choice, though, she's not sure she's made a good decision and may want to change her mind.

- Not as close to her parents and more independent; possibly ambivalent in her feelings toward her parents—showing strong likes and dislikes almost at the same time.

- Often insecure and in need of reassurance from her parents that she is still loved.

At seven, she is . . .

- Surprisingly subdued and often withdrawn—particularly in social situations.
- Frequently complaining that others don't like her or that others are unfairly picking on her.
- Frequently worried about all sorts of things at home, school, or with peers.
- Still in many ways a delightful child as she is more reasonable and more willing to listen to someone else's point of view.
- Often a perfectionist who gets angry with herself when she can't do things the way she wants to.

At eight, she is . . .

- Active, self-critical, dramatic, and outgoing.
- More lively with a higher energy level and, therefore, more willing to try things.
- Careless and prone to make mistakes—often because that's what her liveliness leads to.
- Reflective of her own performance and often hard on herself.
- Sensitive to criticism and concerned about how others feel about her.
- Talkative, willing to share things, and receptive to hearing others talk.

At nine, she is . . .

- More independent and self-motivated.
- Less dependent on Mother and preferring to do things on her own without interference.
- Full of interests, wanting to do everything, and sometimes finding it hard to fit everything in.

- Sometimes unpredictable with wide mood swings; enthusiastic and positive one minute, grumpy and making excuses for herself the next.
- Into collecting and categorizing things.
- Concerned about fairness; she likes reasons and will accept reasons for rules and limits if they seem fair.

Parents can deal better with the oppositionalism and negativism of these years by:

- Talking about the problems of independence when there is conflict over issues of freedom and independence.
- Using reasoning to explain their decisions about the limits they place on her independence.
- Practicing good communication skills, such as listening in a reflective way and acknowledging a child's feelings.
- Giving children of this age sound reasons for all their rules and expectations.
- Allowing as much freedom as a child needs while still protecting her.

The difficult school-age child can be best helped when you:

- Realize she is becoming more highly skilled at detecting loopholes in rules and limits set by you.
- Are consistent and firm; use the principles set forth in the acronym S.M.I.L.E. to remind you to be more consistent and firm.

CHAPTER 11

Understanding and Disciplining the Preadolescent: Ages Ten to Thirteen

The Preadolescent

Up until now, a child's growth and development have been relatively steady. Now they are likely to proceed in dramatic leaps and bounds. With a remarkable growth spurt that has begun to take place during the years from ten to thirteen, kids can grow as much as ten or fifteen inches and add many pounds. Such changes in physical growth will usually be accompanied by dramatic changes in attitude and behavior. The rather nice, friendly, accepting ten-year-old frequently turns into a contrary, oppositional, and highly energetic eleven-year-old.

The ten-year-old is usually an outgoing, friendly, cooperative kid who still needs supervision to complete his chores and assignments. A year later you are presented with a child who is on the go, constantly in motion, and shouting at his parents when they don't follow up on all promises to the letter.

Elevens criticize their parents. They've discovered the opposite sex and they make crude jokes. And most of all they like to argue. Their behavior is often at its worst at school. It's enough to discourage parents and prompt sixth-grade teachers to find another line of work.

Stephen, age eleven, is a good example of this dramatic change. A rather compliant and easy-to-raise child most of his life, during the past few months, his mother says, "You can see the devil in him come out in his behavior."

Instead of always doing exactly what adults want and expect, Stephen shows his individuality and contrariness by defying his mother. If he's been told to clean his room, he resists as long as he can, before taking his good old time getting it done.

Talking to someone besides his mother about it, his eyes twinkle as he says that he "really got her mad this time." However, if asked if he likes to see his mother angry, he says, "Naw, it's just that she's always telling me what to do."

Fortunately twelve-year-olds are more cooperative and less rebellious. More likely to go along with the program at home, they show enthusiasm and interest, and concern about how others feel.

Twelve-year-old Kevin, a typical Twelve, often feels extremely awkward and easily embarrassed.

"My teachers make fun of me," Kevin complained about his seventh-grade teachers.

However, when he thinks more carefully about what he's saying, he changes his mind somewhat. "It's not that they try to embarrass me," he concedes, "it's just that I get embarrassed by most things these days. If I don't answer a question right and the teacher points that out, I feel like he's making fun of me."

Kevin, as is true of many preteens, feels awkward, insecure, and unsure of himself. Sometimes it seems as if almost everything embarrasses him—sexual feelings, growth spurts, pimples, or not getting answers right in class. It's as though he has suddenly been placed in an unfamiliar body with someone else's emotions.

The eleven-year-old often turns into the calmer and sensitive twelve-year-old, who just a year later turns into the more withdrawn and detached thirteen-year-old. The eleven- and thirteen-year-olds look more like the preteens and teens we've come to expect. They are argumentative and display greater than usual oppositionalism, moodiness, and withdrawn behavior.

Thirteen-year-olds resemble seven-year-olds by turning inward, becoming worriers, and communicating much less. They don't want parents prying into their business, and may frequently retreat to their rooms, which they are likely to keep locked against the "intruders" in the family.

In the book *Your Ten- to Fourteen-Year-Old,* Ames, Ilg, and Baker state that a thirteen-year-old is often sad, sour, suspicious, unfriendly, and unhappy. He seems negative and overly sensitive. He's worried about his looks and appearance, and with that worry comes pessimism about his future—which, of course, is moving toward dating, sexuality, and serious life decisions.

Tim is a typical thirteen-year-old. He can be moody and aggressive. He sometimes shows a great sense of humor. But at other times his parents are worried because he appears so depressed. Yet this depression doesn't last long. A day or an hour later he may be talking about how he is going to be "King of the School" now that he's in the ninth grade.

"I can really be mean," Tim admits. "I should become a boxer so I could get paid for socking people—like my brother."

On occasion, Tim seems to be much more serious. "I think I should get a three-point-five average at school this year so I can get a head start on the tenth grade when I have to really start worrying about good grades so I can have my choice of good colleges," Tim says.

Overall, during this stage of development, the biggest issue relates to figuring out "Who am I?" By the time the preadolescent reaches thirteen he will be spending greater amounts of time thinking about who he is and how he fits in. "How do I look?" "Do people like me?" "Am I popular?" "Will I be able to get a date?" "Am I normal sexually?" are all critical concerns of this developmental period.

Nicole, a thirteen-year-old girl in the eighth grade, says that this year has been better than the past two years for her. "I started hanging around with other kids who were popular," she says. "I feel a lot more comfortable and I finally feel like I can say what I want to and no one will laugh at me."

Both boys and girls in this preadolescent phase of development have concerns about social relationships and acceptance by peers. But the differences between Nicole and Tim are apparent in other areas. Nicole's physical development and behavior show greater maturity than Tim's. Tim prefers to talk about sports, science, and math; Nicole is interested in "really getting to know" other people. Nicole will likely want to start dating at an earlier age than Tim, and her ability to size up situations and make mature judgments will make her appear to be older than Tim—even though they are exactly the same age.

At twelve and thirteen, young people like Nicole and Tim worry about schoolwork. Other worries concern their appearance, whether others like them, and, for girls, their relationship with boys.

"I'm really going to try hard at school this year," says Nicole. "I know a lot of kids and that makes it easier for me to go to school and do my best."

What Nicole means is that both schoolwork and relationships are important. Having more friends will, for her, lead to greater motivation at school.

Handling the Opposition of the Preadolescent

There are pockets of resistence and rebellion during the preadolescent years starting at age ten.

Ten-year-olds will resist about such things as taking baths, brushing their teeth, and going to bed. However, during this developmental stage there is usually no prolonged opposition or rebellion.

It is important for you to remember that if you keep the channels of communication open and if you are respectful and considerate of your child's developing needs at all ages, there is no reason for your preteenager or, later, your teenager to ever become rebellious.

Also, keep in mind that each age or stage since fifteen months has its areas of stubbornness, negativism, and oppositionalism. The preadolescent years are no exception.

However, you may be reassured that with careful attention to understanding the developmental needs at this stage, you can prevent these age-appropriate strivings for autonomy and independence from turning into pitched battles or defiant rebellions.

As a rule, ten-year-olds don't give parents much resistance, although they still need supervision. A ten-year-old tends to continue the maturity and friendliness he exhibited at age nine, but that doesn't mean he has enough enthusiasm or motivation to do everything he is supposed to. Parents almost always have to provide some monitoring, supervision, support, and direction.

Nor is it true that Tens can't get angry or boil over in rage. They are prone to do this if they think they've been treated unfairly. Parents do well to appeal to their continuing passion for fairness. Reasoning that invokes principles of fairness works rather well with Tens. And when they get over their anger, they are likely to show you lots of affection.

The eleven-year-old, on the other hand, is more rebellious and resistant. He is pulling away from his parents. To do this, he has to be his own person and show his independence—much as he did as a toddler. The eleven-year-old simply can't afford to go along with everything his parents or teachers want. His rebellion against assigned chores or duties is part of a demonstration of self-determination and assertiveness. If he is to figure out "Who am I?" he must figure out who he is not. He begins to break free from his parents by showing some opposition.

Eleven-year-olds like Stephen tend to be fairly adept at rebellion. They will set up challenges that are designed to provoke responses from parents and teachers.

Is Stephen's goal simply to be stubborn or rebellious? No. He presents these challenges as a way of ascertaining who he is and who others are. Parents can assist in this process.

Establishing Limits

One way for parents to help children through this process is to establish limits and rules. Most Elevens are going to test the limits a little just as Stephen does. He teases his sister and tends to defy his mother by not doing what she has asked. While these responses may be within normal boundaries for preadolescents, still she must remind him of what she expects of him. She can remind him that hostile or aggressive teasing of his sister is off-limits, and despite how he feels he must still clean his room sometimes.

When he gets angry, expect a more violent explosion from an Eleven than a Ten. Elevens tend to react in physical ways when angry—slamming doors, hitting walls, and kicking at sisters (or brothers).

He may suddenly present problems over bedtime. Stephen knows perfectly well that his regular bedtime is 9:30 P.M., yet now it seems to slip his mind on a daily basis. When he's reminded he appears to be shocked that bedtime is so early. This is just another way for Stephen to assert his independence.

Dealing with Outbursts

How can Stephen's mother and father best handle the challenges, declarations of independence, or angry outbursts when limits are set or enforced? Three points are useful to keep in mind:

- **Remain calm.** The best approach to these challenges of the rules and expectations is to remain calm. Parents can be calm and allow oppositional or angry behavior without backing down on a rule or expectation.

- **Don't take it personally.** It's important to remember that negative, resistant, or oppositional behavior is a part of this stage of development. As kids between ten and thirteen try to figure out who they are they must rebel at times. This has nothing to do with you, or what they feel about you no matter what they may say to the contrary.

- **Sidestep arguments.** Since children must assert their independence at times, you should expect this to happen. It's often easier to deal with if you take care not to escalate the conflict. So, whether it's rebellion related to bedtime, friends, or chores, a parent's best approach is usually to sidestep a potential argument.

An incident with twelve-year-old Kevin provides an example of how to sidestep an argument. Kevin's father expected him to help in cleaning the basement. His father had already done the preliminary work by boxing up books, magazines, old appliances, and other items that were to be transferred to the garage or to the street for garbage pickup.

Kevin trudged reluctantly to the basement. When it came time to actually carry boxes up the steps and out to the garage, Kevin began to resist: "I don't want to do this today," he said.

"It's too hot and these boxes are too heavy. I don't see why we have to do this today. Can't we do this next Saturday?"

Instead of responding to Kevin's opening salvo, his dad neatly sidestepped the argument and avoided any escalation of the conflict. "I've marked the lightest boxes for you," he replied. "They are over here in this corner. I'll see you upstairs." With that, his father picked up a heavy box and took it up the steps. Since Kevin had no one to argue with, he grabbed a light box and took it up the stairs as well.

After they both made several trips, Kevin, passing his dad on the steps, asked if he would take him to the video store when they were finished.

"Boy, you've earned it," his dad said. "You've been a big help."

"Look at this heavy box I'm carrying," Kevin replied.

Offering Compromises

When your child is in the preadolescent phase of development and approaching the teenage years, compromise assumes greater importance. While I frequently take the position that parents must be firm and stick to their guns over rules and expectations, I also believe that parents can best handle certain kinds of resistant and oppositional behavior through compromise.

There are many areas in which flexibility and compromise can demonstrate that you appreciate your child's maturity and are aware of his need for greater freedom and independence. The time he goes to bed, the time he comes in from play, the style of haircut, brand of shoes, style of clothes, and the time he does homework can all be negotiated with eventual compromise agreements reached. There are other areas that will not be negotiated or compromised: whether he completes school assignments, is aggressive, hangs out with peers who are much older, goes to parties without adult supervision, smokes, or experiments with alcohol or drugs.

To strike the right balance between rigid adherence to a set of rules and standards and overly permissive behavior is often very difficult for parents today. It is indeed a delicate balancing act. When parents are too permissive, it is often for the wrong reasons.

Michelle's mother, Renae, offers an example of this challenge.

Michelle is thirteen years old and demands more freedom and more privileges than her mother would like to give her. Renae prides herself on having a close relationship with Michelle. "We are just like sisters," she has boasted to friends. "I can't remember the last time we had an argument."

But Michelle stays up as late as she wants, frequently fails to complete school assignments, and complains about doing any household chores. Renae admits that maybe she should take a firm stance with Michelle. "But we've got a very close relationship," Renae says, "and I wouldn't want to spoil this with fights or arguments."

The only way Renae has been able to avoid arguments and conflicts is by giving in to Michelle. Renae is more concerned about being close to Michelle than setting limits, establishing standards, or engaging in the kind of conflict that happens when parents let kids know about the boundaries.

Ann, the mother of another thirteen-year-old girl, recently told me that she overheard her daughter telling a girlfriend that her mother was a bitch. "I must be doing something right," Ann remarked, "if she doesn't always think I'm wonderful."

The fact is, preadolescents don't think that parents who *fail* to take stands on limits and rules are wonderful either. Parents can avoid the worst conflicts through communication and compromise, but they have to set some standards. This is one of the main ways children learn self-discipline.

Creating a Safe Family Atmosphere

Although there's a lot about preadolescents you can't change, there is something vital you can do. You can create a family atmosphere that allows your preteen to rebel. You can do this by always letting children know that they can talk openly with you about any topic. It also helps, as I mentioned, if you don't take their opposition or resistance personally. The same goes for complaints and requests. If your preteen wants to ask about dating at age twelve, you can always be willing to talk about it.

This doesn't mean that you will give in to or agree with the request. It does mean you will be sensitive to the young person's needs and desires—however transitory. A sensitive response, even if it is negative, paves the way for more communication.

For instance, when thirteen-year-old Nicole asks if she can go to an R-rated movie with friends, her mother can hear her out, listen to her arguments, and give her a decision. She can do this in a way that does not embarrass Nicole for asking or appear to be saying no just to be mean—although Nicole's immediate reaction may be to think so.

Nicole's mother could say, "I know you want to see this movie because all the other kids are seeing it. But I read the reviews and there are very violent scenes in this movie I can't give my permission for you to see. There are other movies I could approve and if you and your friends want to go to one of those, you have my permission. Thanks for coming and asking first, though. I appreciate that."

Let's say that Nicole, who is usually compliant and responsible, takes exception to this refusal. She might say, "That's not fair! All the kids have seen it and I'll be the only one in the whole school who isn't allowed to go. And if you don't let me go, I'll go anyway. I just won't tell you! You can't stop me if I really want to go."

Her mother can respond with, "You're absolutely right. I can't stop you. And you might also be right that you're the only kid in school not allowed to go this movie. But I have to do what I think is right. I believe that after you think about what I've said you'll do the right thing."

In a family in which the general atmosphere allows for rebellion, Nicole will be unlikely to decide to rebel and go to this movie. If she does, and her mother finds out, Nicole is not going to be rejected or made to feel as if she is a defiant or oppositional youngster. Her mother might express disappointment by saying, "I'm disappointed that you didn't accept my decision. I thought I could trust you to do what is right."

But no matter what happens, her mother will be there to offer forgiveness, affection, and encouragement—regardless of a specific instance of rebellion or defiance. That's one of the really tough parts about being a parent. You put up with a lot and then you are expected to be loving and giving of your time and affection when needed!

It's helpful to ask yourself at least one question: Is my child rebelling against me or trying to assert independence in a rather crude and inexperienced way?

If you can remember that he's trying to cope with the beginning stages of adolescence (and if you can remember some of the difficulties of your own adolescent years), you're likely to answer this question in the right way and offer him what he needs.

Acknowledging Feelings

Throughout this phase of development from ten to thirteen children have interpersonal difficulties. They may feel that teachers are picking on them or making fun of them. If they see two people whispering in the hallway at school, they may be sure it's directed at them. If they have heard a rumor about themselves, they are likely to believe that it was started with malicious intent.

During ages twelve and thirteen particularly, young people are very sensitive to what others think or say about them. As a result, they may display considerable emotion, have intense dislikes, or be involved in arguments, fights, or threats.

As a result, parents can feel as if they are living with an emotional time bomb. On the one hand, your sympathies are aroused when your daughter tells you that she's the object of rumors and scapegoating. On the other hand, you may feel great distress when you suspect that her emotional highs and lows related to friendships and peer relationships are evidence of either active hormones or disturbed perceptions.

Because you can't change what's going on socially, you can try to stay neutral and not overreact to her charges, suspicions, or intense disappointments. That's where acknowledging feelings and reflective listening can be helpful.

As mentioned earlier, in reflective listening you try to mirror what your child is feeling. You can say, for instance, "It sounds like you and Trisha aren't getting along so well" or, "It seems as if you're awfully angry with Trisha for talking behind your back." By using this technique, you not only help her identify her feelings but also help her to talk about them.

Your goal is not to solve the problem for her or tell her what to do. After all, even if she is telling you about her problem it doesn't mean she wants advice or suggestions. The best thing you can do is be a sympathetic listener who helps her come to her own decisions and choose a course of action for herself. By asking her what she thinks she ought to do, you can help her brainstorm solutions and plan a reaction—one that is not impulsive or ill-considered.

In acknowledging feelings and being a reflective listener it's important to remember that problems in interpersonal relationships change quickly. Nicole, for example, was on the outs with her best friend, Debby, and said she would "never talk to her again." The next week, however, they had made up and Nicole was planning to stay overnight to help Debby solve her problems with a new boyfriend.

By not getting overly involved in these particular disputes, parents save themselves a lot of emotional turmoil and confusion. Keeping track of who is a good friend and who isn't can be very demanding work for a parent!

Handling the More Difficult Preadolescent

Thirteen-year-old Damian is a difficult youngster. He doesn't come home from school on time, talks back to teachers, and fails to obey most requests or orders from his mother and stepfather. He's also been in trouble with the police for stealing. He's generally angry at his teachers and his parents and says he wishes they would "just stop yelling at me."

When his parents try to restrict him, Damian tells them it's unfair. He says that being grounded or restricted to the house doesn't do any good. "It just makes me hyper and I get into more trouble," Damian contends.

His parents have tried other punishments to attempt to get Damian to conform to the rules and to their expectations. They've taken away his bike, the use of the phone, his TV, and his radio. Damian says he has to be good for a "little while" and then he gets his belongings back. He adds, "My dad softens up after a while no matter how long he said he was going to keep my stuff. My ma just can't handle it when I give her a hard time, so my dad lets me go out so my ma isn't upset."

Damian has learned to work the system without really changing any of his behavior. All he has to do is yell at his mother or destroy something in the house (like a door or a lamp) and "my dad wants me out of the house because he can't stand me anymore."

When young people who have been stubborn, oppositional, or defiant for several years get to be twelve or thirteen, and their parents have not had the training or skills to deal appropriately with them, they're likely to be much like Damian. Given his problems at home and at school, and given his consistent anger along with his ability to "work the system," it seems clear that he will be in further trouble and may well end up in juvenile court.

For some parents this development may actually come as a welcome relief. They may feel they can no longer cope with their preadolescent child. The reality is that a juvenile or family court can only offer some support and structure, and it's not likely it will be able to undo everything that has led the youngster to this pass.

There are, of course, other alternatives. Seeking professional help and having the young person attend a therapy group may be useful. Even more useful is family therapy, which is frequently valuable in opening up lines of communication, changing the reinforcement patterns in the family, and decreasing negative and critical interactions.

If a child is presenting more serious and persistent stubborn, resistant, and oppositional behaviors, parents must examine, with or without the assistance of professionals, their own role in the development of the problem, and accept the fact that they will have to make some changes. If a youngster has reached age twelve or thirteen and is as out of control as Damian is, it very likely means that there have been too many ongoing conflicts and battles in the family, and too little parental understanding of children and how they express negativism and independence. If your youngster resembles Damian, then you have very likely mishandled at least some aspects of discipline.

What can you do at this point? Start by reviewing the previous chapters. Understand that there is no magic solution to getting a difficult preadolescent under control. It will take courage, strength, determination, and careful adherence to the following points:

1. **Preadolescents, as much as other young people, need to have clear limits and rules set for them.**

   These must be communicated in an atmosphere that is calm and reasonable.

   For example, Amy is an eleven-year-old child who has been difficult because she is hyperactive, intense, and demanding. She readily admits she's used to getting her own way with her parents, who are divorced.

   One weekend she was visiting her father and asked to go to the state fair. Her father said he couldn't take her that weekend, although he would take her someplace special the next weekend they were together.

   That wasn't good enough for Amy, and she kept asking him to take her to the state fair "this weekend." Not only was she pestering him by asking frequently, but she put signs and notes around the apartment that said such things as "Amy really wants to go to the state fair."

   When her father tried to be firm about his decision, Amy increased the pressure. She said she hated him and told him she would never come back for another weekend visit. Her father finally got angry and said he couldn't take her bugging him and he didn't care if she never came back.

   It would have been much more helpful for Amy's father to state calmly and clearly what the rules and expectations were for asking for something. He could have said, "You can ask me once for anything. But after I give you an answer, the rule is no more asking in any way." If Amy doesn't stop asking or pressuring her father, he can use the broken-record technique ("Sorry, Amy, not this weekend"), which involves him repeating his final position. Or, he can set a limit with an attached enforcement. For instance, he could say, "You've asked me enough. You have to drop this now. If you ask me again, I may reconsider taking you to the fair next week."

2. **Parents must be consistent in communicating rules and expectations as well as in enforcing them.**

The rules can't change from day to day, and neither can the way you enforce the rules.

In the case of Amy and her father, the rule about asking one time and respecting her father's decision is an all-the-time rule. It should not change from one weekend visit to the next. If he forgets about it or doesn't enforce it, Amy will return to her old ways of asking many times and turning up the heat to try to get her way.

3. **Consistency and firmness are required in enforcing rules and expectations.**

How consistent you are able to be depends in part on what sorts of consequences you decide on. They must be clear, reasonable, and enforceable. Firmness lets kids know that their parents will stick to consequences and punishments once given. Unlike Damian's parents, you can't be put off by a youngster's difficult behavior. If you announce a punishment (say, restricting his ability to leave the house), then you can't soften when he turns up the heat.

Make no mistake: Difficult youngsters will still act in obnoxious and irritating ways even when there are negative consequences to their actions. It's up to parents to stand firm and make sure that kids serve out those punishments.

4. **More oppositional, defiant, and stubborn preadolescents need monitoring and supervision.**

This will require time, effort, and determination on the part of parents. When preteens let you know that they can't be trusted, then it's up to you to monitor their behavior and check on their promises, actions, and intentions.

From time to time you can give them a chance to demonstrate that they are trustworthy and that they can stick to agreements. If they blow such a chance, then monitoring and supervision become the order of the day until you're ready to give them another chance.

Twelve-year-old Daniel, while out playing with neighborhood friends, went into a neighbor's garage. In the garage, the boys spilled gasoline on the floor, broke clay flowerpots, took a pair of tennis shoes, and sampled beer in a refrigerator.

Daniel's parents were shocked by his behavior, as he had never done anything illegal before. They responded by making Daniel apologize to the neighbors when they returned home and make restitution out of his allowance money, and by restricting his activities for two weeks, during which time he was given extra chores.

When the two-week restriction was over, his parents were hesitant about allowing him the free access to the neighborhood he had previously enjoyed. At first, and for a few weeks, they required him to let them know precisely where he was going and who he was with. When Daniel complied with this, they felt more comfortable in gradually easing up on these restrictions.

When children show that they can comply with monitoring and supervision, then they can be given more freedom.

5. **Despite close supervision and monitoring, preteens continue to need communication that is supportive and reflects understanding.**

Although their behavior might not be trustworthy, they are still children who require and deserve respect, approval, acceptance, and encouragement. Your communication must always reflect your efforts to be supportive—even when you are enforcing the breaking of rules with consequences or penalties.

You can say to a youngster like Daniel that you're proud that he has been able to let you know so faithfully where he's going and who he's with. What you say will reflect respect, approval, and encouragement: "Because you've helped build our trust again, we're going to trust you some more. If you keep up the good work, then we'll give you a little more freedom. If we find we can't trust you, then you won't get as much freedom as you'd like."

6. **Finally consider professional help.**

If after reviewing these guidelines and making all the efforts you can make on your own you don't see measurable improvement, then you need to think about seeking professional help. Family therapy (and group therapy when it's available for young people) offers the best chance for changing some of the interaction patterns in the family.

Often parents focus on the child as the problem, and prefer to send the child off by himself to be "fixed" when in fact problems of serious resistance, defiance, and opposition develop in a family setting. These problems are handled most effectively within the context of family therapy.

Summary

During the preadolescent years, ten to thirteen, you can expect the following:

- Growth will proceed in a more dramatic fashion with noticeable changes in physical growth.
- Because of the changes preadolescents will experience, most will feel awkward, insecure, and unsure of themselves.

- Young people will go from rather nice, friendly, accepting ten-year-olds to more contrary, oppositional, and highly energetic eleven-year-olds.

- Children at ages eleven and thirteen will look and act like the preteens we often expect—argumentative, moody, oppositional, and sometimes withdrawn.

- The emerging issue of the preadolescent, an issue that continues into middle adolescence, is "Who am I?"

- Young people of this age period worry about their appearance, social relationships, and school.

Parents can best handle the negativism and oppositionalism of the preadolescent by:

- Keeping the channels of communication open and being respectful and considerate of a child's developing needs between the ages of ten and thirteen.

- Providing supervision, monitoring, support, and direction at each age during the preadolescent years.

- Recognizing that eleven-year-olds are more rebellious and resistant than ten-year-olds; understanding that Elevens can't afford to go along with everything their parents want.

- Remaining calm in the face of oppositional behavior.

- Not taking a child's negative behavior personally.

- Learning to sidestep arguments.

- Offering compromises, but not compromising all limits and rules to ensure peace.

- Creating a family atmosphere that allows some rebellion but lets a preadolescent get stabilized again by coming to a parent for affection and encouragement.

- Acknowledging preadolescents' feelings to help them deal with the insecurities of interpersonal relationships.

Difficult preadolescents may be handled in the following ways:

- Setting clear limits and rules.
- Being consistent not only in setting rules and expectations but in enforcing them.
- Firmly enforcing rules and standards.
- Providing preadolescents with monitoring and supervision.
- Communicating in a way that reflects respect, support, and understanding.
- Seeking professional help when the rebellious and oppositional behavior is ongoing and parental efforts to make changes are unsuccessful.

CHAPTER 12

Understanding and Disciplining the Adolescent: Ages Fourteen to Eighteen

The Adolescent

Fourteen-year-old Paul was ecstatic. "My whole thing has changed," he almost crowed. "It used to be sports and school. Now it's still school . . . and it's friends. I come home and I talk on the phone. It drives my mother crazy, but I love it. I love having friends and I love being in high school. . . . My big thing this year is getting a date."

Entering into adolescence is a journey that is exciting and at the same time ominously frightening.

Paul is excited about friendships, school, growing up, even taking on new responsibilities. What is scary for him is the uncertainty of hitting it off with the opposite sex—definitely a part of growing up in the early adolescent years.

There's uncertainty as kids travel the road between childhood and what lies beyond. Along the way are tasks that must be accomplished in this journey to adulthood. Two of the most important tasks to be dealt with are feeling secure in relationships and settling on a direction for a career.

With the somewhat sudden changes that occur in young people at this age, one of the other tasks has to do with adjusting to a new and different body and an altered body image. Paul sees himself as someone who could be attractive to girls. And like most other adolescents, he is now very much aware of his height and the fact that many girls his age are taller than he is.

As he views himself as a student, a friend, and a potential suitor of girls, he is necessarily engaging in one of the most important developmental tasks: developing a personal sense of identity, that is, figuring out for himself "Who am I?"—a task begun in earnest during preadolescence but one that will require the rest of the teen years (at the very least) to complete.

Fifteen-year-old Laurie counted up all the boys who asked her to her high school's first dance of the year. "Can you believe it?" she rhetorically asked her parents. "Sixteen boys have asked me to go to the school dance."

While this wasn't exactly what her father or mother wanted to hear, they couldn't help but be proud of the popularity of their cheerleader daughter. With this kind of attention, though, it's little wonder that Laurie was becoming more egocentric. That's another thing happening to kids during this stage of development—all they ever seem to do is think about themselves.

Both Laurie and Paul spend a lot of time looking in mirrors and comparing themselves to others. Teenagers typically spend a considerable amount of time speculating about their appearance and whether they will be accepted as part of the crowd.

They spend an enormous amount of time thinking about themselves, and often assume everyone else is as concerned about them as they are. Little flaws (or blemishes) can easily seem catastrophes as a result. While they may think everyone is looking at them and judging them, they are equally certain that their parents have never been through what they are experiencing and have no idea how important the littlest things are to teens. At one time or another almost every adolescent will fling "You just don't understand!" at even the most understanding parents.

One of the most stressful developmental tasks of this adolescent period is the process of becoming independent and separating from one's parents. The same process that started during toddlerhood is now at full throttle.

Buddy, a fourteen-year-old boy whose father left the family when Buddy was very young, had always been close to his mother. One late summer day she told him over breakfast that she had planned a nice day for them. "We can go shopping for school clothes and then go to lunch at that restaurant you like."

Buddy responded with intense anger. "Mom," he shouted, "I'm not you! Don't make plans for me because I've got other things to do today!"

Even while seeking psychological freedom from parents, teenagers may still wish to keep the secure, dependent relationships of early and middle childhood.

Heather, a seventeen-year-old, left home after a fight with her parents to live at her boyfriend's house. When she returned home six weeks later her mother knew that changes would have to be made because "she left a little girl and returned a young lady."

"You'll probably want to fix your own breakfast and things like that," her mother suggested.

"Oh no," replied Heather, "I missed the great meals you make. You make an awesome breakfast."

Many adolescents like Heather want to feel and act like adults while maintaining an escape hatch—the option of retreating to the security of a dependent relationship with their parents. Therefore, it is not unusual for teenagers like Cliff, a fifteen-year-old I know, to hug his mom or want to tell her secrets one day, and the next angrily denounce her for treating him like a little kid.

So, teens frequently vacillate between a desire for independence and their still-great need for dependence. One way that adolescents show their desire to be independent is by being hostile, uncooperative, and stubbornly resistant to adults—especially their parents.

What is so difficult for parents is to know how to interpret their teens' behavior, when and how much to exert control, and when to step back and allow them to make their own, autonomous decisions.

While trying to separate from parents, adolescents are moving toward their peers. At the same they are looking for freedom from adult influence, they want to conform to the rules and expectations of a peer group. The peer group offers a sort of protection in that it is often more accepting of teenagers' experimentation with roles and value systems.

Fifteen-year-old Rachel can dye her hair orange and know she's going to be accepted by her friends. Toby, a sixteen-year-old boy, can proudly display his pierced nipple to his pals. His friends think an earring on his nipple is cool; his parents are disgusted and angry with him for "mutilating" his body.

As a teen tries out new roles in her quest to be her own person, parents frequently see this transition as anything but smooth. In fact, they may see their adolescent as immature, deviant, or in need of more control. For their part, adolescents may feel that any attempt by parents to exert control is a way of keeping them in a child-like, dependent relationship.

This transition is often difficult on parents, who may actually experience psychological problems during their children's adolescent years. Laurence Steinberg, the director of the developmental psychology department at Temple University, has found that bickering and squabbling between parents and their teenagers contribute to parents' psychological problems and even to worsening marriages.

On the other hand, parents who have enjoyed a close relationship with a child miss the time spent together as the young person becomes more interested in being with friends.

Rachel's mother felt abandoned on weekends—a time when they used to do things together—and applied pressure on Rachel to spend more time at home. As a result, they frequently bickered about the amount of time Rachel spent at home versus the amount of time she was with her friends.

Cooperation and agreeableness between parent and teen may be relics of the past now. Emancipation requires a moving away. But parents may feel that the way the youth is disrupting previously secure and dependable family life is a grim sign for the future. They may assume their kid is going to continue being uncooperative and resistant.

While arguments and conflict are real, they reflect the teen's attempts to establish her personal identity. So while most parents recognize a young person's need to be autonomous, many find that the adolescent's lack of cooperation, rejection of responsibility, and hostility create troubling conflict in the family.

By adopting an uncooperative, oppositional stance, a teenager can feel more like a unique person. With the rejection of the previous dependent relationship, teens like Buddy and Rachel announce they are individuals and not their parents' clones.

While peers are becoming the predominant influence in a teenager's life, parents continue to play an important role. Most adolescents still express a strong attachment to their parents. Although they do not want a dependent relationship, they do need a relationship. This necessarily means that roles and relationships between parents and adolescents require refinement and readaptation.

Before Heather moved out to live at her boyfriend's house, she had a dependent relationship with her mother, and her interaction with her father, who was used to giving orders and ultimatums, was filled with steadily increasing conflict. When she returned home, it was agreed that "things will have to change."

"You can't tell me what to do anymore," she told her father. "There can't be any more ultimatums." Her father had to agree that she was in fact too big to be ordered around. For Heather and her parents, this marked the beginning of the readaptation of the relationships within the family.

Although teenagers like Heather, Paul, Rachel, and Buddy may protest limitations and controls on their behavior, controls and supervision still represent parental love, concern, and affection to them. And as much as each of these adolescents wants to be his or her own person, they all want more than anything to be able to talk to their parents.

One constant in my work with adolescents over the past three decades has been the complaint that they can't talk to their parents. It is one of their biggest complaints. Sixteen-year-old James, who has violent arguments with his mother and claims that she still treats him like a little kid because she won't give him more freedom, also complains that he and his mother can't talk. One day in a therapy session with James, when he was telling me about his relationship with his girlfriend and his views on religion, he suddenly said, "I wish I could talk to my mother like this."

Psychological researchers have determined that the family atmosphere, the quality of communication between parent and teens, and the influence of parents in adolescents' lives may make the biggest deciding factor in whether young people resolve the tasks of adolescence poorly or well.

Handling the Opposition of the Adolescent

"Sometimes she acts like a baby," Rebecca complained about her fifteen-year-old daughter, Rachel.

And in many ways she's right. The early years of adolescence have a lot in common with the toddler years. Toddlers, as you may recall, are obstinate and push for greater freedom. At the same time they are attempting to learn a large variety of new skills. Teenagers show similar qualities, although at a more complex level. Many of them go through a negative and oppositional period with their parents. And as their bodies become more adult and the social pressures on them to behave more like grown-ups increase, their demands for independence become strong and persistent. They want to stay up later, come and go when they please, borrow the family car, listen to the music they like at the volume they like, and wear the clothing and hairstyles that are currently in vogue. While this push for more freedom and independence is going on, they are also facing a new set of demands and skills to be learned. High school demands more complex thinking; summer jobs demand new levels of responsibility; maturing sexuality must be dealt with; decisions about their educational future must be made.

Donovan, a fifteen-year-old boy, was going through a trying period in his life—for both his parents and himself. Donovan wanted freedom to make his own decisions about who his friends would be and what he would do with his time. He spent considerable time alone in his room where he thought about everything that was going wrong for him.

"I think and think," he told me, "but I don't come up with any answers. I feel very confused."

Donovan's unsuccessful attempt to solve his own problems—which is a legitimate need teens have—typifies adolescence. He doesn't want his parents to interfere in his efforts to deal with his problems, yet he knows only too well that he isn't doing well on his own.

What, then, are the keys to handling the strivings and the search for autonomy that adolescents display?

Understanding

In large measure, the greatest key to living with and handling the sometimes resistant, rebellious, uncooperative, or tempestuous nature of the adolescent is understanding. When parents can understand the developmental tasks of the teenage years, they are likely to find the difficulties of these years easier to handle.

The quickest and most direct path to this understanding is to remember that so much of what adolescents do is related to their increasing struggle to find the answer to the old question "Who am I?"

Buddy's mother had trouble with this. Much of the time she could only focus on his anger, the names he called her, and his resistance to the kind of life she wished him to continue to lead. At times she wondered if he had severe emotional problems, and considered putting him in a psychiatric hospital before he hurt someone with his anger. What she usually failed to note were his comments, which should have told her that he wanted his emotional freedom, needed to separate from her, and had to make his own plans for himself.

At age seventeen, Jill, my daughter, insisted on wearing torn jeans, red bandannas tied around her thighs, and sunglasses. As her parent, I was aghast when she planned to wear this getup to her high school graduation ceremony. As much as I and her relatives, who had come to see her graduate, wanted to tell her to change her clothes or to dress more appropriately, no one was judgmental or critical (although I must admit a few of us were certainly embarrassed).

In one way or another, most of us understood that this was Jill's way of making a statement and trying to find her personal identity. Fortunately it was not the identity she settled on and she gave up that style of dress a short time later.

Remember the Past

Beyond understanding, however, it is important that you remember how you handled the stubbornness, independence, autonomy, or resistance of past developmental stages. If you were fairly adept at handling negative behaviors and resistance at earlier ages, you can likely apply some of those same skills and strategies in dealing with your teenager.

Family Values

Just as it's true that parents still exert the greatest influence on teenagers, it is also true that when teenagers rebel against them, the form that this resistance or rebellion takes will likely be determined by the family's behavior and values.

In a family in which there is open communication, parents could find themselves with a fourteen-year-old who is sullen and secretive; a family that values self-control may discover their fifteen-year-old is rowdy and out of control; a family that prides itself on academic accomplishment may become disturbed because their middle-adolescent doesn't seem to care a whit about grades.

Balancing Act

Although adolescent strivings for independence will be less severe and drastic if the family atmosphere has been one in which children were allowed to gradually become independent and autonomous over the years, not every family has developed in this way. Yet even when kids are in the throes of a rebellious period, parents can take steps that will decrease or at least contain their need to act out their rebellion.

The best steps to take include improving communication, offering support through praise and encouragement, and making sure your comments and remarks are nonjudgmental.

Yet another key to riding out these temporary storms associated with the teenage years is balance. Parents can try to maintain a balance between the desire to give an adolescent advice and respect for her privacy; between exerting greater control and allowing her to learn from experience; between monitoring her activities and showing trust; between expressing disapproval and displaying acceptance.

Conflicts and discussions are best handled by all parties when family relationships are based on mutual trust, respect, and communication. Even as a teenager rebels in such a family atmosphere, she may well realize that advice and limits are not meant to curb all her attempts at independence but are evidence of love and concern.

"When I do something wrong," says fifteen-year-old Rachel, "my mother tells me how disappointed she is with me. We both end up crying for hours. You know I don't like to hurt her."

Adopting Nonjudgmental Attitudes

Parents still need to find a balance in coping with their youngsters, but they can do more to aid their adolescents' strivings for independence. A primary step lies in adopting a nonjudgmental attitude toward a teenager's behavior. This means considering the reasons behind what she's doing, and not judging her with a label of "good" or "bad" based on a few actions. Rather, it is important to keep the totality of the young person's life and personality in perspective.

James, sixteen, and his mother have violent arguments when she criticizes his actions. "You're lazy and a bum," Lynne tells him. "You stay up late, keep me awake with your loud music, bring over friends who leave a mess in my house, and you sleep late. Why can't you do something productive?"

When Lynne picks on one aspect of James's life, she makes judgments about him, and she unfairly leaves out some of the positives—like his holding down a job. This infuriates James and inevitably leads to a shouting argument.

It helps if parents keep in mind that each teenager will handle the issue of adolescence in a slightly different way. While some teens seem to breeze through adolescence, taking on new and greater responsibilities, others take a sidestep into a rebellious lifestyle that causes disruptions in the family's life. No matter what the style, however, each teenager deserves individual consideration.

Heather's rebellion was to run away and live with her boyfriend. Donovan spent considerable time alone, kept his thoughts and feelings to himself, and argued with his parents about the rights of children.

Rachel stayed out late at night, sometimes didn't come home at all, and was sexually active. James not only had violent arguments with his mother, but had physical confrontations with her during which he slapped her and called her a bitch. He also stayed up late, brought unsavory kinds of friends to the house, and swore at his mother, telling her she had no right to tell him what to do.

Each of these teenagers has taken a different approach to expressing independence through rebellion. The parental response, then, will be based on the child, taking into account the child's history and temperament, and not on an idealized or standardized image of what an adolescent should be, or how a parent should handle a rebellious or oppositional teenager.

Accepting Conflict and Confrontation

It helps, too, to remember that conflict, confrontation, and anger are almost inevitable between parents (and other adults) and teens during the years from thirteen to eighteen. Here's an example of what goes on between fifteen-year-old Donovan and his teacher.

Donovan was whispering in his science class one day. His teacher, Mrs. Colman, had put up with his whispering too much lately and said to him, "Donovan, please move your seat over here."

Donovan stood up and asked, "Why do you want me to move?"

Mrs. Colman snapped back: "You don't ask why. Just do it!"

"I have a right to ask why," Donovan countered.

"Why don't you just leave and go out in the hall," Mrs. Colman said, raising her voice perhaps a bit louder than she intended. Donovan slammed the door on his way out.

After class, he went back in when all the other kids had left and told Mrs. Colman he didn't want to argue or cause problems. Mrs. Colman reiterated to Donovan that when she asked him to do something, she expected him to obey.

In telling his uncle about what happened in science, Donovan was sure he was right in how he handled the situation. "If I didn't question what people wanted me to do," he said, "I would be just like my parents. I have a right to be an individual."

And that was what this incident was all about for Donovan. For him it was about being an individual. Such conflict and questioning of authority are quite normal in adolescence, and parents (and teachers) must realize and accept this.

Even anger is a normal emotion that can be healthy. When it is communicated openly—rather than suppressed—and discussed, resentments and greater anger (as well as the acting out of anger) will be avoided.

Showing Tolerance for Experimentation

Parents must also bear in mind that a young person's identity cannot be handed to her or imposed upon her. She must work it out— from her past and present and from her own unique dreams, fantasies, goals, and abilities. What parents can best do while this identity is being worked out is provide support. That means a consistent, reassuring family atmosphere, and the tolerance that allows a teenager to experiment with roles and identities until she finds one that suits her.

Parents can express tolerance, even if not approval, for rebellion. And when they disagree or need to set limits, they can say so without judgment or rejection.

One way to do this is the way we handled Jill and her nonconforming ways of dressing. Most of the time nothing was said about the black T-shirts she wore, her hairstyles, or her constant mirrored sunglasses. When it was seriously inappropriate, then we said something like: "Jill, you know I don't care how you dress most of the time. However, that's not appropriate for this occasion. I would appreciate it if you dressed in the more traditional way for my sake." While she might complain or grumble, that's as far as it usually went.

Parents can set limits in this reasonably respectful, nonjudgmental way without condemnation, criticism, or arguments. Generally, if you respect the teenager's right to be an individual and to experiment, you will get respect in return. This happened when Heather's parents desperately wanted to force her to return home from her boyfriend's house.

Instead of setting a limit they couldn't enforce (such as "You must come home immediately or else we're coming with the police and forcing you to come home"), they dealt with more manageable limits in ways that preserved Heather's self-respect. For instance, they told her that it was her decision as to whether she came back home to live. "However," her mother told her one day, "your car insurance specifies that you live at our address. We haven't notified the insurance company about this, but we will have to soon. If you would like to take out car insurance in your own name at a new address, you are welcome to. I would like you to look into this and make a decision soon."

Heather wasn't forced or coerced in any way that implied that her parents didn't respect her or that they were rejecting her. Heather understood her mother was being reasonable, and after looking into it she let her parents know that she couldn't afford car insurance on her own.

Disciplining the Adolescent

Finding a style of discipline that works well with adolescents is a common problem for parents. Often this means making changes and adaptations from previous years. When children were younger, parents may have been relatively controlling and authoritarian. When Dad wakes up one day to find his son is now two inches taller than he is and outweighs him by forty pounds, however, the idea of parenting by an autocratic or authoritarian method begins to look ridiculous.

The purpose of discipline during the adolescent years is not to affirm the power and control of parents. The purpose is to offer guidance when it's needed and set limits when the young person is not able to set them for herself. Discipline is also a way to provide reminders of the family's standards, expectations, and rules.

When Jill needed reminders about what was appropriate, I tried to provide them. However, it's when parents attempt to exert control over teenagers that they most often have unpleasant and counterproductive confrontations. For example, when Donovan's teacher Mrs. Colman attempted to affirm her power and control over Donovan, she succeeded only in having Donovan angrily leave the classroom. When Donovan asked her why he had to move his seat, she attempted to use a form of control. But that's not what Donovan needed then. He needed a teacher who understood that at that moment in his striving to assert his own identity, he had to question what she was asking him to do. It didn't mean he was rebelling and would refuse. He would very likely have complied if she had answered his question forthrightly. For instance, she could have said, "You were whispering and I just want you to sit over here for the rest of the hour." He might have found that reasonable and responded with less anger.

Many times, the purpose of discipline may be more a matter of guiding the adolescent through a tricky period of experimentation as she finds herself and becomes independent.

Parents cannot and should not let go completely. Yet they must give up some control. The need for balance arises again in terms of discipline. What has to be balanced now is control and concern. While it is difficult to stand by and watch a teenager make poor decisions, sometimes you don't have much of a choice. Privately Heather's parents thought her decision to move out for six weeks was very unwise. One day her mother told her husband that Heather "is making a mistake she will regret her whole life."

While Heather's decision to live away from home for six weeks seems pretty foolhardy and immature, it was not quite as dangerous as her mother thought it was. Moreover if teenagers don't learn to make their own decisions, they will not be independent and successful adults.

There may be times, however, when young people make decisions that have potentially tragic consequences. These can include decisions related to drugs, alcohol, smoking, unprotected sex, relationships with violent individuals, and criminal behavior. However, even when more serious and dangerous behaviors are involved parents cannot use force. What they can do is raise questions, provide indirect guidance, give choices, or set firm limits.

Here is an example of a parent who used these methods rather than trying to coerce or force a teenager to do what the parent thought was best:

John was patiently waiting up for his sixteen-year-old son, Alex, who was late coming home. It was after midnight when Alex stumbled in the front door. He looked up, saw his father sitting in the living room, and glibly said, "Hi, Pops."

John, who had never been called "Pops" by his son, knew there was something wrong. Alex walked as quickly as he could past his father and into his bedroom. His father followed him.

"What'cha doing?" John asked. Alex was struggling to get out of his shirt.

"Nothin'," said Alex. "I'm just trying to take my shirt off." John nodded silently and continued to watch. After a few minutes, with Alex still trying to maneuver out of the shirt, John asked, "Want to talk?"

To John's surprise, Alex replied, "Yeah, I want to talk." Alex finally got the T-shirt over his head and threw it on the floor. "Go to the kitchen," he said to his father, "I'll be right there."

John went to the kitchen, poured both of them a glass of milk, and waited for Alex. Ten minutes later, wrapped in a bathrobe, Alex came into the kitchen and sat down across from his father.

"Do you mind if we talk?" John asked.

"Not really," said Alex. "As long as you don't yell at me. I've got a headache."

"I'm concerned about you drinking, you know," John said.

"What drinking?" Alex said.

"Don't pull that, Alex," John said, fearful that this would degenerate into one of their usual nonproductive "talks." "Your drinking tonight, for starters. I was young once, too. I know about teenage boys and their drinking."

"It wasn't much," replied Alex. "Just some beer."

"I worry about you when you're out with your friends and there's drinking going on," John said. "I worry that something could happen to you."

"You do?" said Alex. "Don't worry. I can take care of myself."

"I said," repeated John, "that I worry about you. Do you understand what I'm saying?"

"Yeah, I guess," said Alex.

"What?"

"Don't ask me hard questions," Alex said, smiling.

"I'm asking you to tell me what I mean when I say that I worry about you."

"I guess you care about me," replied Alex.

"That's right," said John. "I do care. Do you know that?"

"Sometimes I don't think you care," said Alex.

"I admit I'm pretty rough on you sometimes and I yell too much, but I always care," said John. "I love you and worry about you."

"I love you, too, Dad," said Alex. This was the first time he told his dad he loved him in several years.

"What about your drinking?" John asked.

"It's hard to explain," said Alex.

"Try me," replied his father.

"There's a lot going on," began Alex. "I mean with school and friends and everything."

With the lowered resistance of the beer he had been drinking, Alex was able to talk more openly than ever before about his friends, peer pressures, the drinking habits of his crowd, and the stress of maintaining good grades. John listened attentively, occasionally asking questions. Secretly John was overjoyed that they could have this conversation after all the conflict, aborted previous attempts to talk, and hostility between them in the last year or so. But he wanted to stay focused on his major concern.

"What shall we do about your drinking?" he asked.

"I don't know," replied Alex. "I know I've got to stop drinking so much. But it's hard."

"I know," said John sympathetically. "But you know both your mother and I love you and we'll do anything to help."

"I know, Dad," said Alex. "I know."

"Well?" John asked, pressing for a commitment. "I need your support and I want to stop," Alex said. "But I also know I'm saying this now and I don't know what I will think or say tomorrow."

"Fair enough," said his father. "Let's get some rest and talk about this tomorrow. Let's get your mother in on this, too. Okay?"

"Yeah, sure," said Alex.

"No. I'm serious," said John. "We all have to talk about this and decide what to do. Before you go out again. Okay?"

"Okay."

John set some limits (we have to talk; we have to decide; we have to get your mother involved) but asked questions and guided the discussion toward the end he wanted: that there would be continued discussion about doing something about Alex's drinking. Alex could make his own choices and his own decisions, but his father was not going to let him off the hook or avoid dealing with the problem. In providing discipline and guidance in this interchange, John did the following things which are useful techniques for parents of adolescents:

1. He raised important questions.
2. He guided discussion toward a constructive conclusion.
3. He allowed his son to make his own choices and decisions.
4. He set limits and boundaries.

Setting Rules and Limits

An aspect of discipline during the adolescent years concerns rules and limits. While there will generally be fewer rules, there still will be some that impose limits. Rules that impose limits include those that set curfews, regulate driving privileges, restrict certain behaviors in the home, and arrange for keeping parents informed of a young person's whereabouts.

Again balance is the key: successful rules and limits will preserve a teenager's self-respect while offering controls over her activities. When Rachel persistently stayed out later than her curfew, her mother called a conference with her to talk about agreeing on a new rule.

"Rachel," her mother began, "the curfew we agreed upon is just not working. You stay out later than you said you would and when you finally come home I'm so mad I usually yell at you. I don't like doing that and I'm sure you don't like hearing it."

When Rachel agreed, her mother continued: "I'd like to forget about the curfew we set before and think about a new way of dealing with this situation so you're home at a reasonable time and I'm not mad and yelling at you." After talking, the result was that Rachel agreed she wasn't handling her freedom in a responsible way. The new rule was that she would have friends come over rather than going out with them—an appropriate compromise for a fifteen-year-old.

Each family must decide on the rules that preserve balance and respect within that family. At the same time, rules may be evaluated by asking some of the following questions:

- Will this rule allow my teenager to maintain self-respect?
- Will this rule help her to become independent?
- Would this rule be one I would make for a teenager of the opposite sex?
- Is this rule based on a real danger or an exaggerated fear?
- Have I as parent provided a model for my teenager in following this rule?
- Has she had a chance to talk about and express her feelings about this rule?
- Has the rule been clearly stated and explained to my teenager?
- What will I do if the rule is broken?

Heather's parents at one time had a rule that she could not get a job as long as she was in high school. When they evaluated the rule with these questions, they found that they had to answer no to several of them. For instance, when they asked themselves if not allowing her to work would help her maintain her self-respect, they said they didn't actually see how it could. Similarly, when they looked at the question, "Will this rule help her to become independent?" they agreed it might actually do just the opposite. Finally, when they got to the third question ("Would this rule be one I would make for a teenager of the opposite sex?"), they agreed that the rule needed to be reconsidered. It was changed so Heather could go to work.

Because teenagers are trying to find their identity and because experimentation goes along with striving for autonomy and independence during these years, a parent can expect that a teenager will test limits and break rules. Parents who are caught off guard are those who didn't think their teenager "would ever do that." If you just assume that at some time most rules will be broken or violated in some way, then you can be prepared to answer the question "What will I do if she breaks this rule?"

In general, a consistent approach is required. That is, how you respond in one case should be consistent with how you respond in others. But there should be some response, and young people need to know and be able to predict what their parents will do if and when a rule is broken.

Just as when they were younger, teenagers, too, need to experience consequences when they go beyond agreed upon limits. Consequences should be fair and related to the broken rule or offense. They should be moderate consequences, and usually involve restrictions on privileges and activities.

If an adolescent rebels beyond safe territory, and seems to be acting in a way that endangers physical or mental health, confrontation is needed. Good parents confront openly and then give help and emotional support.

Dealing with the More Difficult Adolescent

Carl, a fourteen-year-old, lies to his parents about where he goes, who he's with, and what he does. He lies about his homework, saying it's done when it isn't. He shoplifts from stores and lies about where he got items that turn up in his room.

Stephanie, a fifteen-year-old, told her mother she was going to her friend Brenda's house. When her mother called Brenda's house to ask Stephanie to be home earlier than planned because of the sudden visit of an aunt, she discovered that Stephanie wasn't there. Brenda's mother informed her that Stephanie had left with a nineteen-year-old young man. She didn't return home that night until after midnight, and then swore up and down that she was at Brenda's the whole time.

David, an often rebellious and oppositional fourteen-year-old, seemed to get considerable pleasure from defying adults. At school, he annoyed teachers by talking out loud in class, blatantly disregarding school rules, and being generally insubordinate to adults. In addition, he was disrespectful to his mother, and sometimes hit her during arguments.

All three of these adolescents are more difficult than the typical teenager. All have been viewed as stubborn, oppositional, defiant, and difficult for several years. All frequently push the limits further and more often than most of their peers.

One of the things that characterize difficult youngsters at almost every age is that they don't seem to learn from consequences and continue to defy adults by demanding more freedom.

Fourteen-year-old Julian is a prime example of a difficult teenager. When he came into one of my therapy groups, he made himself as obnoxious as possible. He was determined to make sure that I would act like other adults in his life. His defiance and oppositional behavior provoked adults to react to him in critical and punitive ways.

One day in group therapy Julian related an incident from his middle school. A counselor had come up to Julian in the hall and asked, "When are you going to quit and get out of our hair?"

Julian said that he responded to Mr. Ramos with his typical attitude and manner. "Why don't you shove it up your ass?" Julian had said.

In an equally provocative way the counselor had replied, "What did you say, punk?"

Julian repeated what he'd said, then stared defiantly at Mr. Ramos.

"You've got a big chip on your shoulder and I'm just the guy to knock it off," Mr. Ramos had said, moving closer to Julian.

Julian had laughed derisively and said, "You can try any day, man."

Mr. Ramos was now red in the face and he'd looked as though he wanted to teach Julian a lesson. Instead, he'd turned around and said, "See you around, punk."

Julian told the group he was disappointed that the incident ended there, because he enjoyed these kinds of confrontations. They were a way to release his resentment and aggressiveness and gave him a sense of power. But they did nothing to enhance his status with adults. All they did was reinforce his image as an angry, rebellious, stubborn, and defiant troublemaker.

Julian expected to use the same tactics in group therapy. One day in group when it was time for a short break in the two-hour session, Julian got up to leave like everyone else.

I told him he wouldn't be able to go on break that day. "You misused the break time last session, and instead of coming back on time you were over ten minutes late," I said. "So today you'll be staying in the group room.

"You all know what I've said before about the privilege of going on break," I said to Julian and the other teenagers in the group. "If you abuse this privilege, you get it taken away."

Julian was outraged. "No break! That's not fair. I wasn't late coming back from break last time! At least not that much. . . . Why don't you give me another chance?"

"You can have another chance next group," I said. "This is an important privilege and I want you to learn to be responsible when I give you a break. You'll get a second chance next week. If you handle it well next time, you can continue to have the opportunity of going on break during group."

But Julian was not going to be put off this easily. He was developing a strategy to deal with this "unfairness."

"I'm going anyway," he announced. "What are you going to do if I just walk out?"

Julian, who is taller and stockier than I, stared me in the eye, clearly expecting a response.

I tried not to look ruffled by this. In a calm, measured tone I replied, "It's your choice. However, if you leave, you'll lose your break time for a lot longer than one week."

Julian apparently wasn't willing to test that out. He sat down in his seat and pulled out a pack of cigarettes from his shirt pocket. With deliberate and greatly exaggerated gestures, Julian took a cigarette out and stuck it in his mouth. He started fiddling with his lighter and, holding it up, looked around at the other kids in the room. "Let's light up, everybody," he said. "Who's going to join me?"

None of the other teenagers in the group made a move to do the same, but everyone's attention was fixed on Julian and, alternately, me. I looked directly at him.

When I didn't say anything, Julian filled the void, "What would you do if I lit this in here?"

After a few more seconds of my staring and the silence, Julian answered the question himself.

"I suppose you'd turn me over to security and then I'd get busted or something, huh?"

As I remained unruffled, Julian slowly put the cigarette back in the pack. The other kids filed out on break.

It was just me and Julian then, and he put his head down on the table as we waited for break to end and the other kids to return. Not surprisingly, everyone came back on time and resumed their seats around the table. Julian looked up as the others got settled and said, "This whole things sucks." As we began to talk about issues concerning others in the group, Julian slipped out of his chair and said, "I'm bored. I'm going to sit on the floor." He looked around at the other teens, most of whom were listening to a girl talk about her problems with her father.

"Let's all sit on the floor and really piss him off," he said as he slid to the floor.

The girl stopped talking and all eyes were once again on Julian and his attempted insurrection. He sat on the floor, but again no one joined him. The girl started telling about her father again. After five more minutes, Julian said he had to go to the bathroom. "It's not fair if we have to really use the bathroom, and you won't let us leave the room," he said.

"That's right," I said. "If you have to go, then one person at a time and no more than two minutes." I looked at my watch. "Julian, you have two minutes."

"Shit, man, I can't even get it out in two minutes," Julian said swaggering toward the door.

I shrugged. Julian left.

He returned in two minutes and found that the other kids were talking about drinking and alcoholism. He couldn't resist getting involved and joined in. The insurrection was over.

Julian, in this instance, didn't get what he wanted. What he wanted was a fight with an unreasonable adult. Not getting that, he had no place to go with his oppositional behavior and he eventually dropped it.

What did I do to deal with Julian's defiant and stubbornly opposi-tional behavior?

I did several things that tend to work well with difficult teenagers:

1. I made sure that the rules and limits were reasonable, clearly stated, and understood.

2. I made sure the consequences for not following the rules or limits were clear but fair.

3. My responses were calm and reasonable, and they showed respect for Julian. There was no attempt to undermine his autonomy and self-respect.

4. I gave him choices and allowed him to make decisions based on an understanding of the possible outcomes for what-ever choices he made.

5. I never delivered an ultimatum or used a threat.

6. I allowed him to save face each time he tried to rebel but backed down; he was not made to look foolish or weak by giving in or changing his mind.

7. I put a certain amount of trust in him, although this might not have been obvious to an onlooker, and I displayed the expectation that he would make a reasonable decision.

8. Never once did I degrade him or label him unfairly.

9. I allowed him to rejoin the group without condemnation and without reference to an incident that, for all practical purposes, was resolved.

Sally, age seventeen, was another adolescent who was more difficult than the typical teenager. She had already run away from home once, although she stoutly disputed having run away. What was not in doubt, however, was the fact that she had left home for three days after an argument with her parents.

When she came back home, her parents wanted to have a talk with her and she wanted to avoid such a discussion. In fact, she said she had just come home to get a shower, get some fresh clothes, and be on her way again "to stay with a friend."

Her parents refused to give her permission to go. "We were worried about you and wanted to be sure you were safe," they told her. "We're certainly not going to approve of you leaving again."

To try to enforce what they were saying, they took her car keys from her and told her she could not use her car.

"You can't take away my car," she shouted. "I work to pay back the loan and I pay the insurance."

"But we're responsible for you and can't have you living out on the streets," her mother said, trying to counter Sally's remarks.

"Look," Sally said. "Just let me go out tonight. I swear I'll come back later on and I won't go out again. I'll stay home. But I just want to go out tonight."

Her parents didn't know what to do. They both knew they really couldn't stop her from leaving if she had made up her mind. On the other hand, they thought she might not come home if she left—no matter what she was promising.

"Give us a chance to talk about this alone," her father said.

"Whatever," Sally said shrugging.

Her mother and father left the room and sat on the back deck. They took turns verbalizing what they were both thinking. While they desperately wanted her safe, they were beyond trying to force her to obey.

"Let's let her go," her father said. "If she doesn't come home, we could refuse to let her back in the house when she decides to come back."

"I agree," Sally's mother said. "I'm tired of trying to decide what's best for her. She's got to make decisions for herself."

They told Sally that while they thought she should stay home and work out any problems they had, they couldn't stop her from going. "You've got to make your own decisions," her mother said.

Sally went to her room. Her parents later heard her taking a shower. Two hours later, Sally came downstairs and asked about dinner. "Why don't you give me a hand with it?" her mother suggested.

"Okay," Sally said, and pitched in to assist.

After dinner nothing was said about going out. And Sally didn't go anywhere. She went to bed early that night. The next day, her father remarked to her that he was surprised that she didn't go out with her friends.

"I just wanted to see if you'd let me go," Sally said. "I can take care of myself, you know. You guys have got to realize I'm growing up and have to make my own decisions. If you had told me I couldn't go, I would have gone . . . and maybe I wouldn't have come home. But because you said I could go, it didn't seem so important anymore."

It doesn't matter what difficulties an adolescent is presenting. Certainly some parents reading this will be concerned about worse behavior and more defiant, dangerous, or oppositional teenagers. But whether a teenager is carrying a gun, belongs to a gang, uses drugs, is seriously delinquent, or is a home truant, like Sally, parents will have to use the same guidelines I used with Julian and Sally's parents used with Sally. It is unfortunately true that some adolescents will be so alienated from their families that they are beyond reach. When this is so, parents may have little choice but to use the legal system to remedy a very difficult and serious situation.

It seems clear in this situation that Sally's parents followed, without knowing it at the time, some of the points I made regarding the incident with Julian. They let her know their wishes, but gave her a chance to make her own decision. They did that without an argument, without accusations, and without threats or ultimatums. As a result, Sally was able to make her own decision without being backed into rebelling against her parents.

Summary

Adolescents are embarking on a journey that:

- **Is an exciting adventure, but sometimes ominously frightening.**
- **Is about school, friendships, an altered body, and taking on new responsibilities.**
- **Will take them from childhood to adulthood in a relatively short period of time.**

- Concerns three very important developmental tasks: developing a personal sense of identity, dealing with more mature relationships, and becoming independent and separating from parents.

- Entails a conflict between wanting to keep the secure, dependent relationship of the middle childhood years and yearning to be adult and independent.

- Is often characterized by attempts to demonstrate independence through hostility, lack of cooperation, and stubborn resistance to adults—especially their parents.

- Is influenced more and more by peers, even though parents still play an important role in their lives.

- Will require relationships between parents and adolescents to be refined and readapted.

Parents can better handle the independence and the adolescent's striving for autonomy if they:

- Understand the developmental tasks of the teenage years.

- Remember how they handled independence and striving for autonomy during earlier developmental stages.

- Keep in mind that when teenagers rebel, the form the resistance takes is a reversal or negation of the family's values.

- Maintain a balance between the desire to give teens advice and respect for their privacy; between exerting greater control and allowing them to learn from experience; between monitoring their activities and showing trust.

- Can adopt a nonjudgmental attitude toward teens' behavior.

- Remember that conflict, confrontation, and anger are almost inevitable between parents and teens.

- Show tolerance for rebellion and for experiments with roles and identities.
- Recall that the purpose of parental discipline during the adolescent years is to guide the teenager through a tricky period toward independence.
- Continues to use rules and limits and keep in mind that successful rules and limits with teenagers will preserve their self-respect while offering a measure of control over their activities.
- Understand that some rules and limits will be tested and be prepared to deal with the breaking of rules.
- Use fair consequences when rules are broken.

Parents can cope better with more difficult and oppositional adolescents by:

- Making sure rules and limits are reasonable, clearly stated, and understood.
- Letting adolescents know about the consequences for rule violations, making sure the consequences are always fair and related to the offense.
- Having calm, reasonable, and respectful responses to teenagers' oppositional and defiant behavior.
- Giving teenagers choices and allowing them to make their decisions.
- Avoiding the use of threats or ultimatums.
- Allowing them to save face; not making them look foolish when they back down.
- Trusting that they will make reasonable decisions.
- Avoiding condemnation, labeling, or unfair judgments of the adolescent as a person because of present oppositional or defiant behavior.

CHAPTER 13

How to Tell Your Child No

Did we once have the ability as a society to say no only to lose that skill? There are some indications that this is exactly what happened in America in the 1960s and 1970s.

During those years we lived through a time of revolution and change. There was active rebellion by young people against the established order. One of the themes of that revolution was "do your own thing," another, "if it feels good, do it." Living free was extolled as the good life.

Parents who were young and greatly influenced by this revolution often tried to raise their children in the same way. They believed that children should be free and unrestricted.

With the advantage and the hindsight of about thirty years, however, we can see that permissiveness and freedom from all restrictions didn't lead to a generation of happier and healthier people. Instead, it often led to people confused about their values and all too willing to take risks that turn out to be harmful to their minds and their bodies.

Parents today need to make sure that they learn from the lessons of the past. When parents have been too broadly permissive, children have been harmed. On the other hand, evidence shows that parents who have been too restrictive and repressive also damage the healthy development of children.

Whose Problem Is It?

Is it your child's problem or your problem when you have to say no? Very likely it is both. If you don't like to say no, it probably makes you feel mean, depriving, and unkind, while children who are told no sometimes feel deprived or believe their parents are being intentionally and unnecessarily mean. Both you and your child have to learn to deal with those feelings.

Being able to set limits on children is an essential aspect of being a competent and effective parent. In the long run, setting limits and enforcing rules makes children and teens happier and more responsible.

Learning to accept limits and a little deprivation now is more likely to lead to greater happiness and more contentment in the future than grasping for immediate gratification. In fact, psychologists say that one of the ways to judge the level of maturity of an individual is this: Is he able to postpone present wants and happiness for future gain?

In order to grow up healthy, well socialized, and able to take their place in this world with all of its difficulties and frequent frustrations, children have to learn to handle the denial of their requests and wants. If they can do this at an early age, they will be able to follow rules, accept that they can't have everything they desire, and be able to tolerate boundaries, limits, and disappointments. Good, kind, loving, and successful parents have mastered the art of setting limits.

Some recent research indicates that one of the main differences between parents of adolescent alcohol and drug users and parents of teenagers who don't use these substances is this: parents of non-using adolescents are able to control their teens. That means that as these kids were growing up, their parents demonstrated that they were willing to set limits and enforce them.

The trick is to make sure we say no only as often as the child needs to hear it.

When to Say No

Parents have to be clear about when and where to use no. There are four basic times it's called for.

1. Children should hear no when their health or safety is in danger.

Children do need the freedom to explore, experiment, and try new things in the world, but as parents, you have a responsibility to protect them from physical and mental harm and danger.

Obviously, parents must say no if their child is about to ingest lead-based paint flakes off the wall, wants to taste something toxic he finds in the garage, or runs in a busy parking lot instead of holding on to his mother's hand. Children must also be told no when they want to stay up late on a school night to watch television or watch an adult movie. When they want to try cigarettes, alcohol, or illegal drugs, their health and safety are too important not to say no.

2. **Children should hear no when they are about to break an important rule.**

Some people may see rules as being made to be broken, but when it comes to raising children, rules are made to teach important facts about the world and how to get along in it.

Rules are to protect children and teach them what's right and necessary in order to lead a happy life. Families establish rules because rules let everyone know how the family can get along well. Rules teach kids how to respect property, the rights and boundaries of other people. They teach kids how to respect others. Most important, having rules teaches children how to follow and obey rules—an essential and critical social skill for living in a moral, lawful, and orderly society.

When children learn how to accept no at home and live within the rules, then they will be able to leave home and go out in the bigger world where they will be expected to follow yet more rules. Those rules, if obeyed, lead to a society that functions better and protects the property and rights of everyone.

There is a difference between a rule-driven, authoritarian household and one in which the rules are used reasonably and wisely. You've already come across many examples in this book—starting with the toddler who is allowed to do things (such as sleep in a T-shirt instead of pajamas) because there is no hard-and-fast or important rule that will be broken. In Chapter 12 there is a specific list of questions that can help you determine if your rules are fair and in the best interests of your child.

When deciding on family rules, parents should always consider whether they are making rules to help a child function better at home and in society, or to impose their will over a child.

3. **Children should hear no when they are acting aggressively or violently.**

Everyone is concerned about the level of aggression and violence in this society—especially violence committed by young people. But in order to teach children how to be nonviolent and to solve problems in nonviolent and nonaggressive ways, children have to hear the word "no" and be taught how to accept it.

Hearing no and accepting limits means that over time the child becomes socialized, civilized, and able to solve problems in a variety of nonaggressive and nonviolent ways. Children who are violent and aggressive were not necessarily raised in permissive ways (a few were, though). More likely they were not taught how to live with limits and were not trained to discipline themselves by exercising self-control. In many cases, aggressive and violent individuals, instead of being taught self-restraint and appropriate ways to deal with aggressive urges, have had violent and angry behavior modeled for them by adults.

Self-disciplined young people know how to accept limits and they know how to deal with it after being told no. They have learned ways of managing their feelings, even when disappointed. This learning takes place over a period of time and begins early in life. A few tantrums at the toddler stage are a small price to pay for good self-discipline later.

4. Children need to hear no in order to be responsible.

What does it mean to be responsible? A responsible person is one who is able to respond—to controls, demands, obligations, trust. The responsible child is one who knows his duties and lives up to them.

The responsible child does not do what he wants when he wants. He will say no to himself or his friends (or even his parents or other adults) when what is asked of him is not in his or society's best interests. We can trust such a child to respond in acceptable ways.

How does a child get to be responsible? By hearing the word "no" when he should hear it and having parents willing to back up their no's with action and enforcement. Children learn to be responsible through watching responsible parents, being reinforced in positive and encouraging ways when they do the responsible thing, and knowing that the parents who love them and care about what's best for them won't let them do something that isn't right. Those parents will say no and mean it.

How to Say No

The ability to say no in effective and appropriate ways requires some self-discipline on your part. It's helpful to keep in mind, first of all, the obvious fact that children rarely if ever like to be told no. Most of us don't, when we have our hearts set on doing something.

Secondly, you must deal with your own ambivalent feelings about saying no. It is essential that you resolve your own feelings of guilt, anxiety, inadequacy, and reluctance to be the "heavy."

One way for parents to do this is by believing in their hearts that setting limits is not mean. You must convince yourself that it is essential to raising a healthy, competent, and responsible child. And you must remember that saying no doesn't make you the bad guy except, possibly, in your own eyes.

Some of the more passive parents I've worked with over the years were nonassertive not only with their children but with many other people in their lives. If you are one of these parents, it's a good idea to learn to be a no-ing parent through practice. Practice saying no to lots of people in your life. See it not as a "parent problem" but as a communication problem.

Nonassertive and passive people usually have to learn to stand up to others—even if those others are their own kids. Practice saying no. It's important to get to know what it means to be assertive and to learn the basic principles of assertiveness. Many people have difficulty distinguishing between asserting themselves and acting out aggressive urges. By being aggressive, particularly as a parent dealing with your children, it's vital to learn the basic rights of assertiveness. Those include the right to be your best self ("I'm not going to feel comfortable letting you go out with friends who drink"), the right to make a request and to refuse a request ("You asked me if you could go to the school dance and the answer is no, you cannot go this time"), the right not to be intimidated or pushed to do something you don't feel right about ("You've asked me several times to borrow the car, but I've given you my reason and that is that I don't feel good about you driving in these wintry conditions, and I don't want you to ask again"), and the right to make a mistake and change your mind ("You pressured me into saying you could go to the movies this Friday night. But I've thought it over and decided I made a mistake by saying yes. The answer now is no because I've changed my mind"). Learning how to use these principles takes study and practice. You might begin by reading a book like *Your Perfect Right* by Robert E. Alberti and Michael L. Emmons (which is listed in the Appendix) or by taking an assertiveness training class.

You must also sincerely believe that children need someone to put limits on them and that they will feel safer and more secure when someone stops them from behaving in ways that violate rules or standards.

You have to learn to deal with a child's angry reactions when told no. Notice I said "learn." This means that you don't necessarily come into parenthood with the inborn ability to deal well with an angry child. Most learning takes practice and this does, too.

When told no, children may react with rebellion, outrage, tantrums, anger, criticism, withdrawal, pouting, stubbornness, or resistance. These are typical reactions. To accept that children will have adverse reactions is a first step toward dealing with those reactions.

It's important to understand why children react in these ways. Basically that's what this book is all about—how and why children react with anger, rebellion, and stubbornness. When you understand, you can accept, and when you accept that these reactions are a normal and even necessary part of growth and development, then you are well on your way to putting aside your own unhelpful emotions (such as guilt, anger, anxiety, and fear) and dealing with your child in a rational, realistic way.

Clarify your rules, expectations, limits, and the boundaries you think are important for your children. If you are unclear about some of them or feel weak about enforcing them, then talk to experienced, successful parents, or join a parent support group. They'll give you straight, no-nonsense feedback most of the time.

After you are sure what you want to say no about, you can learn how to say no in ways that are more acceptable to your children and create fewer stubborn or oppositional responses from your child. While you will need to get used to occasional angry reactions from your kids, when rules, expectations, and limits are clear and reasonable, when you are consistent in setting them, and when your children know you mean to enforce them, an amazing thing happens: children come to accept your authority and the reality of the limits. And they get angry far less frequently.

Ten Ways to Say No

Here are ten tips for saying no in more effective ways:

1. **Don't overuse the word "no."**

   Any child (or adult for that matter) will resent it (and you) if all they ever hear from you is "Don't."

   "Don't jump on the couch"; "No, you can't touch the VCR"; "Don't spill your milk"; "No talking back"; "Don't slam the door." I think you get the point. If children think all you ever say is no, then they will resent you and the reaction to the next no may be quite angry, violent, or excessive. And who can really blame them?

Particularly the toddler and preschooler, but also the adolescent, is barraged with the word "no." Try to figure out other ways of getting your point across without using no.

Try explanations and reasons that start out like, "You know I'd love to let you do this, but the reason I can't this time is because I'd be worried the whole time you were gone."

Or try, "I can't let you jump on the couch, but I can let you bounce around on that old tire I have in the garage."

Or, "Remember the rule we have about swearing. Try letting me know how you feel without using any bad words. Okay?"

Or, "I don't think that would be a good idea. Can you think of something else you can do that would be a good idea?"

Or, "You can't do that. But there is something you can do. Let's look in the basement for something that you will enjoy doing."

In these examples, the word "no" was avoided or at least camouflaged, but they still conveyed the idea that there are limits and rules that prevent certain behavior. You can say no in many different ways without actually coming out and saying it.

And make sure you say yes once in a while, too.

2. **Let kids make some of the decisions themselves.**

One of the central themes of this book is that as kids are striving for greater independence and autonomy, they need to have more opportunities to show they are getting more mature and more responsible. One way to let them do this is by helping them make their own decisions.

You can encourage them to make their own choices and decisions by teaching them to think and reason. One approach to this is by asking "think questions."

If your child asks if she can go to the mall to hang out with friends and you've never allowed this before, you might use a think question. For example, you could ask, "What do you think I'm going to say to a question like that?"

This gives the young person a chance to say, "Well, you've never let me any other time I asked, so I guess you're going to say no."

To which you can reply, "That's right. However, if you want to have some friends over today, you can ask them to meet you here."

Or you could respond, "I have to go to the mall myself and if you want to ask a friend to go with us, I'd be glad to go to the mall with you for a while."

Another way to phrase a think question in this kind of situation is to ask, "Why do you think I would have to say no?" This gives the youngster the chance to actually give the reason for the expected negative response: "Because it's dangerous for kids to walk around the mall by themselves." Your job or response to a good answer is to give praise and positive feedback: "Exactly. Very good answer. That shows that you're really thinking."

3. Make an appeal.

Another way to get kids to think is to use an appeal. In an appeal, you remind your child of his own values or standards. For example, if your daughter asked if she could walk to a friend's house after dark, you could say, "I know you would like to do this because you want to spend time with your friend. However, I know you to be a pretty smart girl and I bet you would probably not think it safe for a girl to walk alone at night down a dark road."

Here's another example of the use of an appeal: Your son Michael comes from school and says he hates Jeffrey, a boy at his bus stop. "He was calling me names on the bus today," says Michael angrily. "I'm going to beat his face in tomorrow if he does it again."

To use an appeal, you would say, "I see that Jeffrey really makes you mad. Isn't he that skinny kid who you said was so much smaller than you? I wonder if you would really feel good about yourself if you beat up someone who wasn't as big and strong as you?"

After making an appeal, you can let what you said sink in or you can ask what your child thinks. "Well, what do you think about what I said?" In many instances, kids will agree that yes, they do indeed think it unfair or unwise. This won't always happen, of course, because children's emotions and strivings for independence and freedom can easily get in the way of clear, logical thinking. In the end, you may still have to say that "As a parent of a son I want to bring up right, I just can't feel right about letting you do that. I'm sorry."

4. Reframe situations.

Another way to try to defuse some of the anticipated anger or upset at saying no is to teach young people how to reframe situations. Reframing is a means of looking at a disappointing situation from a different angle, in order to turn it into something more positive. For instance, if Bryan is told that he can't have his friends come over in the evening because his mother plans on going to bed early and doesn't wish to be awakened by the clamor of three twelve-year-old boys, Bryan can be helped to reframe the situation.

"I know you don't like it that I told you that you couldn't have your friends over tonight, Bryan. But let's see if we can come up with other things for you to do at home. What do you think you can do instead?"

In this way, Bryan can be assisted in finding a new way of looking at something he disliked. When he can come up with one or two ways of looking at the evening in a new way ("I could just talk on the phone to my friends" or, "I guess we could rent a video and send out for pizza") he will feel less angry and resentful at not being allowed to have his friends over for the evening.

5. Give reasons for saying no.

Young people of various ages can better accept disappointment if a logical and rational reason is given for the no. It used to be much more common than it is today for parents to say, "It's no because I said it's no." Today more parents understand that "because I said so" is not a rational or logical reason.

This means, however, that you have to know why you're turning down a request. If there's no good reason, perhaps what you're doing is trying to control your child or teach him to obey and accept no in an automatic way.

When a child asks, "Can I bounce the tennis ball against the side of the garage?" you ought to have a fairly good reason if your answer is no. Adding that reason to the no might help: "I'd rather you didn't because the noise will bother our neighbors." Or, "I don't really want you to do that because I'm afraid you'll dent the aluminum siding."

6. Invoke a rule.

Again, instead of just saying no, try letting a child know that to do what he's asking will violate an established rule.

If Heather has asked if she can use her father's car to go out on a date, her father could say: "What's the rule we have about you using my car?" Let's say the rule is that Heather is allowed to use her father's car only in an emergency. She might say, "I know the rule is that I only get to use your car when there's a real emergency, but this is sort of one. Chuck's car isn't running and we promised to go to the concert with Jeannie and Phil."

Her father can then say, "I'm sorry, but that's not what the rule is for. You remember why we made that rule? It was because I need my car for my job and if anything happens to it, I won't be able to work. In a true emergency, I'll always let you use it."

7. Let children and teens know your expectations for mature and responsible behavior.

Sometimes without saying no you can point out that you expect your child to make a good decision. When children are becoming more independent, they need practice in making decisions. When you avoid making their decisions, you are giving them an opportunity to live up to your expectations. In other words, you place the responsibility for a mature decision squarely on their shoulders.

Suppose, for instance, a young person asks if she can go to the basketball game at school that night and finish her homework in the morning. You know that the chances of her getting up early to finish an assignment that has to be turned in the next day are slim. Yet, you don't wish to get into an argument that may involve her saying that "You never trust me when I say something."

One way to handle this is to say, "I know that's an important homework assignment and that you have to have it done tomorrow. I also know that going to the basketball game is important to you. I'm going to trust you to make the right decision in this situation. I have faith in you that you'll do the right thing."

Whether she does the "right thing" and gets her school assignment done and turned in is of secondary importance. In this situation you have displayed trust in her judgment and level of responsibility. If she acts in an irresponsible way, she can only blame herself, and that could well require you to make the decision for her next time.

8. Say you're sorry and be empathic when you say no.

Often when parents turn down a request or set a limit, the child feels that his parents don't understand. You can show that you are understanding and that you are well aware of his feelings by acknowledging those feelings in saying no.

If Jennifer wants to spend the night at a motel party after the prom, you can be empathic while saying no. You could say, "I'm awfully sorry about this because I know this is a big night for you, but I can't approve of you doing that. I know you had your heart set on going to this party and if you don't go you'll be disappointed. Despite your feelings of letting down your date and your friends, I can't say yes."

9. Tell the child you're saying no now so you can say yes later.

Sometimes children are misbehaving and we want them to stop. Let's say your child is throwing a ball at a friend who has come to your house for a visit. This is annoying and irritating both to you and your guest.

You could say, "I'm taking your ball away now, so that I can give it back to you. You want to play with this after Marti leaves, right? Well, I'm going to keep it until she leaves. I want her to enjoy her visit with us. Then when she leaves you get to have the ball back to throw it and have fun."

In this way of setting a limit and attempting to stop an annoying behavior the child is told no now but with the idea that there will be a future yes.

10. Use humor.

If one thing helped me and both my children, Jill and Jason, survive their adolescent years it was a sense of humor. Even when I said no to them—which I did often—I tried to inject a sense of humor. Never did I want either one to think that I was rejecting a request just because I was angry.

One example of this that Jill can still recall is the time when she was fifteen and she told me she was going to sleep out in front of a large arena in downtown Detroit. She wanted to spend the night there so she'd be one of the first in line to get tickets to a favorite heavy metal rock band. Never mind that she was supposed to ask permission before going out at night at all!

"That's radical, dude!" I said in mock seriousness and with my best Valley Dude (or whatever it was) imitation. "I think, like, that would be, you know, like total fun. I mean I really would like to, like, you know, read the headlines in the newspaper tomorrow morning about how my only totally dudical daughter was killed on Detroit's riverfront at three o'clock in the morning by a roving gang of killers who prey on young girls who hang out down there at night. Total blast, man!"

"I take it you don't think this is a good idea, right?" she said.

"Like, no," I replied.

"I didn't think you would let me," she said.

While humor can be very effective in saying no or setting limits, it should never be used in such a way that it pokes fun at the child or implies disrespect.

Putting some of these ten tips for saying no into practice can help you say no without triggering angry rebellion and defiance. The knowing parent is an expert at saying no in ways that help children to accept it.

Summary

Being able to say no and set limits on children is an essential aspect of being a competent and effective parent. In the long run, setting limits and enforcing rules makes children and teens happier and more responsible.

There are four basic times to say no to your children:

1. When their health or safety is in danger.
2. When they are about to break an important rule.
3. When they are acting violently or aggressively.
4. When they are learning to be responsible.

The ability to say no in effective and appropriate ways requires some self-discipline on a parent's part. It's helpful to keep in mind, first of all, the obvious fact that children rarely if ever like to be told no.

You must deal with any ambivalent feelings you may have about saying no. If you are to be effective, it is essential that you resolve your own feelings of guilt, anxiety, inadequacy, and reluctance to be the "heavy."

Ten tips for parents in saying no more effectively:

1. Don't overuse the word "no."
2. Let kids make some of the decisions themselves.
3. Make an appeal.
4. Reframe situations.
5. Give reasons for saying no.
6. Invoke a rule.
7. Let children and teens know your expectations for mature and responsible behavior.
8. Say you're sorry and be empathic when you say no.
9. Tell the child you're saying no now so you can say yes later.
10. Use humor.

PART III

Stubborn Behavior in Special Situations

CHAPTER 14

The Occasionally Stubborn Youngster

Romeo and Juliet are classic examples of occasionally stubborn adolescents. They might be called situationally oppositional young people. Thwarted in their burning childhood affection for one another, they went the distance to defy their families.

In life as well as in fiction, passionate young love is a situation that may lead an otherwise compliant teenager to be defiant. This one issue may become so important to preadolescents and adolescents that it transcends all others. Such situational defiance is not a temperamental trait, nor is it the youngster's typical response.

Because adolescents need to establish their independence from their parents, all you have to do is insist that two teenagers not fall in love and they will. In the musical *The Fantastiks*, this is what the two fathers count on: They tell their children—one a boy, the other a girl—not to have anything to do with each other. Of course, that ensures that the two young people are attracted to each other.

As a therapist, I've had occasion to work with dozens of families in which the parents were opposed to the love object of their teenagers. Stephanie Holder was a sixteen-year-old in one such family. She usually did what her parents wanted her to do. The one exception caused a major crisis in the household.

When I met with Stephanie's parents they described her as a liar and thief. She had secretly used her father's credit card to run up hundreds of dollars worth of phone bills over several months before it was discovered by his office staff in an audit.

Stephanie had lied about whom she was calling. And she was lying to her parents about whom she was dating. Her parents were incensed about her secretive behavior and said she needed psychotherapeutic help.

When I first met Stephanie, I couldn't believe that this was the same girl her parents had described. She had just come from cheerleading practice and was still dressed in her cheerleading outfit. A National Honor Society student who was attractive and popular with classmates, she had caused relatively few problems with her parents—until Bill came into Stephanie's life.

Things had started innocently enough. In June of the previous summer, Stephanie met Bill at a party. She was a sophomore in high school and he was a sophomore in college. They were immediately attracted to each other. When Stephanie hinted she was thinking about dating an older boy she met, her father's first question was, "How old is he?"

Stephanie decided then and there to keep her relationship a secret. Every so often she would test the atmosphere by talking about "friends" who were dating older boys. When she got the usual response from her parents, she would argue with them on a more personal level about "What if I met someone who was older?"

"Don't even bother bringing an older boy home for me to meet," her father declared. "You bring home a boy your own age and then we'll talk."

"But that's not fair," countered Stephanie. "Why can't you judge people after getting to know them rather than just going by their age?"

"I don't have to," said her father. Stephanie knew the time was not right to let her parents in on what was happening.

Stephanie, however, was convinced that Bill was right for her. She was in love, and continued to see Bill behind her parents' backs. She lied about overnights at girlfriends' houses and nights out with the girls, while she spent as much time as possible with Bill. When he was in college, he came home as many weekends as he could, and they managed to find ways to see each other.

Mr. and Mrs. Holder believed that Stephanie was playing the field and was spending a lot of time with her girlfriends—until the extra charges on the telephone bills began to show up on the office account.

It wasn't like Stephanie to lie or "steal" from her parents. And Mr. Holder was quite adamant that using his office credit card number without permission was stealing. "That boy put you up to it, didn't he?" he badgered his daughter. After expressing her guilt and sorrow at "stealing" from her parents Stephanie was unwilling to back down or give up her interest in Bill. Her position had all the characteristics of a stone wall: "I like him and I'm going to continue to see him and you can't stop me!"

Her father took an equally stubborn position: "Oh yeah, we'll see about that!" he thundered in hurt rage.

Stephanie also justified her behavior: "If you had understood my feelings and trusted me," she said to her parents in family counseling sessions, "none of this would have happened."

And indeed, Stephanie had a good point. Forced to contend with parents who took unyielding positions about age differences, she stubbornly justified all subsequent behavior.

"It's all right to go behind the backs of people who don't care about you," Stephanie seemed to be saying.

The battle lines were drawn. Stephanie's father said she couldn't see Bill and he would try to find legal ways of preventing them from having any further contact. He also verbally slammed Bill whenever he could in front of Stephanie. "What kind of boy would let a girl use her father's charge card to make long distance calls?" he asked. "You know a boy who is twenty has just one thing on his mind when it comes to girls." And, "If he was any kind of decent boy, he would have come to me and tried to work this out!"

Stephanie maintained her position: "There isn't anything you can do to stop us from seeing each other. As soon as I graduate and go to college, I'll do whatever I want and you'll have no say in the matter!"

How did a bright, studious, compliant teenager get herself into this situation? One view would be that her love of a boy had transcended her usual common sense and practical ways of approaching life. Another view would be that her father's intransigence, refusal to compromise, and failure to take her feelings or judgment into consideration had forced this classic confrontation between parent and child.

This is not an atypical impasse. A previously model child can easily become caught up in a situation in which she adopts a defiant and stubborn stance. Shakespeare would not have written so eloquently about it in *Romeo and Juliet* if it were not a universal dilemma.

Nor are such clashes confined to romance and boyfriend/girlfriend situations. There are also those that concern school, work, career, college courses, sports, and other decisions. Kids who are determined, against their parents' wishes, to play football, work part-time, have certain friends, adopt a particular lifestyle, or drop out of school are familiar to all of us.

What leads to these kinds of one-incident defiances? Let's examine the standoff in Stephanie Holder's family. If you asked her father to describe the problem, he would say that Stephanie decided to be stubborn, or that she was influenced by an older boy, or that she lost her common sense with a summer romance.

If you talked to Stephanie, she would say that it was her father's failure to understand her and trust her that led to her position.

Maybe both are right. From my point of view, the whole situation could have been avoided. The one thing that always happens when this kind of stalemate develops is that someone—either the parent or the child—loses sight of a very important goal. In my opinion, the most important goal of a parent or a young person is to maintain family relationships and communication.

As the father of a daughter who has dated boys I didn't like, I found that I often had to remind myself of what was most important. Was it to force my will, my opinions, my viewpoint on my daughter? Or was it to keep a good relationship with someone that I loved and respected?

I always opted for the latter. My reasoning went like this: Okay, I don't like this guy. If I actively oppose him, or my daughter's decision, I could alienate her. Then I might lose her companionship and friendship. If I let her make her own decisions, I might lose on this and she might bring herself some unhappiness. But in the long run, because she is a bright and perceptive person, she will figure out what's best for her. And we will still be friends. More importantly, if she needs me to get through this situation, we will still have a close relationship and she can come to me for support and even advice.

That's what always won out—my reasoning, and my keeping in mind what is of supreme importance: that I have the respect and friendship of a daughter I love. And in the end, that's the way it has always worked out. My daughter Jill's boyfriends have come and gone (and even a marriage I couldn't wholeheartedly approve), but our friendship and love have remained constant. Throughout all of her relationships with boys and men, we could always turn to each other.

How Situational Stubbornness Arises

For a problem with situational stubbornness to occur, then, two things have to happen:

First, parents have to lose sight of what is most important—the continuing relationship with a child. Instead of focusing on that, they look at other issues—issues I see as minor compared to what's at stake.

Of course, there are some issues that are of major-league dimensions, and they call for strong measures. For instance, when a young person is using dangerous drugs, is addicted to substances, or is involved in criminal behavior, the parent has to be tough. That will mean that the choices given the young person may be very limited.

For instance, if your son has been picked up for driving under the influence of alcohol, the choices may be as follows: "You can either give us your driver's license or you can get help for your drinking problem."

Similarly, if you discover that your daughter has been stealing from stores, the choice is: "Either you turn yourself in to the police or get better. We're on your side either way and we'd be happy to go with you to see a therapist or to the police. You decide which way you want this to be handled."

The issues that I think often hang up parents and other adults who live or work closely with children relate to the following:

- The anticipated catastrophic consequences or outcomes for the young person ("This will ruin her life").

- Their own expectations for their offspring ("This isn't what I brought him up for").

- Their dismay over the defiance of parental advice or authority ("How could she turn against me in this way?").

The second thing that gives rise to situational stubbornness is that the parent overlooks the feelings, emotions, and positive traits of the child.

In one way or another, the parent says to the child, "I don't trust you to make good decisions in your life and besides that I know better about these things than you do." It's as if the parent says (actually Mr. Holder did say this): "I don't care how you feel. This is the way I want it and that's the way it's going to be." That sets up a tug-of-war between parent and child. It's the parent's will and power versus the child's ability to defy.

Some parents look at the situation as a catastrophe, believing that their children are making enormous and irrevocable mistakes. This may happen because they've gotten caught up in their own expectations for their children. If a youngster makes a decision on her own that goes against the life plan or expectation of the parent it can throw the parent a real curve. Often parents aren't able to adjust to the child's alteration of the course of events. They may interpret this as defiance.

How to Avoid a Battle of Wills

This can be handled if the parent stops and considers the situation as rationally and as realistically as possible. What is the likely outcome? What is the worst thing that could happen? Looking at the worst possible outcome may give you a chance to realize that even if a child's decision leads to that result, you'll be able to cope with it.

You can also help yourself if you make a list of your child's positive and admirable traits. Remind yourself of what the young person does well and what you have taught her. On that list will often appear such things as "good judgment," "honest," "compassionate," "friendly," "loving," and "capable." Reminding yourself of a child's best traits helps you keep in mind that even when she seems to be making a mistake, in the long run she will be able to use her positive qualities to deal with that mistake—and more importantly, learn from it.

The keys to avoiding such a battle of wills, then, come down to these essentials:

1. Parents must keep the importance of maintaining a relationship with their child squarely in mind as they set limits and impose rules.
2. Parents must try to understand and acknowledge the feelings of their child.
3. The child or adolescent must end up feeling that she is understood and that her parents have respect for her feelings, opinions, and needs.

Mr. and Mrs. Holder could have avoided the problem they had with Stephanie right in the beginning by following these three key steps. When Stephanie came to them and said she wanted to date an older boy, they could have expressed their displeasure and their concerns in this way:

MR. HOLDER: A twenty-year-old, eh? Well, that bothers me. He might not have the same interests as you. Also, he's going to college and you're still in high school and I think you might miss out on a lot of fun with your friends. Have you really thought this through?

STEPHANIE: I've thought about those things and I think it's worth it. I really like him.

MR. HOLDER: Well, I can't just let you go out with an older boy. After all, we haven't even met him yet.

STEPHANIE: I know, Dad. I'd be glad to introduce you. Then you can get to know him before you give your approval. Okay?

MR. HOLDER: I don't know, honey. These things bother me. You're sure you like him that much?

STEPHANIE: Yes, Daddy.

MR. HOLDER: Okay. This is the deal. He can come over and we'll meet him. If he makes a good impression on us, we'll let you continue to have him over. As for you actually going on a date, let's wait and see. First we'll meet him and then we'll take things a step at a time. Agreed?

STEPHANIE: It's a deal! Thanks, Dad.

Now, let's say Bill makes a good impression. After a few visits, Bill may fit in with the family. Stephanie, a bright, perceptive girl, will have a chance to figure this out, just as her parents will. If they feel comfortable with her going out with him, then they could set up situations where the dating was fairly controlled ("Why don't we all go out to that concert and have dinner afterward this weekend?" Or, "You two can go to a movie Saturday night. Be home by 11 P.M.").

But what if he doesn't make a good impression? We want Stephanie to be able to see this and see why. Maybe he's just nervous. Or maybe he is very different from her family and does not share the family's beliefs and values. Dad could ask her some questions when they have a chance to talk:

MR. HOLDER: How do you think it's working out with Bill?

STEPHANIE: Oh, fine. He wants us to go out on a real date sometime.

MR. HOLDER: I'm sure he gets tired just seeing you here, doesn't he?

STEPHANIE: Yeah, and me, too. Don't you think we could go to a movie or something?

MR. HOLDER: Do you still like him as much as you did before we met him?

STEPHANIE: Yeah . . . I guess so.

MR. HOLDER: Sounds like you aren't really sure.

STEPHANIE: I don't know. Sometimes it's like he doesn't fit in here. You know what I mean?

MR. HOLDER: Yeah, I've noticed that, too. Why do you suppose that is?

STEPHANIE: I don't know. Maybe he's nervous here. Or he doesn't feel right with our family.

MR. HOLDER: I think we've tried to make him feel comfortable. Is there something more we should be doing?

STEPHANIE: Gee, no, Dad. I think everyone has treated him nicely. It was great when we took him out to dinner and he came over when we had that barbecue. You were really nice to him.

MR. HOLDER: Well, what do you think you should do?

STEPHANIE: I'd like to go out with him a couple of times and maybe take him to a party with my friends and see if he fits in with them. Then I'll decide.

Mr. Holder: I think that's an excellent idea. Let me know how it's working out, okay?

Stephanie: Thanks, Dad, I love you.

Mr. Holder: I love you, too, honey.

In this dialogue, Stephanie would know her father's main concern was her happiness and well-being. She would understand that he wanted the best for her and was not trying to dominate her or impose his will on her. She would sense that he had an understanding of her feelings and that those feelings were important. She would also know that her father respected her, saw her as a bright, capable person, and trusted that she could make adequate and capable decisions on her own.

But no matter what the outcome of Stephanie's relationship with Bill, she and her dad would still be working together and could be friends. Even if she made the "wrong" decision for her, her father would be on her side. That's very important.

Our children will make some wrong decisions, but if you follow this approach they will understand their own responsibility because they will be making some decisions on their own. You will enable them to exercise their responsibility when you allow them some independence and autonomy. They won't have to retreat into defiance and stubbornness in order to prove that they are right, that they are capable, that they are autonomous, or that they have the right to make their own mistakes.

So that this format can be applied to any situation between an adult and a young person, I have put it in a series of steps. Let's take another problem and follow it through these steps, one at a time.

1. **Identify the problem.** Let's suppose that your adolescent son wants to earn some money. He comes to you and says he's thinking about getting a job at McDonald's after school. You identify the problem: He wants to work part-time and you want him to concentrate all of his time and energy on school.

2. **State your concern as parent.** You could say: "My concern here is that you're going to be working afternoons and evenings and you'll be too tired or too busy to finish all your schoolwork. I believe school should come first."

3. **Solicit your child's feelings, opinions, or views.** To get your child's point of view, ask: "What do you think?" Or, "Why is it important for you to get a job now?"

   The child might say: "I've always wanted to get a job. And you know I'm always asking for more money and I hate bothering you guys for extra money when I want to do something with my friends."

4. **Summarize both sides by reflecting how each of you feels.** You could sum up what you each think or feel in the following way: "I guess it's pretty plain that you like the idea of earning your own money so you have enough to spend when you need it. And it sounds as if you would just feel good working. On the other hand, my position is that I'm more concerned with your education and I don't want a job to interfere with you doing a good job at school. Is that the way you see it, too?"

5. **Discuss a compromise.** As the parent you should take responsibility for seeking a solution to the situation and the conflicting points of view. It might well involve a compromise. You could approach it in this way: "Well, I guess we have to work this out. What would you say to just doing some extra chores at home for which we'll pay you?" Or, "What about us increasing your allowance. Would that help out and keep you from taking a job?"

6. **Come to a mutually satisfying agreement.** Your child is unlikely to accept the first (or perhaps even the second or third) proposed solution to the problem. Eventually, though, there has to be a resolution. When that's been reached, it should be stated in a clear and concise way: "Okay, so this is what we're going to do. I agree that you can try to get a job and that you can work up to fifteen hours a week. However, if your grades go down next semester, then you agree that you'll either quit or work fewer hours. Agreed?"

7. **Plan a time in the future when the agreement can be reviewed.** After summing up the agreement, then set a

time for coming back and evaluating how the solution is working: "So we have an agreement. We'll try it out until the end of the semester and you get your report card. That should be about the second week in January. Okay, we'll talk then?"

This series of steps can be applied to any situation in which there may be conflict between a parent and child's positions, needs, or desires. It has the advantages of promoting discussion and communication, shows respect for the young person's feelings and thoughts, and allows for a peaceful solution.

Summary

There are situations that drive ordinarily compliant and not usually stubborn children and adolescents into adopting a defiant position. The ways parents can avoid this are to:

- **Remember one of the main goals in parenting: keeping a relationship with your child.**
- **Understand and acknowledge your child's feelings.**
- **Make sure your child ends up feeling understood and that she believes you consider her emotions, opinions, and needs important.**

A series of steps can be taken in any conflict situation between parents and children in order to communicate and reach a mutually satisfying decision. These steps are:

1. **Identify the problem.**
2. **State your concern as a parent.**
3. **Solicit your child's feelings, opinions, and views.**
4. **Summarize both sides by reflecting how each of you feels.**
5. **Discuss a compromise.**
6. **Come to a mutually satisfying agreement.**
7. **Plan a time in the future to review the agreement.**

CHAPTER 15

The Stubborn Child in the Classroom

"Why do you keep wasting everyone's time by showing up here?" the teacher said to fifteen-year-old Kyle, as Kyle, late again for class, tried to slip in without being seen.

Kyle didn't say anything.

"You haven't done anything since you've been in this class and I doubt you ever will," Mr. Nowicki continued. "I can't wait until you're sixteen so you can drop out and save the taxpayers some money."

"Hey, what's up?" asked Kyle.

"You're disrupting my class, okay?" replied Mr. Nowicki. "I don't need you in here. The office is a better place for you."

"Why don't you just leave me alone?" said Kyle.

"Maybe I don't like your attitude," said the teacher.

"Screw you," muttered Kyle under his breath.

"How'd you like to take a trip to the office, smart guy?" asked Mr. Nowicki.

"How would you like to take a trip to the office, smart guy?" echoed Kyle, as he was now getting laughs from the other students in the class.

"Keep it up, asshole, and we'll see what happens," said Mr. Nowicki.

"Keep it up, asshole, and we'll see what happens," again said Kyle in imitation of the teacher's threat.

Mr. Nowicki was red in the face and didn't want to let Kyle get away with his insubordination. He wasn't sure what would happen next if he tried to make Kyle, a stocky, six-foot-tall teenager, leave the class. He decided to change the subject and asked the class to take out the assignment from the previous day.

Kyle, also, decided not to pursue this, although he looked daggers at the teacher for the rest of the hour.

When Kyle told this story at home, both he and his parents were incensed that a teacher would provoke this kind of confrontation. At the same time, his parents were also aware that Kyle started it by coming to class late. Still, they thought, Mr. Nowicki wasn't handling Kyle in a professional way.

Over the years, I've heard many stories from children and teens that describe situations in which they are in some way picked on, harassed, or provoked into insubordination or oppositional behavior. Most of the young people who relate these kinds of incidents are far from innocent angels. And while their behavior may have precipitated the original comment or remark from the educator, the kids weren't looking for a confrontation in the beginning. Ultimately, however, they reacted in the only way they knew how to an adult authority figure who was treating them with disrespect.

Then there are children like ten-year-old Ricky. A fourth-grader, Ricky often refuses to complete schoolwork assignments. He displays poor work habits and can't seem to stick with a task. In addition, he breaks rules by talking out of turn, playing with pencils when he should be working, and asking to go to the rest room at inappropriate times. When confronted about his wasting time when all the other kids are busily working on assignments at their seats, Ricky just puts his head down and ignores requests. His teacher sees him as a very stubborn, belligerent, disruptive child.

Five-year-old Melanie has been called stubborn by her kindergarten teacher, also. She seems to go out of her way to frustrate her teacher, Mrs. Carmichael, who is generally very quiet, loving, and kind to her kindergarten class.

When the first students come into her class in the morning they are encouraged to go to the bookshelf and choose a book to read or look at while everyone is coming into the room and getting settled. Melanie is usually one of the last children to come into the room. She putters around and sits down in her seat. When Mrs. Carmichael announces that the class should begin putting their books back on the shelf, Melanie goes up to get one, brings it back to her seat, and starts looking at the pictures.

So intent does she become that she fails to hear Mrs. Carmichael tell everyone that their time is up and all books must be back on the shelf. Mrs. Carmichael comes over to Melanie's table and tells her to return the book to the shelf. Melanie may or may not immediately comply, although eventually she returns the book to the shelf.

So the day goes for Melanie in Mrs. Carmichael's kindergarten room. The five-year-old either doesn't comply or is very slow to do so. While never directly disobedient, she seems to march to her own beat and always (or so it seems to a frustrated Mrs. Carmichael) appears intent on doing just the opposite of what is required.

When others are putting scissors and crayons away, Melanie is beginning to work. When it's cleanup time and Melanie is supposed to be wiping off her worktable with a paper towel, she's whirling around and staring at Mrs. Carmichael.

Stubborn, oppositional, and noncompliant children come in all shapes and sizes at school—from kindergartners to strapping high school students. But they all share in common—in one way or another—refusing to do work, defying authority, ignoring requests or orders, breaking rules, or quietly and resolutely failing to complete tasks.

Like Melanie, some oppositional and stubborn youngsters at school seem to be following their own agendas, while others, like Kyle, may react with belligerence and outright defiance ("Go ahead, kick me out of class!").

No matter which style a child uses, to the teachers who try to educate and discipline them, such youngsters seem to be poorly motivated when it comes to schoolwork and completely uncooperative when it comes to adherence to school rules and routines.

Socially these youngsters may not care to succeed in the way the teacher would like. And sometimes the teacher has little understanding of such a child's "agenda." To educators, it often looks as if these kids are out to frustrate, defy, or even manipulate their teachers into acting in authoritarian ways.

The students who continue into middle school and high school behaving in stubborn, defiant, and oppositional ways are the ones most likely to fail or drop out before graduation. Such young people find school an unrewarding experience. Some derive satisfaction from frustrating and defying teachers and administrators. Schoolwork and compliance with rules hold very little intrinsic satisfaction for them. If they can get suspended or sent to the office, they can avoid doing schoolwork and following routines for a few more hours or days.

Often when parents get negative reports from the school about behavioral or academic difficulties, they are perplexed about what is actually going on. Parents wonder if their child really has a serious problem. Or they are confused about how they should get involved or in what way they could either support their youngster or punish him.

Parents usually make an attempt to cooperate with the teacher—especially when they understand their child presents some challenging problems. And most teachers are willing to collaborate with parents to solve school-related difficulties. What happens all too often, however, is that more difficult children and teens are scapegoated by teachers and are frequently suspended or asked to leave school (especially when the child is in a day care center, preschool, or a private school). Prior to this parents may have been strongly advised to get psychiatric help for their child or have the child put on medication.

While this may be useful advice, I often find that schoolteachers and administrators have little tolerance for working with more challenging youngsters. And I've also observed that a great many teachers are inadequately trained to deal with oppositional children or the teacher may be stressed by having to teach in an overcrowded classroom. On occasion they may even be provoking oppositional behaviors.

Teacher Behavior that Promotes Stubbornness

As Mr. Nowicki demonstrates, teachers and other educators are not always innocent bystanders in the matter of provoking or reinforcing stubborn and defiant behaviors. Some educators have their own hang-ups when it comes to issues of authority and relationships with young people.

Children and teens who come to school with already-formed stubborn or oppositional behavior will often come into direct contact with the teachers and school administrators who have the most difficulty with such young people. It is like an accident waiting to happen. Sooner or later there will be a clash. And it can be provoked by a student, a teacher, or an otherwise competent administrator.

Many teachers resent giving undue amounts of attention and assistance to children and teens who are oppositional and stubborn. They may feel it's an imposition on their real duties and responsibilities to have to devote time and effort to youngsters who appear capable of success but who are not able to comply with routines, assignments, and directions. Teachers frequently see such young people as having choices and clearly choosing the wrong path.

It is also clear that dealing with hundreds of children each day (as middle school and high school teachers do) is difficult. There are daily frustrations and always a certain number of youngsters who are defiant or oppositional. If the teacher isn't able to control his own authority problems, these students will bring out the worst in him, arousing anger or dislike. When children and teens sense a teacher dislikes them, the stage is set for yet more willful, oppositional, or defiant behavior. Young people in general just don't respond well to teachers who give off hostile signals. And who does? Such a situation paves the way for those children with authority problems to act out their worst tendencies, and school will become an even more unfulfilling arena.

Active provocation of kids ("Miss Roberson, if you think you can teach this class better than I can, suppose you get up and take over" or, "You're going to flunk this class, young man. I knew it from the first day I saw you here") is one thing, but less directly expressed attitudes teachers bring into the classroom can be just as provoking to children. Even very subtle attitudes have the potential for sparking the oppositional and defiant behaviors of some youngsters.

Those attitudes are sometimes formed in the teacher's lounge, a place where teachers talk about their students, compare notes about them, and pass along their opinions and impressions. Attitudes formed in the teacher's lounge can become attitudes carried into the unsuspecting student's next class.

A teacher's or educator's own temperament and personality may play an important role in the educator-student relationship (just as it does in the parent-child relationship). If a teacher places high value on submission to authority, then a more assertive or outspoken youngster may have a difficult row to hoe. Similarly, a well-organized teacher may have particular difficulty with a disorganized child; or a teacher who is less impulsive may have a great deal of difficulty with an active and impulsive young person.

Why Are Kids Stubborn and Oppositional in School?

Children display oppositional, stubborn, and defiant behavior at school for a variety of reasons—just as they display those same behaviors elsewhere in their lives. Those reasons are as follows:

- They've developed problems with oppositional, stubborn, or noncompliant behavior prior to coming to school.
- They have learning disabilities that stubborn and oppositional behaviors help to cover up.
- They are poorly disciplined.
- They have Attention Deficit Hyperactivity Disorder.
- They are in general poorly adjusted and unhappy young people.
- They are provoked into such behavior by teachers and other school personnel.
- They are divergent-thinking youngsters; that is, they are bright and gifted children who think differently.

Some children are oppositional and defiant long before they get to the classroom. For whatever reasons, perhaps a difficult temperament, poor discipline from their parents, or other causes, they are stubborn and oppositional when they arrive. They aren't created by the educational system or poor teaching, although their worst stubborn behaviors may be triggered by the wrong handling at school.

Then there are children who have learning disabilities. These are often youngsters who do fairly well until they get into the classroom, but then they begin a long and treacherous adventure trying to deal with an educational system that is frequently unable to reach them or teach them well enough so that they are able to keep up with age mates and classmates.

Students with learning problems don't catch on as quickly or as well as their peers, and begin to feel different from other kids as early as the first grade. To cope with this they may become defensive, withdrawn, or disillusioned with school. Their self-esteem may suffer early on in their education, and out of frustration and a deepening sense of inadequacy they project their unhappiness onto teachers and the system as a whole.

One of the ways that children with learning disabilities attempt to cope with a system that seems unresponsive to their needs and learning styles is to become stubborn, defiant, and oppositional. Many attempt to cover over their feelings and their crippled sense of their own competence with behavior that becomes increasingly belligerent and defiant.

Then there is the poorly disciplined child. Again, this youngster's stubborn or oppositional behavior wasn't created by the school system, but since this is where he spends a good part of his day, the behavior is displayed here just as it is at home.

In previous chapters we have talked about the discipline methods that tend to play a part in the development of stubborn, oppositional, and defiant youngsters. Such behavior becomes ingrained when parents don't handle age-appropriate negative or oppositional behaviors in the best way or provide appropriate and consistent discipline.

These children will characteristically manifest the same types of behavior at school that they do at home unless they meet up with very understanding and skillful teachers who know how to handle difficult children.

Children and teens who have been diagnosed with Attention Deficit Hyperactivity Disorder may also show up as stubborn, strong-willed, and oppositional children in the classroom. Because they often have difficult temperaments and because they have at least some kinds of learning problems (a short attention span and high distractibility, if nothing else), they will display stubborn behaviors the same way some learning-disabled or poorly disciplined children do.

The ADHD students usually experience difficulties learning and have trouble paying attention to instruction and to classroom assignments. In addition, they may be impulsive and hyperactive. As a result, they are likely to behave in stubborn and oppositional ways, or to be stuck with negative labels.

Poorly adjusted and unhappy youngsters will tend to bring difficulties from their home life into the classroom. If they are unable to concentrate on or complete their schoolwork, they may appear to be defiant, rebellious, passive-aggressive, or stubborn. When kids don't complete assignments, they are frequently labeled as stubborn by both teachers and parents. However, these are youngsters who need to be distinguished from other children and to be handled in a different way from other children. For instance, they should be referred for counseling services.

Finally there are those kids that I have referred to as divergent thinkers. They may be bright, gifted, or highly creative, individualistic thinkers who view situations in a different way. Sometimes these youngsters don't like to do things the way other people do them; in this case, think of teachers as those "other people."

Teachers who are used to handing out dittos or photocopied classwork may encounter a minor rebellion from divergent thinkers who find such work boring, routine, silly, or beneath them. Such kids may question the teacher and act defiant more frequently than other students. They may rebel against doing work they see as meaningless or unproductive. Teachers may see their questions, comments, and debates with them as provocation or evidence of oppositional tendencies and bad attitudes.

When divergent thinkers meet teachers who place high value on submissive or subordinate and compliant behavior, there is certain to be trouble. One such boy I knew was refusing to do any work for his sixth-grade teacher. The teacher referred him to the school psychologist, stating in her referral that he was stubborn, oppositional, and "refused to do assigned work."

The psychologist, however, immediately recognized a bright, talented boy who was creative and liked to do things his way. While the boy cooperated with him, he also showed that he had a creative way of looking at the world. This was evident in the boy's unique and original sense of humor, his artistic ability when the psychologist asked him to draw a picture, and his creative ways of putting together diverse concepts. Having such a student presented difficulties for a teacher who expected things to be done her way. When the boy was moved to another class with a more flexible teacher, the fit was a lot better and the young man was no longer viewed as "stubborn."

How Can Parents Handle a Poor Fit Between Teacher and Child?

What can you do if your child is a difficult youngster and is presenting problems that the teacher is not handling well?

It's usually best to anticipate this problem before you start getting calls from the teacher or you are asked to come to a conference. One thing you can do if you anticipate that your youngster will be a challenge to a teacher is to work with the principal before a teacher assignment is made. Many elementary school principals are willing to work with parents to decide which teacher is most likely to be able to deal with a particular difficult child.

Occasionally, however, principals are reluctant to give parents choices or a voice in the selection of a teacher. When this happens, parents can go over the principal's head to the director of elementary education in the school district. Often I have found such directors to be most accommodating and willing to assist parents in helping to choose their child's next teacher.

Establishing a working relationship with the principal is undoubtedly the best option, when this is available, because then you can work with both the principal and the classroom teacher throughout the year. When parents are willing to admit to educators that their child presents difficulties in the classroom, educators tend to be more inclined to participate in a team effort—rather than to view the situation from an adversarial, "us versus them" point of view.

Whether you are able to find a good match for your child or whether you are already well into a new school year with problems, one of the best things you can do is share your expertise with the teacher. Parents are not always aware of the expertise they have in dealing with their own children. While some parents may feel just as perplexed as the teacher or school staff about how to deal with a child, most have figured out at least a few ways to handle the difficult child effectively. When you have a working relationship with the teacher, you can teach him how to handle your child.

Parents frequently assume that because a teacher is experienced or competent in some ways, he is a behavioral expert capable of managing all children. Sometimes this just isn't the case.

Jeanette, the mother of nine-year-old Edward, is an expert on her own son. She wasn't always so, but after taking a parenting class and doing as much reading about oppositional and defiant children as she could, she learned new and effective ways of disciplining Edward. She wanted her son to be handled well by the school staff, too. When Jeanette discovered that a teacher was mishandling Edward, she politely but assertively made observations and suggestions.

"Edward has to learn to follow rules," Edward's teacher told Jeanette in a conference.

Jeanette's response was: "No, you have to learn how to handle Edward. He follows rules, especially when you don't let rules slide. Sometimes you let rules slide and that works well with a lot of your students, but it won't with Edward. You have to hold fast to a rule every time with him."

Another time, his teacher sent a note home about Edward playing with Pogs in the class when he was bored. Jeanette went to school the next morning to talk to the teacher.

"You have a problem with Edward playing with Pogs when he's supposed to be working?" she asked.

When the teacher said this was true, Jeanette said, "Okay, here's the situation with Edward. You have to structure things for him. If you let him play with Pogs, he will keep doing that. I would recommend that you take his Pogs away and suggest to him that he should read when his work is done. You can return the Pogs at recess or after school."

"But he argues with me," his teacher said.

"I know," said Jeanette. "He argues with me, too. I find that keeping my voice low, using an authoritative voice, and being clear about what I want him to do works well. If he argues about it not being fair when you take away his Pogs, you can tell him that he will get the game back at recess, but you do not allow children to play with Pogs in class."

When Jeanette checked back with the teacher a week later, the teacher thanked her. "Those things you told me really do work well," she said.

Again, a working relationship featuring open communication with the teacher helps. Together you may be able to figure out how to solve the problem. Sometimes it turns out that there is a poor fit or a personality clash between the teacher and the child.

In such a situation, you have two choices: You can request a change to a different teacher, or you can work with your child to learn to deal with a teacher he doesn't particularly like. I have seen both approaches produce successful results, but you must decide which option to pursue.

Certainly there are reasons to teach children to learn to cope with people they don't like. Asking a child to figure out ways of getting along better with a teacher can be good training in problem solving for other kinds of situations that are sure to come up in a child's life.

Sometimes there are teachers, like Mr. Nowicki, who should not be working with young people. If your child is having difficulty with a particular teacher, it helps to talk to other parents who have had children taught by the same teacher. When you start talking to other parents, you will find out quickly whether the teacher has some serious defects or problems. If you learn that a teacher is burned out, is emotionally disturbed, or has character defects that lead to verbal or physical abuse of children, not only should a child be removed immediately from that class, but it is time to deal with the school's administration.

I know of situations where principals and other administrators have tried to protect such teachers, and I also know of cases where a principal was open in admitting a teacher should not be working with children but felt powerless to do anything about it. Parents who protest loud enough can make a difference. By organizing protests to make their complaints known to the school board parents can sometimes exert enough pressure to have such teachers removed from direct contact with young people.

How to Recognize Adequate Teachers

As a parent, whether of a compliant and easy to get along with child or of a stubborn and oppositional youngster, you will want to be able to evaluate the type of teacher your child has. Here are some pointers to help:

- The ideal teacher is one who views all young people as individuals and responds sensitively to each child in his class. Such a teacher, when faced with noncompliant and oppositional behavior, will examine himself, the child, and the setting as he attempts to determine the reasons for such behavior. Once a reason, however tentative, is found, the ideal teacher will attempt to change his approach to suit that child.

  When a teacher is unable to find a better way of reducing noncompliant and oppositional behavior on his own, he should make a referral to the school psychologist or a treatment team for a consultation or evaluation.

- Young people in general, even those with difficult temperaments or problems of an oppositional, defiant, or stubborn nature, respond best to a warm, respectful, and honest style. A teacher who exhibits these characteristics is on the right track.

  Approaches that are disrespectful, demeaning, accusatory, belittling, or demanding are usually doomed to failure. It's important to listen to what your child reports at home about his teacher.

- Teachers and educators must have their own authority needs under control so that those needs don't unduly influence their view of noncompliant behavior as a personal insult or affront.

When a teacher takes a child's stubborn or oppositional behavior personally (and as a threat to his authority, a rejection of his values, or a black mark against his ability and competence), then it is inevitable that he will respond in more authority-laden, heavy-handed, and forceful ways. Treating children and teens with respect means allowing them to function on their own terms. They are entitled to express themselves, have (and express) opinions, have (and be able to express) likes and dislikes (even about a teacher's special field of study), and have the opportunity to make choices.

Listening to what your child tells you about what goes on in the classroom is an invaluable first step. Checking with your child's friends and classmates can be a useful way of validating what you hear from your child. When there are too many frustrated youngsters, or when too many children are sent to the office, it is usually an indication of authority problems in the classroom.

• Young people in school, just as at home, need to know what the rules and limits are, what the school's or teacher's expectations are, and what the consequences will be for noncompliance and more oppositional behavior.

A teacher must make sure that consequences are not only clear, but reasonable and fair. And they have to be consistently administered to all children in the classroom— independent of the kinds of difficulties presented by a particular youngster.

Teachers who start out a class with well-defined rules and limits, a basic understanding of each child's abilities and disabilities (both in regard to learning and dealing with authority), and a knowledge of fair and reasonable consequences, are unlikely to encounter individual or group rebellion.

This will remain true as long as the teacher continues to be a fair, responsive, and respectful authority figure to his students.

How does your child's teacher measure up in each of these areas? Assessing a teacher's performance according to these points will help you determine if classroom problems belong to the teacher, to your child, or to a combination of the two. Not every school difficulty is a "teacher problem" or the result of a poor fit between your child and his teacher. Most teachers are competent, decent people who despite the often unrealistic expectations we have for them actually do a fine job of teaching young people. As I have met and talked to teachers around the country, I have discovered that most are delighted to work with parents who are interested and involved in their child's education. A great many teachers want nothing more than to help children and teens get the most of their experience at school.

Summary

Children and teenagers can display stubborn and oppositional behaviors at school just as they will at home. Teacher behaviors that lead to more stubborn and oppositional behaviors include:

- Resentment and hostility toward students with behavioral problems.
- A teacher's inability to control his own authority and control problems.
- Active provocation of young people by threatening their self-esteem or self-image.
- Having temperament or personality conflicts with students.

Children show stubborn and oppositional behaviors in the classroom for the following reasons:

- They have problems of oppositional, stubborn, or noncompliant behavior at home.

- They have learning disabilities that they attempt to cover up through disruptive behavior.
- They are, in general, poorly disciplined children.
- They are, in general, poorly adjusted and unhappy children.
- They are provoked into such behavior by educators.
- They are divergent thinkers.

You can evaluate the competence of your child's teacher by asking these questions:

- Does he view all children as individuals and does he respond to each child in a sensitive way?
- Does he adjust his style to the needs of a particular student?
- Does he make referrals, when necessary, to the school psychologist or a treatment team?
- Does he use a warm, respectful, and honest style of teaching and communicating?
- Does he avoid disrespectful, belittling, demeaning, or accusatory approaches to students?
- Does he avoid taking a student's stubborn and oppositional behavior personally?
- Does he teach children the rules and expectations, making sure they are clear and reasonable?
- Does he spell out the consequences for violations of rules, expectations, and limits?

CHAPTER 16

Oppositional Defiant and Conduct Disorder Adolescents

Adolescents

John is a seventeen-year-old who has been diagnosed by a psychologist as exhibiting Oppositional Defiant Disorder. What this means is that John persistently defies authority figures and breaks rules. You can easily see this in John's behavior and in his relationship with his mother.

John and his mother have been in conflict about friends, freedom, school grades, clothes, and his girlfriend for at least three years. After one argument, John said to his mother, "Haven't you figured it out yet? If you're for something, I'm going to be against it."

And that's the way John typically reacts to his mother, to teachers, and to rules at home and at school. John's whole purpose in life, at this point, seems to be to defy adults.

"I'm good at frustrating adults," John has said.

That pretty much defines what an Oppositional Defiant Disorder child or teenager is all about. They make it a point—or so it seems—to go against established rules and the wishes of adults, especially parents and teachers. In the most severe forms, they may have run-ins with the police or commit minor delinquencies—such as running away, skipping school, physically fighting with parents, or shoplifting.

While they don't get involved in the degree of criminal behavior that young people diagnosed with Conduct Disorder do, oppositional defiant children and teens like to upset adults and will do so in a variety of ways. They often go to great lengths to prove themselves right and to make adults look stupid or feel in the wrong.

"If I'm right and I know it," said fourteen-year-old Allyson, "I'll do anything to prove my father wrong just to get the satisfaction of him knowing I was right."

If kids like Allyson or John are threatened by an adult, that's just the sort of motivation they need.

"When I get threatened," says Allyson, "it makes me feel like I have to do something. I'll argue or do something so he'll know he can't control me."

The Diagnostic and Statistical Manual of Mental Disorders of the American Psychiatric Association (DSM IV) defines an Oppositional Defiant Disorder as a disorder in which there is a pattern of negativistic, hostile, and defiant behavior. Children and adolescents who are given this diagnosis commonly are argumentative with their parents or other adults, lose their temper, swear, and show their anger, annoyance, and resentment. They do this quickly, without much provocation, and with little apparent regard for the feelings or rights of others.

Besides all that, the manual of the APA says, they defy adult requests and rules and blame others for their own mistakes or difficulties. And the interesting thing is that young people given the label of Oppositional Defiant Disorder don't necessarily show this behavior in all areas of their life. Often it may be just with their parents. Or it may start at home and gradually extend to school or to other adults or even to their friends and peers.

Children and teens with a diagnosis of Conduct Disorder, on the other hand, may show more serious negative and oppositional behaviors. In addition to those described under Oppositional Defiant Disorder, they exhibit behavior that violates the basic rights of others and shows a disregard for the rules of society. Such young people may be aggressive and threaten, bully, or assault other people (or animals), cause property damage, steal, lie, or be deceitful—and do these things repeatedly, without displaying guilt or anxiety.

Such young people have very little empathy or feeling for others. They usually don't think about how their behavior will affect other people, and often deny responsibility for their actions, blame others, or find what seem to them to be plausible reasons to justify their own behavior.

Oppositional Young People

Cecilia is a girl with an Oppositional Defiant Disorder. It was, for the most part, confined to her behavior at home, but by the time Cecilia was three years of age it was apparent to her parents that they had a "contrary and controlling child." Her parents described her as headstrong and stubborn and they said her stubbornness got worse over the years.

When she was thirteen years old, they first took her to see a psychologist. They told the first therapist that Cecilia was mouthy and disrespectful, always wanted more attention, and got angry very easily. Her teachers had also complained that she was obstinate and stubborn, often refusing to do schoolwork she didn't like.

When Cecilia was sixteen, her parents were frustrated with trying to manage her and asked a psychologist for help in placing her in a psychiatric hospital. "If we ground her," her mother said, "she runs out of the house. If we try to make her follow the rules, she throws a temper tantrum like a two-year-old and breaks things. And then she leaves."

Her parents said that they had taken away "everything" as punishments, but that didn't do any good. "If we don't allow her to watch TV," her father said, "she sneaks around to watch it. There is no punishment that works with Cecilia."

On the positive side, Cecilia could be very focused. When she made up her mind about something, she would focus on that thing and stick to it. At eleven, she had decided to become a vegetarian, and at fourteen, three years later, she had not reneged on this promise to herself. She would never touch meat. At fifteen, she was determined to get on the swim team at school, and she did.

Her parents, though, were fearful of her violent reactions. "I've never met a child as stubborn as Cecilia," her mother said. "When you try to talk to her, she gets angry and swears at us. The only time she's nice to us is when we give her more freedom and independence. But if you say no to her or try to talk about her feelings, she'll flare up and get angry. I just try to get out of her way. I'm afraid she'll attack me when she's angry."

Mark, a fifteen-year-old high school freshman with Oppositional Defiant Disorder, displayed stubborn, oppositional behavior both at home and at school. "My teachers said I was pigheaded," Mark explained one day. "And my mother says I have a hard head. I guess I've always been that way and I know it gets me in trouble. Mostly, I keep going until I get my way. Sometimes, I don't get my way and I just give in, but I don't like giving in."

A Boy Diagnosed with a Conduct Disorder

Then there's Devon. A sixteen-year-old who came into the juvenile court because he was caught with a gun at school, he has been oppositional at home and at school, too. However, Devon has been diagnosed by a court psychologist as having a Conduct Disorder.

At age five, Devon first ran away from home. When he was in first grade, he fought with children and stole money from them. One day, when he was eight, he got mad at his mother and set her bed on fire. Another time, he slashed clothes in her closet with a knife he got from a kitchen drawer.

Devon's aggressive behavior became worse as he got older. He collected weapons and joined a gang known for its violence. At fourteen he was arrested after he and a friend talked their way into a man's apartment in a senior citizens' complex by pretending to be part of the maintenance crew. Inside, they knocked the man down and took his money and the keys to his car. After driving the man's car for several days, they abandoned it in a field. Later, when Devon was arrested for the crime, he told the police that the man should be more careful about who he lets into his apartment.

A report written by a juvenile court psychologist who had conducted a psychological evaluation of Devon said that Devon was "highly delinquent" and that he did not have any remorse for his actions or feelings of empathy for the victims of his crimes. "This boy is diagnosed as a Conduct Disorder," the report concluded, "and there is a likelihood of more criminal behavior in the future."

The Statistics

It's been estimated that approximately 10 million children and adolescents are in need of mental health services in this country. Of those 10 million, some experts suggest that as many as two-thirds (or about 6.5 million young people) have Oppositional Defiant Disorders or the more severe diagnosis of Conduct Disorder. When it is considered that about a third of all referrals of children to mental health agencies and clinics involve problems of out-of-control behavior or unmanageability, then we begin to get a picture of how serious the problem of stubborn and oppositional children is in the United States.

Treating Young People with Oppositional Defiant Disorders

While a variety of treatment methods have been proposed and tried over the years, traditional psychotherapy involving one-on-one treatment by a therapist (psychologist, counselor, psychiatrist, or social worker) hasn't proved very successful with either the oppositional defiant young person or the one with a Conduct Disorder. In fact, some research suggests that traditional approaches may only make the child's behavior worse.

Neither has medication or psychopharmacology proved beneficial in treating oppositional young people. And residential treatment centers have not been found to have a lasting effect, although most oppositional young people do well as long as they're living in a psychiatric treatment center. When they return home, however, their behavior worsens again.

So what are the best approaches?

In almost all research, successful programs were those that involved the parents and the family. In successful approaches parents are taught behavioral principles and trained in the proper use of rewards and consequences to change the behavior of the children in the family. In effect, parents are taught to be teachers of their children.

One aspect of family life that goes wrong when young people behave in an oppositional defiant way is that parents give rewards and reinforcements despite the child's behavior. There is, I believe, a particular sequence that occurs when children develop oppositional problems. It starts with children with a difficult temperament. Such children present a considerable challenge to their parents. In an effort to curb their stubborn and defiant behaviors, parents use discipline methods that lead to more behavioral problems. Those behavioral problems create stress in the parents, who are then even less able to provide effective discipline. The result—several years later—is an oppositional and defiant youngster or, in the worst case, a child with a serious Conduct Disorder.

For a stubborn and temperamentally difficult child to become oppositional and defiant, "training" has to take place. Children literally have to be trained to be oppositional. The training occurs when parents continue to give rewards, privileges, and reinforcements despite unmanageable and oppositional behavior.

The two most successful approaches to treating families in which there are children or teens with Oppositional Defiant Disorders are group parent-training classes and family therapy. Both help parents set specific behavioral goals and teach them to apply rewards and reinforcements consistently, but only when children behave in acceptable ways.

Group Parent-Training Classes

While many specific parenting and discipline skills may be taught in parent-training classes, almost all such programs teach parents to increase their monitoring and control as well as to improve communication skills. In addition, group parent training may give parents information about why children misbehave, help them learn how to distinguish misbehavior from developmentally appropriate and age-appropriate behavior, and teach them the discipline techniques or skills that are effective in managing difficult child behaviors.

Family Therapy

The other category of successful treatment programs is family therapy. Employing systems theory, in which child behavior problems are seen as caused by family tension and conflict, family therapy helps the parents learn why the child became oppositional within the context of therapy sessions that include the child. Parents learn to change their own behavior and to alter interaction patterns within the family. Again, although there are different specific approaches to family therapy, all are similar in that they view the problem as having developed within the family and proceed from the assumption that the solution must therefore involve all the family working together with a trained family therapist.

Treating Adolescents Diagnosed with Conduct Disorder

No one approach has been shown to be highly successful with young people diagnosed with a Conduct Disorder. However, as the DSM IV points out, in a good many individuals the symptoms decrease in adulthood. When the symptoms of a Conduct Disorder are present early in life—by age ten—the prognosis is worse. A substantial proportion continue to show behaviors in adulthood that lead to a diagnosis of Antisocial Personality Disorder.

Group therapy with young people exhibiting more severe behavior disorders has shown a great deal of promise. Although various kinds of group therapies (such as discussion groups, psychoanalytic groups, client-centered groups, and teaching groups) have been tried with conduct disordered youth, the ones that have been shown to be most successful since the early 1980s are those emphasizing social skills training, anger replacement, and moral reasoning.

It has been found that adolescents with serious behavior problems have deficient problem-solving skills, inadequate social skills, a poor ability to consider consequences, and low levels of moral reasoning. Adolescent group therapy that teaches social skills, helps teens to have better control over their impulses, and instructs them to reason in moral ways have all shown promise in treating youth with Conduct Disorders.

One thing seems certain, however: There are a number of different factors associated with oppositional, defiant, stubborn, and aggressive children. The approaches that seem to be most successful in treating such children and teens take all these factors into consideration.

Factors Associated with Oppositional and Conduct Disorders

Some of the parental and family factors that are frequently associated with Oppositional Defiant Disorders and with Conduct Disorders are these:

- Poor parental supervision of children.
- Lack of parent involvement in the children's activities.
- Harsh or abusive forms of discipline.
- Inconsistent discipline.
- Parental antisocial personalities.
- Substance abuse by parents.

Although these factors are associated with both oppositional defiant problems and Conduct Disorders, not all families with a stubborn, oppositional, or defiant child or adolescent exhibit all of these factors. But it is likely that at least some of these factors are present.

In the studies that I have reviewed, at least four of these factors stand out:

1. Parents of children who are most oppositional and defiant or have serious behavior disorders are not very good at supervising their children. That is, they do not pay strict attention to what their children are doing, who they're with, and when they are expected to be back home.

2. Parents of oppositional and defiant young people are usually inconsistent in applying discipline. Such parents change in their application of discipline from day to day. Some days they are able to be firm and strict in making sure their children follow the rules, and other days they let the rules slide. Parents of the most oppositional children do not enforce rules and limits with consequences and punishments very well.

3. Parents of oppositional and defiant children tend to have substance abuse problems. We don't necessarily know if this is a cause of the children's problems or an effect. It could be one or the other.

4. Parents of oppositional and defiant children and adolescents often use harsh and coercive discipline methods. Unable to tolerate strivings for autonomy or the child's more difficult temperament, they may respond with fear-inducing, forceful, and punitive discipline. In the long run this creates more defiance and opposition rather than gaining compliance.

The Best Approaches to Treatment Recognize These Factors

As I indicated, the best approaches to treating oppositional, stubborn, aggressive, and defiant youngsters are those that involve the parents or the whole family. This has been shown in a number of research studies. These approaches are designed to deal with the factors that lead to such disorders in the first place.

If you're going to look for assistance and treatment outside the family, then it is important to select a therapist, social service agency, psychological or psychiatric clinic, or other treatment program that will utilize an effective treatment approach. Look for treatment programs that emphasize parent training or family therapy. Additionally, you will want to be certain that the program, therapist, or clinic has experience in treating children or teens who have been diagnosed as Oppositional Defiant. Such programs are most likely to address the critical factors that lead to stubbornness and defiance. Check the credentials of any therapist recommended or assigned to you to make sure he or she is licensed as a psychologist, social worker, psychiatrist, or counselor. A family therapist may have almost any combination of credentials because the designation "family therapist" is not licensed in most states. Perhaps the best credential is being a clinical member of the American Association of Marriage and Family Therapists. Then, ask questions about the therapist's background, fields of study, experience, and approach to handling your case.

Summary

An Oppositional Defiant Disorder is defined as a disorder of childhood and adolescence in which there is a pattern of negativistic, hostile, and defiant behavior. Nearly 6.5 million young people are estimated to have an Oppositional Defiant Disorder or Conduct Disorder. The most effective treatments have been those that involve parent group training or family therapy.

Parental factors associated with Oppositional Defiant Disorder and more severe Conduct Disorders are:

• Poor parental supervision of children.

• Lack of parent involvement in the activities of their children.

• Harsh or abusive forms of discipline.

• Parental antisocial personalities.

• Substance abuse by parents.

The most effective treatment approaches will take these factors into consideration.

CHAPTER 17

Living with Stubborn Children

In this chapter I want to summarize some of the most important points I have previously made about how parents can best deal with children's independence and their stubborn and oppositional behavior.

Three points especially need to be emphasized:

1. Parents must train themselves to be highly skilled in raising children.

2. Parents must learn as much as they can about child development.

3. Parents should develop a repertoire of positive discipline techniques.

When children develop normally, going from one age or stage to another, they are expected to assert their independence and to some degree resist the direction and instructions of adults. Children can, when they have the proper guidance and discipline from knowledgeable and loving parents, move fairly effortlessly through the various phases of development. On the other hand, they can be stagnated in one or more of them if parents do not handle them well. When parents show understanding and sensitivity regarding the stages of development that produce negativism, opposition, and defiance, they will handle their children in respectful and acceptable ways. However, this requires knowledge of the developmental stages of childhood and adolescence.

At the present time in our society, this generally means that if you want to be a knowledgeable parent (or teacher) you will have to take the initiative. You will need to actively seek out information on

understanding children and normal child development. That development will include oppositional behavior as part of a child's healthy striving for independence and self-assertion.

You also need to know how best to respond to children when they
are asserting themselves and resisting adult requests and direction. This
means learning effective discipline techniques and methods. Again, in
our society parents must take the initiative and educate themselves
about how best to deal with children.

Fortunately there are a great many books and magazines available
that give parents assistance. A little education and basic grounding in
advance is the best route. Finding the exact book or article at the exact
time you need it can be chancy. I have included in the Appendix a list of
some of the best books available to parents; these may help.

In Chapter 15, I listed some of the parental factors associated with
oppositional and defiant children. If you want to avoid creating a more
difficult and more noncompliant child, or if you have a child like this
and want to change that child, you will need to pay attention to your
own traits, characteristics, and behaviors that might be causing or
maintaining oppositional or stubborn behavior in your child.

Commit Yourself to Being an Excellent Parent

In particular, to raise your child most effectively, you must have four
important "abilities":

1. **The ability to commit yourself to provide appropriate consequences or rewards for positive, compliant,
   and nonresistant behavior.**

   The first requirement is always your motivation and desire
   to respond in appropriate ways to positive (which generally means nonstubborn and compliant) behavior.
   This means a commitment to being a good parent and a
   real desire to handle your child in ways that bring out the
   best in him.

   When parents are trained in positive and effective discipline techniques, they know that reinforcement works

wonderfully well with children of all ages. They know that when children are positively rewarded through verbal praise, attention, and encouragement, it usually ensures that more compliant behavior will result.

If having the will and motivation comes first, next is the ability to respond well to your child. When you have the motivation to raise children well, you will be child-focused and interested. But do you have the ability?

Generally the parents who are not able to respond in appropriate ways are those who are temporarily "disabled" by depression, stress, anxiety, substance abuse, or a current crisis that prevents them from focusing on the best interest of the child. Sometimes the stress stems from the hectic pace of contemporary life, or it may be related to trying to raise more than one child while maintaining other life roles. In addition, some parents are overly anxious, fearful, overprotective, or even highly distracted—perhaps with an attention deficit disorder condition themselves. If you are a parent who is experiencing any of these "disabling" conditions, you must get help.

That means seeking out professional mental health treatment or professional counseling to better handle your stress, depression, substance abuse, or current crisis so that you can be a parent in the best possible way. A great deal is at stake in being able to carry out your commitment to yourself and your child.

2. **The ability to respond to children's behavior consistently.**

I cannot emphasize enough how important and vital consistency is in making the world predictable for children. When the world is highly predictable, children feel safer and more secure and are likely to develop in healthy ways. As part of that healthy development, they will learn to recognize what is expected of them and what the consequences will be for their actions.

Many of the children I have seen and worked with who might be viewed as stubborn, spoiled, bratty, or seriously noncompliant have been dealt an unfortunate hand by their parents. They have been treated with considerable inconsistency. When parents handle children inconsistently, their children become insecure about their parents' responses. They fail to realize where the limits are, and feel stubbornly compelled to push the boundaries.

We want children to know exactly how we will respond to given behavior. That, however, requires consistency. When we always (or at least nearly always) act in a predictable way, our kids know what to depend on from us. They won't have to test the limits and push us until we are angry, frustrated, or exasperated.

3. **The ability to use discipline that is age-appropriate and is not harsh, punitive, or physically inhumane.**

Children are most likely to develop into stubborn, oppositional, resistant, and severely noncompliant young people when they have been subjected to harsh and punitive discipline. Of this there is no question. The research in the past few years has simply reinforced what we have known or suspected for decades. (Parents of the nineteenth century and earlier will not be remembered for their enlightened view of raising children—even if a popular misconception about Victorian times is that it was a more genteel era.)

Harsh discipline, which usually means overly punitive, demeaning, and abusive discipline (either verbal or physical), will result in children who are angry, resentful, and resistant. There is no way that harsh discipline methods can lead to more compliance—except in the sense that children become conforming out of fear and intimidation. Children raised with fear do not become healthy individuals.

There is a whole body of research and psychological studies that demonstrate very clearly that delinquent teenagers and those diagnosed with Conduct Disorders grow up, more often than not, in families in which there is coercive (fear-inducing, forceful, and punitive) discipline.

While it often seems that young hoodlums, adolescent criminals, and delinquents need or deserve harsh and punitive discipline, the fact is that most of them grew up in families in which they were subjected to harshness, physical discipline, spanking, hitting, and attempts to control them through fear, nagging, yelling, and intimidation. It didn't work to control them. It doesn't teach them to control themselves as they are growing up, and it doesn't work after they've become teens.

This applies to all other children as well. Physical discipline in even a minimal amount creates the potential risk of increasing—rather than decreasing—stubborn and oppositional behavior. Schools in this country are on the right track, as most of them forbid spanking or hitting students.

4. **The ability to use positive communication skills in being responsive and supportive to children.**

While this includes many of the principles covered above, good communication skills also involve broader aspects of parenting. Skillful communication involves the ability to talk and reason instead of yelling, scolding, or nagging. It also includes the ability to listen to children and respond sympathetically and empathically. And it involves being able to teach children how to solve problems.

All of these aspects of communication are necessary in raising children to become emotionally strong individuals with a positive self-image—without their having to actively resist and go against adults.

These four "abilities" are important for all parents. They become more critical for the parents faced with the challenge of a difficult child. When children don't easily listen, don't respond in a compliant way quickly, and seemingly refuse to learn from experience in the parent-child relationship, these four abilities become absolutely vital. There is no doubt from recent research (especially the research done by Rolf Loeber mentioned in Chapter 2) that children who demonstrate authority conflict problems at a very young age (by being stubborn and oppositional, by failing to mind, and not responding well to punishment or attempts at correction) are at high risk for developing more serious behavior problems. If left unchecked, these problems can become so serious in adolescence that young people may engage in delinquent or criminal behavior.

If temperamentally stubborn and oppositional children are most likely to develop behavior and management problems for their parents and for society, then we as a society have an obligation to work with those children and especially with their parents.

What Can Society Do?

It is evident that the parents of difficult and stubborn children will have frustrating and unrewarding "careers" as parents.

Studies done over the past two decades have shown that one of the best, most productive, and effective ways of working with delinquents is by training their parents for the job. Gerald Patterson, the great researcher at the Oregon Social Research Institute, has made a career of establishing just this fact. When parents are trained in the "abilities" given above, they stand a chance of changing their acting-out and poorly managed adolescents.

More than this, though, if such parents don't get assistance when their children are young, those children may end up as unhappy, maladjusted individuals who are a drain on a society already overburdened by delinquents and criminals.

How can society intervene?

Unfortunately useful books on parenting do not find their way into everyone's hands. The parent who buys them is likely to be already reasonably well motivated and informed.

But all parents—especially very young and inexperienced ones— need to know the warning signs of a child at risk. They need to learn while children are just infants or toddlers how to recognize signs that they may be at high risk for serious behavior problems in the future.

If parents, especially inexperienced parents, knew the warning signs and then were taught what steps to take, they could take appropriate action. We have accepted and taken to heart information from the American Cancer Society and the American Heart Association. Every adult in our society has read or heard about the "seven warning signs" of cancer as well as the risk factors for heart disease, high blood pressure, and diabetes. Why have we never warned parents about the risks of certain childhood behaviors and certain parenting styles? Why have we not promoted national goals and guidelines for parenting? The stakes are just as high.

When parents have been given information about which children are likely to develop serious difficulties and eventual conflicts with school and legal authorities, then those parents can choose to seek help.

This is only part of the equation, of course. The other part is the question of where to go for help. Where can parents find appropriate information and assistance?

Unfortunately at present most parents will have a hard time finding parenting classes, seminars, or workshops that give them the kind of help and training they really need. Even going to licensed or certified psychologists, counselors, social workers, or psychiatrists is chancy. Do they have any knowledge about parenting? Have they ever had a course in raising children? Do they know about dealing with difficult children? To what methods and theories do they subscribe? In many instances, a license, degree, or certification in a mental health specialty is no guarantee that the professional has been trained in child development or parenting.

It is informative and instructive to look at what other countries have done to ensure that children are raised more effectively. Sweden was the first country to introduce a national parenting law. In 1979, the Swedish government passed a law outlawing spanking in the country.

Its passage sent a powerful message to parents: No longer was it acceptable to discipline children by physical means. While this was a radical move for Sweden, as there had been little preparation for parents to stop spanking, the government did not just set a standard without providing for parenting services to help parents.

Available to all parents in the country was a pamphlet that described alternative discipline techniques. In addition, visiting nurse services were set up and are widely used by most parents in the country. A nurse visits the homes of all families during the first month of a baby's life, and pays at least one more call by the fourth year, making herself available to help out with parenting problems. Also, the staffs of child care centers—located in nearly every neighborhood in Sweden—are trained and available to teach frustrated parents new discipline skills.

The schools of Sweden likewise had a role. Beginning about 1979, every child at the junior high level and above has a weekly class in parent training. Not only are they taught about the no-spanking law, they are taught other skills that will be valuable when they become parents.

The United States needs a similar effort to promote positive discipline and parent training—not just for parents with difficult children, but for every parent. The research is in place. It just hasn't, until recently, made its way into the popular literature directed at parents and teachers. Nor is parent training based on this research readily available.

Yet it is clear that parents of children considered to be at risk need it. Such training has to be very specific and detailed. It must be dedicated to teaching parents about child development and training them in appropriate steps toward changing a stubborn, oppositional, and resistant child into a compliant and responsible youngster.

Until such training is in place and available to every parent in this society, we will be a nation condemned to repeat past parenting mistakes and we will continue to raise oppositional and defiant children. Until all parents have the know-how and are willing and able to use it, we will continue to raise young people who will become the gang members and the violent criminals of the future.

This book has been about helping children become independent and self-reliant. This is a strong theme in our society. The American people believe in being independent, self-reliant, and autonomous. No one wants the government to intervene in our lives—certainly not in our family lives. Yet, drawing on the Swedish experience, we know that the government can lead the way in setting standards—just as good parents do within a household. A very important standard that our government could establish is that children should be treated with basic dignity and that every child should be guaranteed the right to be raised in an atmosphere free of spanking, hitting, and violence. The health, responsibility, and self-reliance of future generations depend on it.

The government can also set standards by establishing guidelines for states to provide parenting assistance through classes, training, and workshops. State departments of education should be directed to establish parenting classes in all schools for every student, beginning in middle school. Every American student, from junior high through high school, should have classes each year in parenting and discipline.

America, which usually prides itself on being among the world leaders in humanitarian efforts, has fallen behind in this area of raising children—and our crime rate reflects this. All it might really take is as greater emphasis on the education of parents—and the education and training of parents-to-be.

It is time to place the raising of children at the top of the list of what's important in America. We owe it to our children to guarantee them the basic right to grow up in a family in which they are allowed to develop as individuals with decency, dignity, and autonomy.

Summary

Parents will best be prepared to deal with stubborn and oppositional children and teens if they keep these points in mind:

1. **Parents must train themselves to be highly skilled in raising children.**
2. **Parents must learn as much as possible about child development.**
3. **Parents should develop a repertoire of positive discipline skills.**

In order to most effectively raise a child, parents should have four abilities:

1. The ability to commit themselves to providing appropriate consequences for positive, compliant, and nonresistant behavior.

2. The ability to respond to children's behavior in a consistent manner.

3. The ability to use discipline that is age-appropriate and is not harsh, punitive, or physically inhumane.

4. The ability to use positive communication skills in being responsive and supportive to children.

Society has a role to play in helping parents to know the warning signs of a child at risk. In addition, society has a responsibility to set standards for good parenting and to see to it that parents have access to parent-training classes and school courses.

Appendix A

Throughout this book I have suggested various discipline techniques for you to use with children at different ages. In several instances I made mention of discipline methods without either defining or describing them in detail. While it was not usually critical or necessary in the text to give a more complete description, in this appendix I want to go beyond what was in earlier chapters to provide you with more descriptive information about some of those discipline techniques. This will allow you to have a better understanding of the discipline method and give you guidelines for using these techniques more effectively with your children.

Time-out: A discipline technique that involves removing a child from the scene of the action to a dull, nonstimulating place. Often this will be a special time-out chair or place. It can be a chair in a hallway, a place facing a wall, or stair steps on which children are to sit. Since it is a punishment, time-out should be used only to decrease more dangerous or serious behavior. Overuse of this or any other punishment will decrease its effectiveness and children will become immune to your use of it as a negative consequence.

Keep children in time-out only briefly. One rule of thumb is that children should be kept in time-out for only about one minute for each year of age.

You may use a warning before placing a child in time-out. For example, you might say, "If you bite him again, then you will have to go to the time-out chair." Having said this, you must follow through with a time-out the next time that misbehavior occurs.

When children are assigned to time-out, they need be given only a brief statement about why they are receiving the time-out. For instance, you could say, "You crossed the busy and dangerous street after I told you to stay in our yard and now you have to go to time-out." Thereafter, ignore any temper tantrums, shouting, or protests as well as any promises to reform until the time-out is ended.

If a child refuses to comply with time-out or leaves the time-out area, tell her that time-out doesn't begin until she is in the time-out place and quiet. Then, you do not allow her to play or return to her former activity until the time-out is served.

After time-out is over, then the child still must comply with any previous request or order. For example, if she was placed in time-out because she hit you when she got angry because you asked her to pick up her toys, she must still pick up her toys.

Finally, as soon as the child performs a desirable or requested activity after time-out is over, be sure to use praise and attention for her positive behavior. This lets her know you still love her while it tells her how to get positive attention from you.

Ignoring: Ignoring misbehavior means systematically withholding attention from an undesirable or inappropriate behavior. You would never ignore a serious or dangerous behavior, such as biting another child or running into a busy street. However, there are plenty of minor and annoying misbehaviors that often thrive on parental attention but diminish when you don't respond to them. Examples of behaviors that are often best ignored are whining, temper tantrums, swearing, tattling, and sibling arguing.

To systematically withhold attention from a behavior requires you to pick an inappropriate action you would like to decrease or stop and direct no attention to the child or the behavior. Once you start to ignore it, you must do so consistently—even though at least for a short period of time the behavior may get worse before it gets better.

Be sure there is no eye contact or other nonverbal cues that may serve to reinforce a misbehavior. Obviously when you are ignoring you are not talking to the child or otherwise communicating with her.

Sometimes you may have to do find something to distract you from the child's behavior, especially if you have trouble sticking to your decision to ignore a certain annoying or attention-getting behavior.

Once the inappropriate or attention-getting behavior has stopped, then you can resume normal interaction with your child, making sure that you use plenty of praise and positive attention as well as affection for actions you want to encourage.

Reprimands: A reprimand is an expression of disapproval and a very mild verbal punishment. It is a brief scolding done for the purpose of decreasing a misbehavior.

Here is an example of a reprimand: "Jason, I don't like it when you swear. I want you to stop." Or, "I don't allow hitting. I won't allow that when you're angry."

Reprimands are very effective when used properly and when you have a generally positive and loving relationship with your child. As with any punishment, reprimands should be used only with serious and intolerable behaviors and should not be overused. If they are used too often they will lose their effectiveness.

To be most successful with reprimands, follow these guidelines:

- Move closer to the child and establish eye contact.
- Raise your voice slightly and make sure you sound serious and authoritative.
- Make the reprimand brief and to the point: "Jill, I'm very disappointed that you disobeyed and had friends come over after we told you that no one could visit you tonight when we were not at home."
- Do not humiliate or attack the child; stick to the subject of your disapproval of a misbehavior.
- Maintain eye contact for a few seconds after the verbal part of the reprimand is over.
- Conclude the exchange by saying something positive. For instance you could say, "I know that most of the time you follow our rules. I believe that the next time you won't disappoint me. I still love you. Okay?"

Removing Rewards and Privileges: This is a punishment used to reduce or stop a serious or dangerous misbehavior. As children outgrow the use of time-out as a negative consequence, withdrawing privileges, rewards, activities, and opportunities becomes a more frequently used consequence.

It is common for parents to remove some of these rewards and privileges from children and teens: going out to play, spending time with friends, using playthings, receiving an allowance, or earning special privileges or events.

This punishment is more likely to be effective if the removed reward or privilege is related to or nearly equal to the misbehavior. For instance, a youngster who comes home late from play may be restricted from going out to play next time, or a child who uses crayons to draw pictures on the wall may have the use of crayons restricted. Also, this type of negative consequence has a better chance to be successful if the restriction doesn't last too long and has meaning or value to the child.

If you threaten to remove a reward or privilege, be sure that what you threaten is fair and not too harsh or outrageous ("You'll be grounded for the whole semester"), and that you follow through firmly with the threat.

Distraction: Distraction means diverting a child's attention to some other activity or thing in order to avoid a more serious problem or to prevent a misbehavior. Distraction and diversion work well with toddlers and preschoolers, who may easily forget their interest in the undesired or inappropriate behavior. However, older children see through this and it loses its effectiveness as children become more sophisticated.

In most cases being prepared by having special "equipment" with you at the time that you need it can come in handy. For instance, carrying toys in your purse that your child likes can distract her from undesirable pursuits at the doctor's office or in the car. Always, though, you must offer a distraction or diversion that has as much or more appeal than the activity or object the child has her eye on initially.

Substitution: This is virtually the same technique as distraction because with both techniques you are presenting something in exchange for what the child wants to do. Offering to read a story to a toddler who is touching the TV knobs may be an acceptable substitute. Suggesting a child watch a favorite video when she's fighting with a sibling may help to distract her from the annoying behavior to something much more positive. Substitutes, like distractions, avoid a confrontation and may prevent a problem from escalating.

Redirection: Sometimes the best way to handle an infant, toddler, or preschooler's misbehavior is through a process called redirection. In using redirection you move the child or a part of her body—for instance, her hand—in another direction or toward another object. Or you redirect her by pointing her shoulders in another direction. In most instances, the child's actions or energies are redirected toward something more positive without scolding or shouting on your part.

It helps to think of redirection as channeling. We redirect by channeling anger, feelings, or behaviors in new and more positive directions. For example, a child who is hitting another youngster when she's angry can be redirected by having her express her anger in verbal ways. Or, a youngster who is throwing stones at another child can be told that she can punch a punching bag all she wants, but she is not allowed to throw stones. Or, an infant who is grabbing your glasses can be redirected by moving her hand from your face and your glasses to your necklace or a rattle.

Appendix B
For Further Reading

Books for Parents

Here is a listing of parenting books that address the concerns and issues discussed in this book. Each of these books will give you more information in the specific areas indicated by the heading of each section.

Discipline

Lee Canter and Marlene Canter. *Assertive Discipline for Parents.* Santa Monica, Calif.: Canter and Associates, 1982.

Lynn Clark. *The Time-Out Solution: A Parent's Guide for Handling Everyday Behavior Problems.* New York: Contemporary Books, 1989.

Mark Devlin. *Stubborn Child.* New York: Atheneum, 1985.

Don Dinkmeyer, Sr., and Gary D. McKay. *Systematic Training for Effective Parenting.* Circle Pines, Minn.: American Guidance Service, 1989.

Stephen Garber, Marianne Garber, and Robin F. Spizman. *Good Behavior: Over 1200 Sensible Solutions to Your Child's Problems from Birth to Age Twelve.* New York: Villard Books, 1987.

Christopher Green. *Toddler Taming.* New York: Fawcett, 1985.

Thomas Lickona. *Raising Good Children.* New York: Bantam Books, 1985.

Eileen Nechas and Denise Foley. *From Newborn Through 5 Years: What Do You Do Now?* New York: Fireside, 1992.

Michael Popkin. *Active Parenting: Teaching Cooperation, Courage, and Responsibility.* New York: Perennial Library, 1987.

John Rosemond. *Six-Point Plan for Raising Happy, Healthy Children.* Kansas City, Mo.: Andrews and McMeel, 1989.

Charles Schaefer and Theresa Foy DiGeronimo. *Teach Your Child to Behave: Discipline with Love from 2 to 8 Years.* New York: Plume, 1991.

Peter Williamson. *Good Kids, Bad Behavior.* New York: Simon and Schuster, 1990.

James Windell. *Discipline: A Sourcebook of 50 Failsafe Techniques for Parents.* New York: Macmillan, 1991.

James Windell. *8 Weeks to a Well-Behaved Child: A Failsafe Program for Toddlers Through Teens.* New York: Macmillan, 1994.

Child Development

Haig Akmakjian. *The Natural Way to Raise a Healthy Child.* New York: Praeger Publishers, 1975.

Louise Bates Ames, Frances L. Ilg, and Carol Chase Haber. *Your One-Year-Old: The Fun-Loving, Fussy 12- to 24-Month-Old.* New York: Delta, 1982.

Louise Bates Ames and Frances L. Ilg. *Your Two-Year-Old: Terrible or Tender.* New York: Delta, 1976.

Louise Bates Ames and Frances L. Ilg. *Your Three-Year-Old: Friend or Enemy.* New York: Delta, 1976.

Louise Bates Ames and Frances L. Ilg. *Your Four-Year-Old: Wild and Wonderful.* New York: Delta, 1976.

Louise Bates Ames and Frances L. Ilg. *Your Five-Year-Old: Sunny and Serene.* New York: Delacorte Press, 1976.

Louise Bates Ames and Frances L. Ilg. *Your Six-Year-Old: Loving and Defiant.* New York: Delacorte Press, 1976.

Louise Bates Ames and Carol Chase Haber. *Your Seven-Year-Old: Life in a Minor Key.* New York: Delta Books, 1985.

Louise Bates Ames and Carol Chase Haber. *Your Eight-Year-Old: Lively and Outgoing.* New York: Delta Books, 1985.

Louise Bates Ames and Carol Chase Haber. *Your Nine-Year-Old: Thoughtful and Mysterious*. New York: Delta Books, 1985.

Louise Bates Ames, Frances L. Ilg, and Sidney M. Baker. *Your Ten- to Fourteen-Year-Old*. New York: Delacorte Press, 1988.

T. Berry Brazelton. *What Every Baby Knows*. New York: Ballantine, 1988.

Theresa and Frank Caplan. *The Early Childhood Years: The Two- to Six-Year-Old*. New York: Bantam Books, 1984.

Theresa and Frank Caplan. *The Second Twelve Months of Life*. New York: Bantam Books, 1990.

Arlene Eisenberg, Heidi E. Murkoff, and Sandee E. Hathaway. *What to Expect the First Year*. New York: Workman, 1988.

Robin Goldstein. *More Everyday Parenting: The Six- to Nine-Year-Old*. New York: Penguin, 1991.

Robin Goldstein and Janet Gallant. *Everyday Parenting: The First Five Years*. New York: Penguin, 1990.

Penelope Leach. *Your Growing Child: From Babyhood through Adolescence*. New York: Knopf, 1989.

Penelope Leach. *Your Baby and Child: From Birth to Age Five*. New York: Schocken, 1989.

Diane E. Papalia and Sally Wendkos Olds. *A Child's World: Infancy through Adolescence*. New York: McGraw-Hill, 1979.

Adrienne Popper. *Parents Book for the Toddler Years*. New York: Ballantine, 1990.

Laurence Steinberg and Ann Levine. *You and Your Adolescent: A Parent's Guide for Ages 10–20*. New York: Harper and Row, 1990.

Communication

Michael DeSisto. *Decoding Your Teenager*. New York: Quill, 1991.

Adele Faber and Elaine Mazlish. *How to Talk so Kids Will Listen and Listen so Kids Will Talk*. New York: Avon, 1982.

Haim G. Ginott. *Between Parent and Child*. New York: Avon, 1976.

Thomas Gordon. *Parent Effectiveness Training: The Tested Way to Raise Responsible Children*. New York: McKay, 1970.

Temperament

Stella Chess and Alexander Thomas. *Know Your Child: An Authoritative Guide for Today's Parents.* New York: Basic Books, 1987.

Mary Sheedy Kurchinka. *Raising Your Spirited Child: A Guide for Parents Whose Child Is More Intense—Sensitive—Perceptive—Persistent—Energetic.* New York: HarperPerennial, 1991.

Stanley Turecki and Leslie Tonner. *The Difficult Child.* New York: Bantam Books, 1989.

Assertiveness

Robert E. Alberti and Michael L. Emmons. *Your Perfect Right: A Guide to Assertive Living.* San Luis Obispo, Calif.: Impact Publishers, 1987.

Index